D0899963

MISSING ELEMENTS IN POLITICAL INQUIRY

SAGE FOCUS EDITIONS

missing elements in political inquiry
logic and levels of analysis

edited by
Judith A. Gillespie
and Dina A. Zinnes

WITHDRAWN

JA
35
1981

SAGE PUBLICATIONS
Beverly Hills / London / New Delhi

Copyright © 1982 by Sage Publications, Inc.

All rights reserved. No part of this book may be reproduced or utilized in any form or by any means, electronic or mechanical, including photo-copying, recording, or by any information storage and retrieval system, without permission in writing from the publisher.

For information address:

SAGE Publications, Inc.
275 South Beverly Drive
Beverly Hills, California 90212

SAGE Publications India Pvt. Ltd.   SAGE Publications Ltd
    C-236 Defence Colony   28 Banner Street
    New Delhi 110 024, India   London EC1Y 8QE, England

Printed in the United States of America

Library of Congress Cataloging in Publication Data

Main entry under title:

Missing elements in political inquiry.

   (Sage focus editions ; 55)
   Papers presented at the conference held in Bloomington, Ind., Mar. 26-27, 1981 under the sponsorship of Indiana University's College of Arts and Sciences, and others.
   Includes bibliographies.
   1. Political science—Congresses. 2. Political science—Methodology—Congresses. I. Gillespie, Judith A. II. Zinnes, Dina A. III. Indiana University, Bloomington. College of Arts and Sciences.
JA35. 1981   320'.01'8   82-6009
ISBN 0-8039-1802-X   AACR2
ISBN 0-8039-1803-8 (pbk.)

FIRST PRINTING

12/11/85

IN MEMORY OF JOHN GILLESPIE
whose ideas motivated this
volume and whose spirit
continues to enrich our lives

Contents

Preface and Acknowledgments

Missing Elements in Political Inquiry serves as a memorial to the late John V. Gillespie. The volume has been developed by friends wishing to continue a tradition of scholarship and fellowship to which John devoted his personal and professional lives. We hoped to find some nonobvious answers to significant questions. The result was to highlight some missing elements in political inquiry that we feel need to be further explored in current research and teaching.

We began by organizing a conference titled, "New Dimensions in Political Science: How Do We Know What We Know?" The conference was held in Bloomington, March 26-27, 1981, under the sponsorship of Indiana University's College of Arts and Sciences, the Department of Political Science, the Vice-President's office, and the Workshop in Political Theory and Policy Analysis. Many people participated in the conference. The eight papers that were developed into chapters of this book were, in part, written by all those who attended the conference. The panel chairs and discussants, as well as the synthesizers, took part in important discussions during the conference, which stimulated major revisions in the papers. Both the revised papers and the synthesizers' comments are provided in this volume.

Participants in the conference included the authors of chapters, introductions, and syntheses in this volume. They are all indebted to the panel chairpersons: Edwin Fogelman, University of Minnesota; Harvey Starr, Indiana University, Bloomington; John E. Turner, University of Minnesota; and Leroy Rieselbach, Indiana University, Bloomington. Moreover, many stimulating ideas raised by the paper discussants are incorporated in this volume. The discussants were: William H. Baugh, University of Oregon; Maurice A. East, University of Kentucky; Lyndelle Fairlie, San Diego State University; Karen Feste Hanson, University of Denver; Roger A. Hanson, Institute for Court Management, Denver; Marjorie Randon Hershey, Indiana University, Bloomington; William E. Linehan, State

University of New York at Stony Brook; Martin Sampson, University of Minnesota; Roslyn Simowitz, Texas Tech University; John Sprague, Washington University, St. Louis; Ronald E. Weber, Louisiana State University; and Susan O. White, University of New Hampshire.

Royalties from the volume will be donated to the John V. Gillespie Memorial Fund at Indiana University. This fund provides scholarships for advanced graduate students in positive theory and quantitative methods. Anyone wishing to contribute to the Memorial Fund should contact Judith Gillespie.

Finally, we would like to thank the conference participants for contributing to the volume, and to thank John for the ongoing stimulus that he is providing for our professional and personal lives.

—Judith A. Gillespie
—Dina A. Zinnes

Introduction
Some Basic Puzzles in Political Inquiry

JUDITH A. GILLESPIE

When I first moved to the state of Indiana twelve years ago, I didn't know much about it. I knew that Gary was in the north and Bloomington was somewhere south of Indianapolis (how far south I was soon to find out). I needed some shorthand method for figuring out where I was, perhaps so that I could know who I was in the context of this new environment. As a political scientist, I looked for a logic for figuring out this puzzle and turned to the basic organization of counties, townships, and metropolitan areas. I was soon able to define that I was in Monroe County (which is an SMSA) in Bloomington Township and then began to recognize the socio-cultural characteristics of my environment. I was "gown" and *they* were "town," and even before *Breaking Away,* they were stonies (*not* cutters). I was pleased. I could position myself in a new environment through a logic that was familiar to me.

However, I could only get so far in my logical mapping with geographic tools. I went to vote only to find that the logic of understanding voting in election districts was not the same as that in townships and counties. When I changed to a different level, that of the election district, I had to use a new logic in order to determine where I was and who I was as a voter. I soon found that I was a Democrat, but not a Southern Democrat, in an area that was overwhelmingly Republican. Alas, the dominance of the gown geographically in Bloomington would be coupled inextricably with permanent political minority status at the polls.

This small exercise in political inquiry is analogous to the key concerns we have here. The preliminary mapping that someone does when they

11

move to a new area requires the use of multiple logics and levels of analysis. Many times a logic we develop for one level cannot be transposed onto another level of analysis and our logic itself does not allow us to get from one place to the other. Many times our problems are much more complex. It is difficult even to pin down the post holes that will allow us to begin to map conceptually the terrain that we are studying. Therefore, our basic problem is an inquiry problem, one of developing ways of thinking that will allow us to provide new insights into political problems and one of levels of analysis, or how to get from here to there or from one logic to the next as we traverse basic units of analysis.

In this volume we explore some very important puzzles in political inquiry. We feel there are missing elements in the logic people use to approach political problems and in their treatment of levels of analysis. We will try to put together some of the missing pieces in these puzzles in ways that will bridge gaps in our knowledge. In general, we are concerned with four key puzzles here.

First, we explore the role of formalization in political inquiry. Both coherence and precision are important elements that are often overlooked as we approach concepts and theoretical arguments; yet they are basic to our ability to build theory in political science.

Second, we probe some key missing elements in studying the dynamics of political life. While political scientists have long recognized that the logic of the dynamics of political change may be quite different from static models that have been used previously, the development and formalization of a set of dynamic models that take into account both the structure of political action and the interactions of political units have yet to be fully realized.

A third key puzzle involves linkages. If we are concerned about individual behavior as well as macro-unit behavior, we must puzzle fundamentally over aggregation problems of how individual behaviors relate to the composite behaviors of larger units. Many of the tools for linking the behavior of units within and between levels of analysis are still missing from our inquiry skills. Identifying relationships across political units and the sequence of interactions between them are primary questions here. The strength of every political inquiry depends on the continuous search for sound answers to linkage problems.

Finally, we focus specifically on the problem of cumulation in the discipline. We have so little cumulation that it is difficult to find a base to start from, yet we will face this puzzle squarely. The result will be a contribution to our understanding of ways of putting together knowledge that we have and ways of exploring new knowledge in order to help us to synthesize our work. We hope that this will enable us to see the larger picture of where we are and to identify new directions in which we can move to build a coherent body of knowledge about political life.

Each of these ideas is taken up in turn below. Exploring them will help us to find missing elements and identify them in the puzzles of political inquiry. Then we take a look at where we are in working with these missing elements and where we might go in terms of implications for theory, research, and teaching.

Missing Elements in Formal Models

Although political scientists have been doing formal modeling for decades, logical analysis has been adopted as a form of inquiry for even a longer period of time. In general, the two are not separable. Logical analysis involves formalization whether that formalization is precise conceptualization or has a mathematical representation. Formalization provides a way to think through problems. Some may question whether formalization as a tool adds or detracts from our ability to think logically through problems, yet formal modeling does contribute a tool that many have utilized to aid the logical process of political inquiry.

There are a great many cases that could be stated in which formalization has added to our knowledge of political life. International relations studies using formal modeling have developed more complex models and explored interactions in different ways than verbal descriptions have allowed. Formal statistical models at the urban level have added important kinds of insights into public policy problems, such as desegregation, that otherwise were lacking in the literature. Even the most skeptical would have to agree that formalization provides insights or heuristics for many of us to think through problems in significant ways (Langer, 1967).

Yet there are many, many puzzles in the use of formalization in political inquiry. Even if formalization is used well and is not substituted for logical thinking but employed as a tool for advancing knowledge, the number of puzzles is staggering. We cannot deal with the complex number of variables that accurately explain a political situation even with the aid of formalization. There is a whole complex of variables that we do not yet have the capacity to deal with in formal ways without becoming as confused in the analysis as we would without it. Probabilities and dynamics of behavior are rarely captured by the simplistic types of formal models that we use to describe them. Whether the models are formal logical deductions or statistical models, we still run into the problem of making our probability statements or our dynamics accurately fit both the complexity and the irregularity of human behavior. Still another puzzle involves the assumptions that we bring to an analysis any time that it is formalized. These assumptions far from fit reality and, therefore, our models are often hedged with so many caveats that, although the finding may be insightful, we find the method lacks coherence with real-world ideas or events.

Although these kinds of problems are important, there is a basic puzzle that transcends any summary or critique of the literature on formal models. The basic puzzle is found in our own analytical abilities and our use of formalization in order to improve our inquiries. A particular example from my own research on high schools illustrates this point well (Gillespie, 1978).

In Washington, D.C., there is a high school at which we studied the effects of welfare policy on students' attitudes about their future and job careers. In talking with female students whose parents were on welfare, we discovered that these students clearly desired to remain in the welfare system. They saw having children as the primary means of staying on welfare, and 40 percent of them were pregnant or already had children of their own. This finding was not unrelated to those of other scholars who talk about the "welfare syndrome." Yet until I had personally interviewed dozens of women in the high school and heard them talk about their family situations, I did not realize that the rate of pregnancy might not be as directly related to common findings about the welfare syndrome as it was to the desire and need for affection. In fact, women at this particular Washington, D.C., high school, as well as in high schools across the country, were getting pregnant and having children because of family situations that deprived them of a basic need—love. Love ranked above money as a priority for these young women, and explained more of the variance in future expectations than family welfare history. The situation highlights the difficulty of using any type of analysis that relies on our own abilities and skills in conceptualizing basic explanatory variables.

We can think of the basic puzzle as one of seeing, and once we "see," as one of finding some empirical referent for *what* we see. In this case, seeing enough of the whole picture to adequately conceptualize the major explanatory variables underlying the expectations about the future of some women in high schools involved a great deal of both speculation and informal data collection. Second, and as important, it involved operationalizing concepts in ways that would adequately represent "need for affection" in diverse communities of students, determining the complex linkages between the variables we wanted to explore, and deriving the basic propositions that needed testing. It is at this point that many people find or construct empirical indicators and proceed. In so doing, we miss an important element in the inquiry process.

The missing element is one that we will term "coherence." It is a missing element in a great deal of political inquiry. We conceptualize the problem inadequately and then proceed to collect data that have little or nothing to do with the solution to the problem. Our argument is that formalization can help this process, in terms of both the initial conceptualization and the linking of this conceptualization to data collection and analysis.

Formalization can aid us in this process in several ways. First of all, it provides a language for looking at a problem that will enable us to define what we are looking for and its elements. Without this definition, we cannot begin the essential deductive process involved in formalization. If we are looking for an explanation of variance in the future expectations of women in high schools across the country, we must, if we formalize the argument, look for the essential components of the problem. To begin to formalize the model, we must ask what the range of expectations is and why it occurs.

A second way in which formal languages can aid us in political inquiry is that they help us to specify relationships between ideas. Often a formal language will give us some precise logical connection between a and b that allows us to see more clearly what we are talking about and how we are thinking. Once we have linked together ideas, the formal language can help us to derive deductions from them; the formal language also forces us to specify relationships that the English language normally slides over very easily. The word "increase," for example, can be defined using formal logical and statistical languages in quite a few ways that otherwise would not be specified in our common, everyday writing. Therefore, a major contribution formal languages make is helping us to link together our ideas. Once we see a problem, such as the one above, specifying relationships between expectations and the need for affection can be developed within a formal language in ways that will give us a relationship that otherwise would merely stand as an assumed, correlational one.

A third way in which formal languages help us is that they enable us to relate statements to one another. They help us to build a coherent theory from which we can test our ideas. More specifically, the logic of the language helps us to see that not only can a and b be related, but a and b can be related to c and d through a series of steps. In short, the very logic of our argument is tightened from statement to statement in the use of formal languages. We can see not only the relationship between affection, pregnancy, and expectations, but how that relationship relates to expectations through the intervening variable of performance in school. These kinds of logical aids can bring us closer to asking significant questions of our empirical data and to making our operationalizations fit the major connections in the theories we are trying to test.

Finally, formal languages give us a way of making deductions from our ideas that we otherwise might not contemplate. Throughout this volume we will see how the use of formal languages can help us to arrive at conclusions that run against standard assumptions about political problems. In many ways the real fruit of formal analysis is in the kinds of deductions that we can make when this analysis done in a way that allows us to "see" things we would not otherwise see. It provides us with unique empirical tests for our theoretical arguments.

Basically, then, formal languages help us to pinpoint what our inquiry is or what we need to find out. They give us a frame of reference or a way of thinking that helps us through the problem of finding out where we are and what we want to know. In effect, formal languages can create a map that helps us in ways similar to the ways in which the township and county maps helped me to find out about southern Indiana. This is no small blessing if, indeed, formal languages are used to their best advantage.

The basic dimensions of the missing element of coherence are fully discussed in Chapter 1 in this volume. Within the nexus of the problem of coherence rests an issue that is of equal importance to coherence itself. That issue is one of specification. Once we "see" the initial elements of the conceptualization of our inquiry, we need to be able to clarify our thinking and our ideas to a point at which we can not only talk about them to others, but operationalize them in significant ways.

The missing element in a great deal of political inquiry is precision. While there are valid arguments against precision, and we may want to keep the word "specification" or "clarification" rather than "precision," being precise in terms of specifying what we are looking for is a key missing element in a great deal of political inquiry. One need only look at most of the studies of power and influence to determine that specification is clearly an important idea.

An analogy to this particular problem is found when we hear that someone has had a heart attack. The words "heart attack" are a lot like the word influence; both can mean a great many things. A person can have atherosclerosis, a person can have a valve that does not function properly, a person can have nervous angina, and all of these conditions can be classified under the term "heart attack." Clearly, if this happens to someone whom we know rather well, we want to know something besides the fact that he or she has had a heart attack. We want the doctor, in this case, to specify or clarify what it is we are talking about and whether or not it is the result of a disease, life style, or other factors. We are asking no less of political inquiry conducted by political scientists than we ask of the medical community when we have a physical malfunction (Miller, 1977).

In this case, precision means specification. Being precise allows us to be more clear about what it is we are talking about, regardless of whether the language that we use is a formal one or not. In Chapter 2 Barbara Salert discusses the need for specification of the concept "threshold." This concept, not unlike "power" or "influence" or "heart attack," needs a great deal of specification and can mean different things in different situations. Generally speaking, precision enables us to determine whether we are talking about the same concept or about variants of the same idea (which may be two entirely different concepts) when we do our research and teaching.

Precision also helps us to specify relationships between ideas more carefully. Although formal languages give us ways of specifying these relationships, we often do not pay the same kind of attention to precision in relationships as we do to precision in specifying main ideas. Just as we want to know more about the causes of our friend's heart attack than that heart disease is correlated with smoking or tension, we also want to know more about relationships in political science than the fact that they are additive or interrelated. Thinking about precision in terms of specifying relationships helps us to come to conclusions that are more sensitive to the complexities of the problems that we wish to solve.

Precision's most important role often comes in tracing the implications of the ideas we are dealing with. While many political inquirers are very conscious of precision in specifying ideas and their relationships, they often fall short of this standard when they trace the implications of what they are doing. Their conclusions may or may not fit the class of ideas with which they began their inquiry. Their conclusions may also be too broad or too narrow for the individuals who would like to use them in order to solve problems in ongoing political settings.

Both coherence and precision are very important in political inquiry. Both are problems of logic as well as of levels of analysis that are normally not well specified in most research designs or in most teaching enterprises. Laying out the logic of a lecture may be as important to someone's teaching experience as specifying the research design is to a researcher inquiring about political life. In each case, both coherence and precision are twin elements of vital importance to political inquiry.

In Part I, we tackle these two important missing elements in most political inquiry. In Chapter 1, Bob Boynton focuses on coherence, while

Chapter 2, by Barbara Salert, focuses on precision. Both discussions add to our knowledge of the importance of these ideas and contribute ways of utilizing coherence and precision in research and teaching.

Missing Elements in Dynamic Models

Much of the contribution of dynamic models to political science has been to move us from static conceptions of politics to more interactive ones. Where research used to involve mostly static descriptions of the political world, we now deal with political change and do so with more than mere verbal descriptions. Dynamic models allow us to deal more with politics as it is, rather than as slices of reality that do not reflect the heartbeat of political life.

The definition of a dynamic model that will be used here involves two essential elements. First, we are concerned with change or potential change in relationships among individuals or groups. This potential for change involves a core aspect of dynamic models. In effect, politics is dynamic in the same way that human body functions are dynamic. Even when we are standing perfectly still to pose for a picture, biologically we are not standing still at all. Cells are being created and others are dying, and lungs, heart, and stomach are functioning.

Dynamic models also involve a time element. Whenever someone deals with dynamics, they deal with changes in behavior from one time to another. The dynamic models that we talk about here refer to over-time models that reflect changes in attitudes and behaviors of individuals and their aggregate characteristics.

This definition leaves us wide open to discuss a great many types of dynamic models. The most common type is statistical, dealing with multi-variate equations tracing behaviors over time. Other kinds of dynamic models, however, deal with formal logic or with algebraic models that capture the structure and sequence of events over time. In their generic form, dynamic models of all types make similar types of contributions to our efforts to look at politics in terms of its changing elements.

Although there are a great many different types of dynamic models used in the discipline, few take into consideration the many dimensions of the dynamic elements of political life that must be taken into account in order to accurately describe a dynamic mechanism. Most models are simplistic and take into account extremely few variables. If we do not take into account all the dimensions that are parts of the dynamic, and if we do not find ways to accurately integrate those dimensions, then we can model only a "small" world, one that does not capture the true potential for the change of any set of political interactions.

When people do take into account multiple dimensions in political analysis, they often "count" those dimensions in the sense that they assume that relationships are additive. They provide a variable for social conditions and another for economic conditions and another for political decision making, for example. They then proceed to add these dimensions together in some kind of forced integration of a context for political change. Clearly, this tells us very little about the dynamic of political life even though it does take into account multiple dimensions that may influence the dynamic. Dynamic relationships in politics just are not, even occasionally, additive. Much more complex, integrative mechanisms are needed if dynamic models are to prove useful.

The central question regarding dynamic models is not whether or not to use them (although this is an important issue); it is one of process. We need to determine different ways in which the elements of the dynamic come together into something that evolves and changes in ways that describe the truly vital interactions that constitute the core of politics. Unless we can find integrative mechanisms for determining how the dynamic fits together, we are no better off than a person who has all of the parts to a new car and no knowledge of how the gears must fit together. Our problem is much more complex than that of building an automobile engine, but nonetheless, we often fall far short of simply determining which parts are necessary, let alone the relationships among those parts that will allow us to build a functioning automobile.

One example of this phenomenon is found in the voting behavior literature. Here we most often want to know how people are going to vote or why they vote the way they do. Multidimensional techniques examine and evaluate a wide array economic, social, and political factors. Political analysts often simply assign these different weights, and, in effect, add them up. What we really want to know is not how many factors there are or how they are weighted, but how they enter into and affect the decision of the person who is making the voting choice. In order to determine this, we must consider the behavior of the individual in a dynamic model with some knowledge of the dynamic mechanism: how the economic, social, and political dimensions enter into the individual's decision. We want more than a list; we want a set of parts that go together in order to produce a vote, and we want to know how those parts are interrelated.

To do this, we need to focus on behavior. We must seek a behavioral dimension in dynamic modeling. In this case, we need to know something about the nature of the decision process and how that person makes the decision to vote one way or another. Then we can identify the "choice" points in the individual's decision-making process and assign weights to these points, rather than assigning weights to economic, social, and political factors. This is a missing element in most dynamic modeling.

In effect, a dynamic model that considers behavior (in this case, decision-making behavior) would look like a series of prototypic decision trees. One decision tree might look radically different from another. There may be more choice points or fewer in different individuals' decision-making processes. Once the dynamic of this process is determined, we can then give weights to the choice points according to how variables figure in the individual's own decision-making process. Without this type of consideration, we cannot go much farther with dynamic models than we can with any other kind of analysis.

We need to look at dynamics from a point of view that examines the dynamics of the interaction of variables at different points in time when the nature of that interaction itself may change. This is why the "cone of mutual deterrence" described by Brito and Intriligator in Chapter 3 is so important. Where nations position themselves in this cone of mutual deterrence determines which type of decision tree they will use in making decisions about arms control. In effect, in mapping the behavioral dimension of dynamic models, Brito and Intriligator have given us a way to distinguish different types of decision trees and to determine what the nature of the dynamic will be, depending on where nations fall in the cone.

A very important missing piece in the puzzle of dynamic mechanisms is found by exploring the structure of decision-making behaviors. Chapter 3 represents a beginning of this exploration, bringing us one step closer to finding out which integrative mechanisms drive political behavior. The ultimate goal is to develop several logics of behavior that will serve to guide inquiry in a wide range of political activities.

Once the structural dimensions have been mapped and the dynamics of processes are understood, subprocesses need to be considered. Basically, we are talking about interactions between two or more parties that themselves can change in their own dynamic over time. It is one thing to map a nation or an individual in a cone of deterrence; it is another thing to place two individuals or two nations within this cone and to determine the ongoing interactions among those units of analysis. This puzzle involves both logic and levels of analysis.

In Chapter 4, Zinnes et al. map these kinds of interactions. An interaction is a situation in which A and B enter into some type of relationship. There are basically two kinds of motivating factors in this interaction: independent and dependent. For example, A is not feeling well or B just won a million dollars in a sweepstakes. These events are really *independent* of A and B's relationship, and yet they motivate the interaction in important ways. In contrast, motivations can result from the ongoing interaction between A and B: A is angry at B or B is in love with A. These are *dependent* factors. The point is that an explanation must take into account both the independent and dependent motivating forces for the interaction in order for a dynamic model to capture any of the true interactions that go on between two or more parties.

Once we consider the independent reasons for interactions, we run into a problem of levels of analysis: identifying the actor that we are talking about. If A is an individual, then we can talk about individual motivations. If A is an aggregate, such as a nation-state, then representing that aggregate in terms of independent motivations creates an entirely different set of problems. Therefore, in identifying the independent component of any interaction, it is important to specify the level of analysis and to make sure that the interactions that are being studied do not violate the basic principles of studying interactions across multiple levels. The point is that to understand the basic interaction, one must take the internal factors of the individual or group into account.

The external factors are what we normally look at. They can be relatively well specified. Actor A sends a message to actor B and actor B returns another message. These types of interactions have been studied extensively in communications theory as well as international relations.

The basic missing element is that there are also interactions among the internal and external factors that motivate any given actor or actors in a situation. These interactions have not been adequately identified by anyone using dynamic models to date. In effect, the missing element in the puzzle is not the interaction itself, but particular aspects of that interaction that have not been well studied. While we can identify factors in the interaction between nation-states, we have rarely been able to discover the basic dynamic of the relationship between internal and external factors entering into the interaction.

The chapter by Zinnes et al. on crisis interactions represents an initial step toward resolving this problem. The authors generate a series of dynamic models that look at both internal and external factors in decision making. The final model that is presented provides some basic steps for looking at the dynamic of the relationship between internal and external factors. Should this line of inquiry be pursued further, our dynamic models would become much more convincing and our conclusions much more representative of the real dynamics of political activity.

The basic missing elements in dynamic models involve consideration of the integration of behaviors into the structure of political processes and the consideration of internal and external factors in interactions across units of analysis. Most of our exploration of these issues to date has been very superficial. We need to give a harder look at the nature of dynamic models and to pay careful attention to how we elaborate the structure of behaviors and describe the internal and external factors that motivate these behaviors.

The major contribution that dynamic models make, especially if these missing elements are taken into account, is to allow us to understand much more of the interactive process of political activity than otherwise would be the case. The chapters in Part II provide some of the essential elements of dynamic models that are critical to any exploration in political inquiry. They pinpoint these elements in actual studies and will provide us with important insights for research and teaching.

Missing Elements in Linkage Models

Parts I and II focus more on general puzzles about the logic of political inquiry than on the problem of levels of analysis. Questions about levels of analysis are core puzzles of linkage models. For our purposes a linkage model will be defined as any model that maps interactions between two units of analysis. Normally, linkage models stress national units and trade, aid, military, social, or educational types of linkages. However, almost any model is a linkage model if it seeks to map interactions between two units of analysis, regardless of their level of aggregation or complexity.

In linkage models, two units of analysis can be at the same level. We can decide to study two nation-states or two clubs or two states within the United States. Usually, the units that are mapped in linkage models are aggregates, that is, they are treated as individual units of analysis although they are made up of an aggregate of many individual behaviors. One of the basic steps involved in constructing linkage models is to identify the nature of the aggregate. This is very difficult since we do not know the relationship between individual behaviors and aggregate outcomes. Although nation-states are a well-defined geographical unit, they do not tell us anything about the range of opinions and characteristics of individual members of that nation-state.

The puzzle becomes more complex when the two *units* of analysis in a linkage model are at different *levels* of analysis. When we attempt to connect individual behaviors within one nation-state, for example, with behaviors of another nation-state as an aggregate, we encounter problems of composition and aggregation. In effect, we are attempting to map a single unit or composite in one case, with some subsection of an aggregate composed of many individuals. The linkages can be diverse and differentially motivated.

As if these problems were not severe enough, we have, within the last few decades, begun to talk about units that are not geographically or individually defined, but are defined in terms of interactions. In effect, we are talking about transnational relationships or transunit relationships at the microlevel, which are really a set of interactions. The interactions themselves define the unit of analysis. When we are looking at transnational economic relationships, we are looking, basically, at a set of interactions defined not by particular nation-states, but by flows of money, materials, and credit. When we begin to talk about basic units of analysis that transcend geographical boundaries, even the lines defining these units can become blurred. The ability to solve problems created by the complexity of composition and aggregation is another major missing element in most political inquiry.

We can draw an analogy to the problem here. Let us suppose that our friend is buying a car. He or she must make a choice about which car to buy, including whether or not to buy an American car or a foreign car. We will ignore, for the moment, the question of American automobile parts being produced in foreign countries. Let us suppose that because of problems in getting parts with foreign cars and because our friend's local Chevy dealer is a good friend, he or she decides to "buy American." This is all well and good. We can understand the logic of the decision that was made by this individual and why the car was purchased; yet, the minute we attempt to generalize across an aggregate of individuals who are buying both American and foreign cars, we no longer have this advantage. We have a problem because the unit of analysis, let us say, car buyers in the United States, is a diverse aggregate and because the outcomes cannot be predicted by the preferences of a single individual. We have an additional problem in that "foreign" is a diverse aggregate also, so that the linkages between the individual buyer and the foreign aggregate are extremely complex. The key to the puzzle is the linkage between the individual and the subset of the automobile seller aggregate, which produces a decision to buy an American or a foreign car.

When one of the two units is not an individual or nation-state but a transnational aggregate, we encounter further problems (Rosenau, 1980). Let us suppose that one of the units we are looking at is an individual and another one is a transnational unit. We are looking at the individual's identification with transnational units in terms of citizenship. Actually, the individual is not linked to the entire transnational unit of the world or the globe or to a single nation-states but to some subset of those transnational characteristics. Perhaps the individual has an overwhelmingly positive impression of world trade relations and a negative one of world military activities. Based on this subset of possible transnational characteristics, the individual forms a negative attitude about transnational citizenship. A thorny question then arises, for although we may be able to link individuals and aggregate transnational interactions, we have no idea which subset of the multitude of characteristics the individual actually attaches his or her loyalty or opinions or dollars or future aspirations to, much less the *interaction* among those characteristics.

It is necessary to develop some composition rules that can link individuals to parts of aggregates in order to figure out which subset of characteristics is salient to the individual and how these characteristics interact. Those that are salient for one individual may not be for another. The composition rules must be extremely complex. Few people to date have attempted to figure out these basic logical links. In Chapter 5, Rosenau argues that we must come to some conclusions about the logic of the linkage between the individual and the transnational aggregate before we can begin to understand the changing nature of citizenship, trade relations, military activity, or any other kind of configuration of events in politics beyond the national level.

This brings us to an even more complex problem: that of the super-aggregate. This is the case in which we have multiple units linked in multiple transnational interactions at multiple levels of analysis, which we all know is the reality of this world. It is not unlike trying to figure out how to spell the word "antidisestablishmentarianism." Basically, we must divide up the word into syllables in order to understand it at all because the word is so complex that it cannot be characterized by any single spelling rule. Then, we must put those syllables together using multiple rules so that the sequence we arrive at is the one that spells the word that we are after. In considering superaggregates, we have no real conceptual framework within which to analyze multiple units related in multiple transnational interactions. Rosenau attempts to develop some of the conceptual ideas that are necessary in order to understand this complex set of interactions. Without basic aggregation and composition rules, our efforts will suffer from superficial, and probably wrongheaded, analysis of linkages between units.

What we need is a "sorting" process. We need to identify units and linkages and combinations of linkages. The key here is to develop a logic of aggregation that is not just quantitative, but qualitative. We need to be able to understand not only the number of links between units, but the kinds of links that are made and why they are made; without this understanding, we will never go beyond description to explanations of transunit behavior.

When we begin to seek explanations of linkages, we run into another puzzle. To take our previous example, negative attitudes about transnational citizenship may be partially attributable to attitudes about trade relations and military activities. To provide an explanation here we need to determine the interactions between these attitudes and their behavioral bases. Yet we also may find at least part of the explanation in the *sequence* of behaviors. An individual's negative or positive attitude about transnational citizenship may be partially due to whether or not trade opportunities are followed by domestic job opportunities. Both factors may be important, and their sequence may be even more important in the explanation of attitudes about transnational citizenship. Sequence, then, is an important missing link in the explanation of transunit behaviors and attitudes. Studying sequences can also help us see why these behaviors and attitudes change over time.

Changes in transunit behaviors and attitudes can have roots in many sources. The nature of the source may be key to understanding change. The source may lie in an individual, an aggregate, or a superaggregate, depending on which of these units we are analyzing. The determination of the key characteristics of the unit, in general, will help us to identify major sources for change. It is just a beginning, but we may see a behavior or attitude change due to the interaction between a characteristic of the unit and an outside event. The nature of the interrelationships between units may also be a key to understanding change. Once we have mapped the relationships, for example, between the individual and the aggregate, we then need to determine what the nature of that interrelationship is. Is a trade relationship, for example, a long-lasting, firm commitment or is it something that is new and relatively fragile? Can it be changed easily or only with difficulty? What makes the interrelationship strong or weak? Both historical analysis and examination of the points of contact in the interrelationship between the two units may be extremely important in helping to identify why transunit attitudes and behaviors change over time.

Nesvold presents in Chapter 6 a third possible source of change: the *sequence* of interactions (Gurr, 1980). This is another element that is often overlooked in linkage models. In effect, whether or not someone uses coercion prior to or after conflict may be the key to understanding violent behavior. The sequencing or order of events in crises or in peace or in trade relationships may in and of itself form the dynamic for understanding why behaviors change over time.

The nature of the change in linkages across units is probably related to all three of these sources: to the nature of the unit, to the interrelationships among units, and to the sequence or order of behaviors. The problem is to sort through these elements and to determine in any analysis which, if any, of these possible explanations best fits the phenomenon under study. More importantly, we may need to map more than what appear to us to be key characteristics: Some of the causes of a change in relationships may result not from the original interaction, but from these other elements. Therefore, a composite list of characteristics, interrelationships, and sequences is needed in order to understand the possible sources for change.

We need to map a set of potential sources as well as those that form the basis for interaction. Our original mapping may change to include more variables as we get into over-time analysis. The nature of the unit and its aggregate characteristics are important, but the sequence of behaviors is also important. In order for linkage models to be most effective in explaining interactions within and among nation-states or other units of analysis, we must consider these basic elements of aggregation and sequence in defining those models. Chapters 5 and 6 of this volume provide some initial conceptual mapping of the domain of these missing elements.

Missing Elements in Integrative Models

The idea of cumulation is a recurring topic of this volume. People concerned with a wide variety of specific topics in political inquiry are all concerned about the degree to which we can generalize from our research and link together general theories in political science. No matter how eclectic the discipline appears, cumulation matters to all of us.

It is possible to have cumulation without synthesis. If we were to measure how much cumulation and synthesis exist in the discipline at this time, we would probably discover that there is considerably more of the former than of the latter. We have a well-developed body of literature that, although not exactly cumulative in areas such as voting behavior and interstate interactions, is quite extensive, but there is little synthesis of theories based on multiple, disparate studies.

One of the reasons that our discipline lacks both cumulation and synthesis is that the requisites for the development of both are very tough. We are constantly reminded by summarizers of the field that we are dealing with human behavior and not with electrons or rocks and, there-fore, we are excused from the normal natural science requisites of theory development. Yet we often hold those requisites as standards, and mea-sured against these standards our work receives very low grades.

Casting the scientific method aside for the moment, probably the first requisite for cumulation and synthesis is the ability to generalize. Unfortunately, in most research that we pursue, we are interested in specific propositions about microscopic aspects of the discipline rather than fully generalizable theories. Lave and March, in their *Introduction to Models in the Social Sciences* (1975), provide a good example of developing generalizations in social science inquiry. When they talk about an observed pattern of friendship among college students, they start out with the observation that college students who are friends tend to live close to each other. The authors then attempt to build a model that will explain this event, speculate about several processes that might lead to this result, and test those processes. They come to the conclusion that college students come from similar backgrounds and have similar experiences, problems, and values. Therefore, pairs of college students who live near each other will have frequent opportunities for interaction and are likely to discover their common characteristics. Most of us would think this was already a generalizable theory, but not Lave and March. They go on to test the model in terms of neighborhood integration and in other settings. Finally, they extend the theory to include other similarities and differences in experiences and come to the conclusion that most people have sufficient experiences, problems, and values in common to be capable of being friends. (They can also differ and are capable of being enemies.) Pairs of people discover their common and differing characteristics through communication.

Indeed, Lave and March have come up with a general theory with which most research in communication and organization would agree. The real problem is that few of us extend our thinking, let alone our data analysis and experimentation, beyond the initial narrow limits of our investigation to generalize beyond the particular set of data with which we are working. We fail to have cumulation and synthesis in the discipline because we do not meet the first requisite of having truly generalizable theories.

Second, in order to have cumulation and synthesis, we must meet the requisite of linking together generalizations in a theoretical structure. In order to do this, we must combine elements of induction and deduction, logic and statistics, mathematics and matrix algebra. Doing this, however, is not easy when single propositions are tested by research or when the initial construct for the research study does not begin with a serious effort at developing some type of deductive theory. Too often, those of us who are funded to do research are pressed for a product well before we can take the time, let alone the effort, to think through a system of generalizations that if substantiated, would provide us with a theoretical model.

Finally, we normally do not have cumulation and synthesis because we fail to include the bridging elements that are essential to any system of generalizations. In other words, we do not know the elements to add to or subtract from our analysis in order to provide a general synthesis. Without synthesis, however, cumulation in the discipline is relatively meaningless and the kinds of very general theories of human behavior to which Lave and March refer are not found because the dynamic is neither sought for nor possible because of the way we have stated previous generalizations.

In previous research, we have rarely met any of these three requisites. The question "Why?" is worth exploring, at least briefly. Basically, we do not do these things because we have almost as many perspectives or quasi-theoretical frameworks in the discipline as we have people. The ability to generalize beyond one's own work to include the work of others is simply not part of the general intellectual millieu of political science. Because we are eclectic and isolated, there are very large holes in the scope of a field of study. We study some things about judicial behavior and not others and, therefore, when it comes to providing for a general theory of judicial behavior, we are stuck because there are holes that need to be filled before we can get to the point where linking generalizations makes sense. If we cannot generalize, then we cannot get to the first step in cumulation. We have to see others' perspectives, understand their research, and have some sense of the scope of the field of inquiry in which we are interested.

We also do not generalize because we do not start out with what Lave and March would call nouns and verbs that are generalizable. If we cannot extend our descriptions of the types of political actors that we study to include the public in general, then we cannot make very general statements about classes of individuals who fit into our theories. If we cannot find ways of describing behaviors in generic terms, then true generalizations will not result.

We also cannot generalize if we use only one experiment. If we collect or utilize only one set of data in our analysis, we cannot expect to have tests of the experiment that are valid across different types of populations. Most research studies use a narrow range of types of individuals and experiments in order to test whether propositions are true. This is because voters, for example, are classified narrowly, and most voting theories that could relate to human decision making are focused on voting behavior only. Data is collected that is relevant to the vote which, if generalized, might be relevant to whole sets of aggregate decision-making processes in large groups, both local and national.

Finally, we cannot generalize if our data base is so weak that we cannot provide coherence between our basic generalizations and the data that we gather in order to test those generalizations. A good example of this is found in institutional political research that focuses on Congress, the presidency, and the Supreme Court. Because of the protection surrounding current public officials, those wishing to get hard data are often foiled by their inability to get them at the point at which they want to test their generalizations. Yet there are natural laboratories for testing political propositions outside of Capitol Hill that are underutilized by political scientists. Schools are a good example of institutions that exhibit a great many of the characteristics of macropolitical institutions; yet, the data base in school politics research is underutilized by those wishing to test propositions other than those related to socialization theories.

Furthermore, if we are to link generalizations, then we first must find a language that allows us to develop the composition rules that will link together our generalizations. That language may be logical or mathematical or statistical, but without some kind of formalization, it is difficult to imagine linking generalizations into true theoretical constructs. We lack the practice at linking generalizations because so few political scientists pursue languages that allow them to develop theoretical structures.

Krislov surveys this need in Chapter 7 and finds some places where cumulation has occurred and others in which there are huge gaps. He outlines where we need to go and concludes that we need to develop linkages between generalizations and to focus on the composition rules that will allow us to tie together some currently established sets of research studies.

Let us suppose that we could derive some body of generalizations that were interrelated and had achieved cumulation. We would then need to be able to produce concepts and mechanisms that would allow us to link these bodies of generalizations together, in other words, to synthesize. There are a great many reasons why we do not have synthesis in the discipline, the major one being that we have not taken the necessary preliminary steps.

We do not have synthesis because we do not often consider the macrostructure surrounding the theories that we construct. Vincent Ostrom, in Chapter 8, illustrates one kind of concept—constitutional choice—that demonstrates how institutional arrangements can serve as a macrostructure for considering the way polities perform. Institutional arrangements, then, become a key for synthesis in the discipline in important ways. Because they have been ignored in many studies, their advantages will be elaborated here.

Institutional arrangements help us, of course, to see the parameters of the study we are undertaking. We might argue, for example, that voting behavior is defined by party identification and candidate appeal. However, the institutional arrangements through which the individual is voting can have a major impact on which variables have salience in the voting process. By failing to identify major institutional arrangements, we also fail to identify the major context or constructs through which behavior takes place. We argue here that it is this set of parameters that serves as the major source of linkage between alternative theories of voting behavior and political behavior in other areas.

Institutional arrangements also provide a set of rules governing behavior that helps us to identify the mechanism or dynamic of political life. Therefore, we can utilize institutional arrangements to determine why there are similarities or differences in political behavior in different institutional settings.

Institutional arrangements provide a means for revealing the mechanism that is the source of the synthesis across theoretical bodies of knowledge. If we understand, for example, the structure of rules that limit and produce behavior in a type of institution, we can look at the nexus of those rules or at the mechanism for the system and link it through composition rules to the mechanism of other types of institutional arrangements. In effect, we have two wheels, and the cogs in the wheels are the institutional arrangements; the differential can be connected between the two wheels as a way of synchronizing and synthesizing because we have the source that can drive the wheels both forward or backward. Institutional arrangements can fulfill this very real need in theory building in political analysis.

Ostrom focuses on the constitutional level of analysis and institutional arrangements that are related to constitutional choice. This tradition has not been linked to other traditions examining, for example, the behavior of the president versus the Congress or the relationships among institutions of government. The constitutional level of analysis can bridge disparate studies of behavior and organizational functioning to provide us with an understanding of the mechanism that links constitutional theory at the national and state levels or across nations. We can develop through the study of constitutional choice some generic kinds of generalizations that can be linked together to form a general theory of human behavior. This is because the constitutional level is general enough and at the same time, provides sufficient parameters and rules for us to be able to define those composition laws that interrelate behaviors at the macrolevel.

Ostrom's argument is a powerful one. It is certainly true at the constitutional level of analysis in American politics, but it is also true at any level and for any group under study. The same type of thinking and analysis could link together interest groups in a community or family groups and aggregates such as voters. The point is that by including basic institutional arrangements in the analysis of American politics at any level, or international politics generally, our hope for synthesis in the discipline is strengthened by the consideration of macrovariables that provide mechanisms for linking together series of theories.

Thus, to be truly integrative, we must include both cumulation and synthesis. This is a tough charge for a "young" discipline. We must deal with human beings and not with plants or rocks and, therefore, it is also a complex and difficult charge; yet, if we were to advance in these directions and to motivate our research with some of these ideas, we would be closer to general theories of political behavior than we are to date.

Implications for Theory, Research, and Teaching

Throughout this introduction, we have identified a wide range of missing elements in political inquiry including more specifically coherence and precision, structure and interaction, aggregation and sequence, and cumulation and synthesis. It is hard to tell what the study of political science would look like if these elements were in place in our everyday research and teaching. Here, however, we will speculate about what might happen if these elements were fully elaborated.

First of all, there would be a change in the values of those who do research. Research puzzles would be chosen a bit differently. Our values would focus on cumulation and bridging previous inquiries with new ones in order to develop theory in the discipline. We would not choose specific research topics based on particular and distinctive interests that delineate a given political scientist in the field, but rather, we would choose with an eye toward the scope of the field and the needs for the development of bridging ideas and data analyses. This would constitute a basic change in values for most of us doing political inquiry.

There would be a renewed emphasis on the development of theory and how we think about problem solving. Political scientists would, first and foremost, be theorizers. Once a problem was pinpointed, the search would begin for key concepts that would serve to bring together scattered research, and the very nature of our research would be at least 50 percent dependent on the development of adequate theoretical structures.

As we considered the theoretical elements of our problem, we would be concerned, first and foremost, with the logic of our analysis. Forming deductive or inductive or statistical or mathematical structures would be paramount to the beginnings of any research enterprise. Modeling would serve as a major focus of the initial steps in the construction of a research design and the execution of a research project. We would, in effect, be testing deductions from theories as opposed to isolated propositions or sets of propositions about political behavior.

With regard to theory building, at least four major types of logical concerns would surface as paramount. The first would be the definition of terms used in the theory, i.e., precision in terms of adequately defining concepts and making sure that various meanings and interpretations across research studies were given careful consideration and delineation within the definition of major concepts. Precision would be one of the first concerns because without it, the development of key concepts could lead in multiple directions and interpretation of findings would be very difficult.

Another central concern would involve coherence. Once theoretical premises were adequately established, the link between theory and research would be paramount. Political scientists doing research would carefully articulate the relationship between the propositions they were testing and the methodologies and data base for determining the worth of these propositions. This concern goes beyond the basic logic of the argument to include the link between theory and data analysis.

Units of analysis would also be a primary concern. Both the definition of the unit and the consideration of levels of analysis are complex but important parts of the linkage between theory and data collection. Particular attention would be paid to organizational and interorganizational levels of analysis as a primary means for bridging various fields or particular inquiry studies. The "constitutional level" would be rejuvenated as a primary level of analysis. Experiments would be carefully designed in order to determine the relationship between institutional arrangements and political behavior. A major focus for research would be on both composition rules crossing levels of analysis and on comparisons made across multiple units of analysis.

Finally, there would be a concern for the dynamics of theory development and its relationship to theory, in terms of both interactions and over-time stages of development. The consideration of dynamics would go beyond standard concepts of change to include interactional patterns and the potential directions that they can take.

The renewed emphasis on theory and specific puzzles that help us to better define theory building would lead to a new emphasis in methods. Because of the emphasis in formalizing theoretical development, methodologies would stress new modeling techniques. Particular attention would be paid to mathematical modeling, which would enable us to capture more of the dynamics of interactions that we felt were key bridging ideas across research studies more precisely. Typical correlational and cross-unit methods would be replaced by more formal, more theoretical, and more mathematical methodologies that would suit the testing of propositions derived from theoretical structures.

Interpretations of our research would also change. They would stress cumulation of basic ideas in the discipline and possible new linkages across theories and research studies. Cumulation would be a central focus of most research efforts. This, again, would change the kinds of basic evaluations of the value of research studies as well as the kinds of conclusions that would be drawn about future possibilities for research and applications. In effect, a forecasting mode in terms of future research would help political scientists who apply their research to offer practical suggestions to policy-makers that would indicate more about both the dynamics and future directions of policies than the description of actual policy mechanisms. In the long run, both in terms of research and application, this focus on cumulation would bring stronger impetus to both the profession and practical applications.

Teaching would also be affected by this emphasis. It is important to discuss here because in the teaching that researchers do, new professionals are brought into the field and socialized according to changing values and theoretical perspectives. Therefore, as the changes occurred in theory and research, so teaching would take on new dimensions, both at the under-graduate and graduate levels.

First of all, teaching courses from the basic introductory course through the graduate level would have more of an emphasis on concepts and theories. The content of courses would, in effect, evolve around a set of concepts or theoretical approaches. Less concern would be given to description and more concern in terms of the ultimate objectives of teaching with theory and concept development. Students would need to be taught to work with concepts in precise and important ways, not only to improve their own everyday lives, but to move the profession toward a more conceptual orientation that would bridge across theoretical frame-works.

Another focus that would appear in teaching across levels would be the development of skills in analytical thinking. More effort would be made to teach students about the logic of arguments and how to think analytically. This would involve developing some basic skill teaching in undergraduate as well as graduate courses to ensure that the development of arguments as well as the development of theories would occur among all student populations taking political science courses.

An offshoot of this would involve the teaching of modeling at both the undergraduate and graduate levels. This occurs to some extent, but not to the full extent it would if we focused on cumulation in the discipline and on teaching students how to work with modeling situations. Of course, this type of skill development, both in analytical thinking and modeling, would involve the revision of basic textbooks used in courses and the inclusion of basic ideas from texts that were restricted to specific methods courses.

As coherence between theory and data became a chief concern of professionals, the teaching focus at both the undergraduate and graduate levels would change. Most undergraduates political science majors can avoid taking any data analysis or methods courses. This is a problem because this socialization pattern carries over to the graduate level. If major concerns in the discipline focused on the missing elements we have emphasized here, data analysis skills would be a significant part of teaching at all levels in political science.

It would be increasingly important for teachers to teach well, as it always is, but as they form a model for students, teachers would need to rethink the purposes for which they are teaching and, in turn, the model of a political scientist that they present to students. Teachers would integrate more research into their teaching and focusing more on theoretical development. Students' common perceptions of political science would change to that of a theoretical enterprise that had exciting kinds of cumulative potential and intellectual puzzles that would encompass many different fields and disciplines.

In fact, if all of this happened, there would be a veritable revolution in political science. The challenges would be largely puzzles of logic and levels of analysis, and students and professionals would develop models that would give the profession more useful tools than those common descriptive ones I used when I first came to Bloomington. In effect, the kinds of pursuits stressed here would dramatically change both research and teaching in political science. We have created this volume in answer to this challenge, and we hope it will stimulate the reader to think of these challenges and puzzles and to push his or her inquiry toward the goal of cumulation and synthesis in the discipline.

REFERENCES

GILLESPIE, J. A. (1978) School Case Study Research Project. Bloomington: Workshop in Political Theory and Policy Analysis, Indiana University.

GURR, T. R. [ed.] (1980) Handbook of Political Conflict. New York: Macmillan.

LANGER, S. K. (1967) An Introduction to Symbolic Logic. New York: Dover.

LAVE, C. A. and J. G. MARCH (1975) An Introduction to Models in the Social Sciences. New York: Harper & Row.

MILLER, T. (1977) "Conceptualizing inequality," pp. 334-350 in Marcia Guttentag and Shalom Saar (eds.) Evaluation Studies Review Annual, Vol. 2. Beverly Hills, CA: Sage.

ROSENAU, J. N. (1980) The Study of Global Interdependence. New York: Nichols.

PART I

Coherence and Precision in Formal Models

Introduction
Making Sense Out of a Muddle

ELINOR OSTROM

Some of my best memories of John Gillespie are of extended conversations about the state of the discipline of political science. Given John's deep interest in philosophy of science and his broad familiarity with the discipline, the lack of cumulation in political science preoccupied him.

In his chapter in this section, Bob Boynton provides an explanation for the lack of cumulation in political science. He argues that many general perspectives exist in political science but that they are not fully developed. Many of these perspectives are so broadly formulated that no specific interrelated set of hypotheses are directly derived from them. Thus, the general perspectives do not provide a specific rationale for empirical work. On the other hand, many empirical studies in political science are decidedly descriptive. These studies provide data about specific events or relationships but do not relate them to general propositions derived from a theoretical framework. The end result is a muddle:

> As a discipline we have descriptive propositions and we have general perspectives, but the perspectives and propositions are not as tightly connected as we feel they ought to be and the propositions do not cumulate as we feel they ought to. In these respects our work lacks coherence [Boynton, this volume].

Cumulation occurs in a discipline when empirical studies provide evidence that enables scholars to evaluate the validity and usefulness of alternative general perspectives or world views. While several general perspectives may remain in a cumulative discipline at any point in time, an examination of its past history will usually reveal the earlier elimination of some perspectives. One perspective is eliminated when another metaphysical view enables scholars to generate carefully formulated logical structures that explain all of the evidence presented by the eliminated perspective and more (see Watkins, 1975).

A cumulative discipline should be able to point to some metaphysical views previously accepted but now replaced by others judged to provide a more valid base for explanation. Some "dead" perspectives should have been cast off and eliminated. But if tight connections are not constructed linking metaphysics to logical structures and to empirical research, competing perspectives can continue to remain on equal footing. All that is learned from empirical work is specific time and place facts and relationships. Political science may have too many general perspectives retained on equal status and not enough "former" perspectives considered now to be inadequate.

But the key point Boynton makes is that empirical research alone is *not* the means to achieve cumulation. To make sense out of phenomena requires the development of languages adequate for the purpose of describing elements of interest and their relationships under specified conditions. Languages provide the connections between perspectives and descriptions—they help to provide what Boynton terms *coherence*. As long as research describes a wide variety of seemingly unique phenomena, we cannot develop languages to classify events by those aspects that they share in common (even though they are considerably different in other aspects) and by the principles that relate these events to one another. This is an important point made by Susanne Langer and reinforced by Bob Boynton in his important contribution to this volume. As Langer argued, it is often hard to understand how

a scientist has any chance whatever of reducing widely different things to the same category, because they look and "feel" so incommensurable, but he has found a principle by which he can describe them as two forms of one substance, and we are amazed to see how precisely and usefully he then relates them" [Langer, 1967: 26].

Notice that Langer stresses the importance of "finding a principle" by which a scientist can view widely different things as similar for the purpose of explanation, rather than for finding evidence. Language is the key link. Further, Langer argues that the definition of a concept or substance relates to a principle or theory. Events are clustered together as being the same thing depending upon organizing conceptual principles. The creative application of an organizing principle makes seeming incommensurables commensurable. Water and oil do not mix. They are considered different substances for most purposes. However, when one explains the flow of liquids in contained spaces like pipes, water and oil are both included as liquids whose behavior can be explained using the same theoretical laws. Which events are considered to be the same thing is the consequence of the theoretical language developed by scholars.

However, the process of developing a tight connection or theoretical structure between perspectives and empirical events—or coherence—is extremely difficult as Langer beautifully expressed in another volume.

> The process of philosophical thought moves typically from a first, inadequate, but ardent apprehension of some novel idea, figuratively expressed, to more and more precise comprehension, until language catches up to logical insight, the figure is dispensed with, and literal expression takes its place. Really new concepts, having no names in current language, always make their earliest appearance in metaphorical statements; therefore, the beginning of any theoretical structure is inevitably marked by fantastic inventions [Langer, 1951: vi].

Many "fantastic inventions," which Boynton calls perspectives, have been articulated by political theorists. However, the language of political science has not in most cases advanced as far as the logical insights of those who first apprehended novel ideas and expressed them figuratively. Thus an important task of those concerned with developing a cumulative political science is the development of adequate languages for expressing principles derived from general metaphysical perspectives in such a manner that empirical research can examine the validity of propositions derived from those perspectives. This need for an appropriate set of languages in political science leads to three central questions to be addressed in this section:

(1) What are the roles of formal languages in the study of political phenomena?

(2) What are the possible types of relationships between models that are utilized in political science and the phenomena that are studied?

(3) What new insights can be contributed by the use of formal languages and models in political science?

Boynton addresses primarily the first and third questions in his chapter. He argues that formal languages, because of their overt logical rules, are an important mechanism bridging perspectives and empirical research to enable genuine cumulation to occur in political science. Formal languages first require a scholar to think in terms of general categories abstracted from the specific names used in a particular time and place. Furthermore, they may require a scholar to think about ways of articulating the form of the relationships among general categories. X and Y may be "related," but a key question is what is the form of that relationship. While one can formalize an argument and keep this question open, most formal languages require the theorist to specify a particular form.

It is this specification that is essential prior to the conduct and analysis of empirical research. Without it empiricists have found all too frequently that X and Y are not "related" because of the way they have specified the form of the relationship for statistical analysis. Given the complexity of interacting variables of interest to political scientists, the likelihood that all variables are related through simple linear additive relationships is extremely low, but this has been the primary way such relationships have been examined in most empirical work in political science. Until we focus on "*how*" variables are related and not simply *that* they are related, the coherence that Boynton and others seek may continue to be the political scientist's holy grail.

Salert's effort is one of conceptual clarification and primarily addresses the second and third questions. The term "threshold" has been used in a number of different ways in social science. Salert begins the difficult task of sorting out the many ways. She illustrates the power of exploring theoretical questions to organize our understanding of the world. In the process she enables us to see how a number of seemingly unrelated phenomena may be similar in the sense that a similar type of *process* is at work. Joining a social movement, leaving a neighborhood, and voting for a candidate are all seemingly different actions. They look and feel incommensurable. But Salert shows us that they are all discrete acts that may be taken when the value of some event (or complex of events) has reached a threshold that triggers one action or another. Looking at these disparate types of phenomena as if they were forms of one substance, we may be amazed to see how usefully Salert helps us to relate them.

Once she establishes the substance, Salert then clarifies two very different types of thresholds—individual thresholds and aggregate thresholds. She demonstrates the differences in these types of thresholds and their implications in empirical research. The precision with which she develops these definitions allows her to capture the basic dimensions of the concept of threshold and to draw implications consistent with her original conceptualization. In so doing, Salert confronts the missing element of precision in the definition of concepts and problems associated with levels of analysis. Out of a generic definition, then, come two different types of thresholds, each with a different implication, depending on the level of analysis that is being studied. Precision adds an important element to the coherence that Salert is seeking and allows us to see both the generic and particular variations of the concept of threshold.

Both Boynton and Salert demonstrate the value of formal languages in political theory and pinpoint the missing elements of coherence and precision. They are working on the development of theoretical structures that can tightly connect general perspectives to empirical research. Their work and others doing similar work is helping provide some of the essential links for a cumulative political science.

REFERENCES

LANGER, S. K. (1967) An Introduction to Symbolic Logic. New York: Dover Publications.
——— (1951) Philosophy in a New Key. New York: Mentor.
WATKINS, J.W.N. (1975) "Metaphysics and the advancement of science." British Journal for the Philosophy of Science 26: 92-121.

1

Linking Problem Definition and Research Activities

Using Formal Languages

G. R. BOYNTON

Several years ago I spent a considerable amount of time talking to political scientists about cumulation in our discipline (Boynton, 1976). I argued that the accumulation of tools that had become part of our repertoire and the propositions we had advanced (some to be rejected) constituted cumulation. I still believe that argument is correct, but I had no luck "selling" it to the political scientists with whom I talked. Their conception of cumulation incorporated more than a collection of propositions more or less adequately supported. Specifically, they were not happy about the incoherence of the propositions. They argued that a collection of propositions was not enough. There had to be intellectual coherence, and that is what they found missing.

Perspectives provide coherence, at least that is their putative role. Political science has had its share of perspectives; remember Almond, Dahl, Deutsch, Easton, and others. With the exception of "positive theory," however, all of these perspectives seem to be on the wane; they are no longer frequently cited in research publications. And there seems to be nothing arising to take the place of these perspectives of a past decade. Empirical political science has slipped into empiricism. Research reports are replete with findings, but they do not cohere. Lacking any clear vision of how to produce coherence, we continue to produce substantiated descriptive propositions.

The Problem

The problem I would like to address in this chapter arises within the empirical tradition of political science. The nature of the problem can be summarized in the following propositions.

(1) The potential for description of interesting political phenomena is infinite.
(2) We have been very good at developing (largely via the route of borrowing from other disciplines) perspectives that provide an overview for ordering these phenomena.
(3) The perspectives or overviews have rarely, if ever, been effectively integrated with the research enterprise. Research and perspective go their separate ways, joined only in the first paragraphs of research papers.

There is no dearth of empirical work to be done. Each day brings new phenomena that are a challenge to our ability to adequately describe them. There is a certain reassurance in this; we are not going to run out of a job in the near future. However, the wane of the old perspectives and the failure of new perspectives to arise to replace the old has left much of our empirical work with a very descriptive air. Even work that was or is oriented by the perspectives we have utilized is not tightly tied to the perspectives. It has been, at best, difficult to derive hypotheses from the perspectives.

The result is a muddle. Research topics are chosen either because we have "always" investigated the topic or because they are currently important in our political world. Conceptualization of research and statements of hypotheses are largely ad hoc. Research accumulates, we know more, but the findings are inadequately integrated. And conceptualization on a broader level neither guides nor is guided by the ongoing descriptive efforts of the discipline.

I do not mean to denigrate the importance of either description or perspective. We need both, but we badly need them to be joined more effectively. I believe that this is the paramount problem, at this moment in history, for the political science I am interested in pursuing. We need to learn how to theorize in a fashion that more effectively integrates perspectives (ideas) and description.

Let me restate the problem. The problem is the development of a cumulative body of knowledge about political phenomena. For many political scientists this development has not been as rapid as they would have liked. As a discipline we have descriptive propositions and we have general perspectives, but the perspectives and propositions are not as tightly connected as we feel they ought to be and the propositions do not cumulate as we feel they ought to. In these respects our work lacks coherence. In this chapter I suggest that assistance in solving this problem is to be found in using formal languages.

The suggestion I have for bringing ideas and description into a more intimate relationship involves a reorientation of our understanding of theorizing as an activity within the research process. In particular, I will try to show how and where formal languages play a crucial role in a theoretical activity that is able to generate hypotheses that can be empirically tested. I will try to show that the use of formal languages facilitates our ability to join perspectives and empirical findings in a coherent manner.

I will begin with a characterization of theorizing drawn from Susanne Langer's *An Introduction to Symbolic Logic* (1967). I will then show how this characterization of theorizing leads quite naturally to the use of formal languages. This will be followed by a case study, a reworking of a specific piece of research on the incidence of war among nations. Finally, I will suggest wherein lies the utility of formal languages, and what we cannot expect them to do for us.

Theorizing

Susanne Langer gives the following characterization of theorizing:

> Often it is hard to believe that a philosopher or a scientist has any chance whatever of reducing widely different things to the same category, because they look and "feel" so incommensurable, but he has found a principle by which he can describe them as two forms of one substance, and we are amazed to see how precisely and usefully he then relates them [1967: 26].

> Whenever we may truly claim to have a science, we have found some principle by which different things are related to each other as just so many forms of one substrate, or material, and everything that can be treated as a new variation belongs to that science [Langer, 1967: 23].

The key word in this characterization of science is principle. There is a principle that, by its use, brings coherence to the phenomena gathered together in the science. I would like to explicate this use of principle by suggesting three aspects of its meaning in this context.

The first aspect of principle as it is used here is *perspective*. It is only from a particular perspective that all of the phenomena can be seen to be something other than an unrelated collection of disparate events. "See all of this as a system." "See all of this as the result of independent individuals each maximizing their utilities." The perspective points to a way of seeing the incommensurable as commensurable. Surely this was the importance of the work of Easton or Almond or Schattschneider or Edelman. In each case they provided a perspective that helped political scientists see apparently disparate phenomena as one. When Langer says that "he has found a principle by which he can describe them as two forms of one substance," she must surely have meant something like Almond's assertion that rule making goes on in any polity no matter how differently located in institutional structures.

The second aspect of principle is *boundary*. One has to be able to distinguish what is appropriately included within the "science" and what is to be excluded. Not everything will be seen as one, falling under the principle; there will also be phenomena that are excluded. Exclusion as well as inclusion is derived from the principle. Defining the stuff of a particular "science" is a theoretical act, a matter of principle.

The third aspect of principle to be noted is *structure*. In the two quotations above Susanne Langer uses the word "form" as that in which commonality is to be found. In another passage she discusses the meaning of form [Langer, 1967: 24].

> The bridge that connects all of the various meanings of form—from geometric form to the form of ritual or etiquette—is the notion of structure. The logical form of a thing is the way that thing is constructed, the way it is put together. Anything that has a definite form is constructed in a definite way.

Form or structure is the way a thing is put together. Perhaps an example will help clarify the meaning of "put together" in the context of political research. A subject is identified for study, say war. Wars are fought between nations. At any time a given nation is either at war with some other nation or combination of nations or it is not at war. At a subsequent point in time this nation is either at war or not at war. With this specification of the situation, the relevant possible states have been defined. One would like to find a rule that specifies the transition between states (war or not war) from time 1 to time 2. If one can find such a rule, the form or structure of the situation will have been discovered. One should not be misled by the use of "rule" in the singular. Different nations find themselves in different conditions, and the rule one is looking for must surely be flexible enough to incorporate some of these conditions that prove to be relevant. Thus, the rule(s) will have to differentiate nations by conditions at time 1 in order to specify war or not war at time 2.

What is the appropriate form in political research? It must be something like: given this and this and this, that should follow. It is the form of an argument; from these premises this conclusion can be deduced. From this specification of conditions one would expect this nation to be at war (or not at war) during the next time period. And this is precisely the point at which formal languages can be most helpful. The point of a formal language (other than intrinsic interest) is to facilitate deductions or long chains of reasoning.

Here is what is being suggested. One aspect of principle is form or structure, that is, the way things are put together. In understanding political events, the "put together" can be summarized by a rule. This rule takes the form of premises from which further statements can be derived (hypotheses). To the extent to which this rule can be stated in a formal language, derivation of "further statements" is facilitated.

We need to learn how to theorize in a fashion that more effectively integrates perspectives (ideas) and description. That identifies the problem. How does Susanne Langer's characterization of theorizing, and more specifically, how is form or structure, a solution to this problem? The theorizing in political science to which I have alluded included perspective; it suggested a way of looking at disparate phenomena as though they were one. What was not included in these perspectives was rules that specified *how* the phenomena were "put together." Since there were no rules incorporated in the perspectives, no hypotheses could be derived and tested. If one starts with description one gets the reverse problem. There are statements that are tested, but the collection of these statements does not cohere. The answer is a statement of perspective that includes rules from which hypotheses can be derived, and this is facilitated if one uses formal languages.

Wars, Reinforcement, and More Wars

In a recent paper, Most and Starr (1980) suggest that the occurrence of a war at one point may be related to the incidence of war at a previous or subsequent period.

The notion that an event may alter the probability of subsequent events through diffusion or contagion processes is not new. The work of scholars on a variety of topics suggests that wars may also diffuse [Most and Starr, 1980: 932].

They go on to specify the subject of their analysis in the following way:

The general war diffusion hypothesis concerns the possibility that the occurrence of one new war participation will alter the probability of subsequent occurrences. It is helpful, however, to disaggregate this general hypothesis in order to distinguish the four following diffusion-related processes:

- Positive Reinforcement: The process in which the occurrence of a new war participation in a nation increases the likelihood that the same nation will experience subsequent war participations;
- Negative Reinforcement: The process in which the occurrence of a new war participation in a nation decreases the likelihood that the same nation will experience subsequent war participations;
- Positive Spatial Diffusion: The process in which the occurrence of a new war participation in a nation increases the likelihood that other nations will experience subsequent war participations; and,
- Negative Spatial Diffusion: The process in which the occurrence of a new war participation in a nation decreases the likelihood that other nations will experience subsequent war participations [Most and Starr, 1980: 933].

I would like to review the Most-Starr paper, specifically that part of the paper about positive and negative reinforcement. The review will serve as a case study in formal analysis. I chose this paper because of the interesting perspective the authors take on the incidence of war, and because it seemed to lend itself readily to formal treatment. I will attempt to faithfully summarize their argument, add some to the argument, and show that the formalization of the argument yields a set of hypotheses that are consistent with the paper, and that go beyond what is presented there.

Most and Starr begin their analysis with some assumptions about nations engaging in war:

Some initial assumptions can be made about the possible linkages between a nation's own war experiences at one time and some subsequent time:

1. The decision makers in any nation are confronted by an "operational milieu" (Sprout and Sprout, 1965, p. 30) that comprises the risks and opportunities that effectively impinge on the nation in question;
2. The operational milieu (and hence, the perceived risks and opportunities) may change through time, and such changes may induce decision makers to reassess their situations;
3. If decision makers are to protect themselves from the risks or avail themselves of the opportunity they perceive in their environment, they must possess both the capacity and the willingness to do so (Starr, 1978); and
4. Just as changes in decision makers' operational milieus may alter their perceptions of the risks and opportunities, changes in the perceived environment may also result in changes in decision makers' willingness to undertake particular policies in response to the risks and opportunities confronting them.

The importance of these assumptions can be demonstrated by considering Boulding's "theory of viability" (Boulding, 1964). Focusing on zones in which a nation is dominant ("unconditionally viable") and dominated ("conditionally viable), Boulding argues that a nation will increase its defense expenditures in an effort to expand the first area and contract the second. Decisions to arm or disarm at one time thus have some effect on a nation's zones of unconditional and conditional viability at some later time.

The point to be noted, of course, is that an armaments decision is only one factor that may alter a nation's zones of unconditional and conditional viability, and hence, its decision makers' perceptions of risks and opportunities [Most and Starr, 1980: 933-934].

This describes decision makers as operating in an environment of risks and opportunities, and as attempting to increase internal and external viability.

We are given a definition of positive and negative reinforcement and a description of how national decision makers operate within the environment in which war or not-war comes about. These two characterizations of the process do not yet fit neatly together. One manifestation of this "nonfit" is implicit in the test for positive and negative reinforcement. If positive reinforcement "worked," then every nation that was at war initially would also be at war subsequently or the reverse for negative reinforcement. But there is no way to identify nations on which positive (or negative) reinforcement is at work, and one can only look at the results of the transition from time 1 to time 2 to attempt to estimate if either of these processes is at work. We know what the outcome of the process should be: enhanced probability of war or not-war. But the "structure" or "form" of the process is not specified, and, therefore, we cannot specify the nations on which the process ought to be operating.

I would like to use this characterization of national decision making to build a simple structure of positive reinforcement. The result should be a specification of the types of nations that should be at war or not at war at time 2.

Positive reinforcement will operate only on nations that are at war at time 1 and thus are predicted to be at war at time 2. I will use WAR-1 and WAR-2 to represent a nation being at war at time 1 and time 2.

It is hard to understand what it would mean to say that a nation received positive reinforcement from losing a war. There may be reasons that a nation that loses a war at one point is more likely to go to war at a subsequent time, but surely the reasons would not involve what is ordinarily considered positive reinforcement. Thus, winning or not winning must enter into the construction of the structure; let WIN-1 represent this.

The effect of winning a war is very likely to be enhanced internal and external viability, which is the goal postulated for decision makers. Let EIEV represent this.

Having learned that enhanced internal and external viability result from winning wars, decision makers should be looking for subsequent opportunities to realize this goal; SEEK will represent this. The world does not necessarily fit itself to the designs of decision makers, and they may not search successfully. FIND will be used to represent a successful search.

These are all of the terms or propositions (or variables) needed for the structure of positive reinforcement that will be suggested. The formal language to be used is the propositional calculus. Its advantage, in this context, is that it is simple enough to be readily understood but has enough deductive capability to produce hypotheses from the structure. Propositions take only one of two values (true or false, win or not win, and so forth) in the propositional calculus, but that does not seem to do serious violence to this subject.

The first proposition: *A country that engages in a war and wins has its internal and external viability enhanced.*

(1) WAR-1 and WIN-1, then EIEV.

The second proposition: *Enhanced internal and external viability lead to seeking similar opportunities to further enhance internal and external viability.*

(2) EIEV, then SEEK.

The third proposition: *If a country searches for opportunities to enhance its internal and external viability and is successful, then it will engage in war.*

(3) SEEK and FIND, then WAR-2.

These are three simple propositions. I believe they reflect, more or less faithfully, the argument of Most and Starr's paper. At least, on the basis of reading the paper, this is the structure of positive reinforcement as I understand it. And it will generate deductions.

In addition to the basic structure of positive reinforcement, one needs to add some assumptions about the situation of a given nation. First, assume that the country had been at war at time 1 and was successful. Second, assume that it found what appeared to be an opportunity to enhance its internal and external viability through war. With these assumptions one can deduce that the country will engage in war at time 2.

(1)	WAR-1 and WIN-1, then EIEV	
(2)	EIEV, then SEEK	
(3)	SEEK and FIND, then WAR-2	
(4)	WAR-1 and WIN-1	Assumption
(5)	FIND	Assumption
(6)	EIEV	1,4 Modus Ponens
(7)	SEEK	2,6 Modus Ponens
(8)	SEEK and FIND	5,7 Conjunction
(9)	WAR-2	3,8 Modus Ponens

This structure of positive reinforcement produces war given the appropriate assumptions. However, one would be very surprised if it failed this test since it was specifically designed to do this. There are other less direct tests that the structure should be able to pass.

One would not want to assert that every war was the result of positive reinforcement. A nation may be more or less minding its own business and be invaded, for example. This suggests that the structure of positive reinforcement should not predict that a nation would not be at war if positive reinforcement was not at work. If the condition WAR-1 were not true, then positive reinforcement surely would not be operating. But one would not want to be able to deduce, on the basis of not WAR-1, that the nation was not at war (not WAR-2). Unless one can assume that a nation may or may not be at war when positive reinforcement is not operating, it is impossible to assume that spatial diffusion (another hypothesis of the Most-Starr paper) could be operative. This is a characteristic of this suggested structure of positive reinforcement. Unless WAR-1 and WIN-1 are assumed, nothing can be deduced from the structure. Unless FIND is assumed, WAR-2 cannot be deduced. When at least one of WAR-1 or WIN-1 or FIND is not true, one can only assume that the nation may or may not be at war. Thus, "room" is left for other possible explanations of war.

There is a related question that can be addressed given this structure. If a nation was at war at time 1, but is not at war at time 2, what can one assume must be the case?

(1)	WAR-1 and WIN-1, then EIEV	
(2)	EIEV, then SEEK	
(3)	SEEK and FIND, then WAR-2	
(4)	WAR-1 and WIN-1	Assumption
(5)	not WAR-2	Assumption
(6)	WAR-1 and WIN-1, then SEEK	1,2 Hypothetical Syl
(7)	not (SEEK and FIND)	3,5 Modus Tollens
(8)	SEEK	6,4 Modus Ponens
(9)	not SEEK or not FIND	7 DeMorgan
(10)	not FIND	9,8 Disjunctive Syl

This deduction produces two hypotheses that are, within the limits of measurement, testable. One, the nations should have been looking for an opportunity to engage in war (proposition 8). Two, the nations were not able to find a good opportunity (proposition 10).

There are a few more things one could do with this rather simple structure, but that would be beside the point. The point is to see this as an illustration of a mode of theorizing that brings perspective and description together. I suggested that in political science we have had a number of perspectives and a considerable amount of description, but that the two were not joined with the result that there is a feeling of incoherence in our product.

In this case the perspective involves seeing war participation at two time periods as being related, at least some of the time, through positive reinforcement. We know, in a general way, what positive reinforcement is, and we can specify what the outcome should look like if the process is operating in a given setting. When we look at the world (do our empirical research) we cannot specify very well when positive reinforcement is at work and when it is not. And I suggested that this was the result of not having worked out the structure of positive reinforcement in this particular context. I suggested three propositions that I believe could be construed as representing the structure of positive reinforcement for this case. From these propositions and empirical descriptions of specific cases one can generate the deductions given in the Most and Starr paper plus some qualifications and additional propositions.

From this perspective embodied in this structure, testable hypotheses (propositions) flow (can be deduced). Each of the propositions is related to the perspective through the deductive structure. That yields coherence.

Another Perspective

A single perspective will not exhaust everything one can or will want to know about a subject. To illustrate the use of another formal language and how what one learns differs from the previous analysis, I will suggest another perspective on the problem dealt with in the Most-Starr paper.

Most and Starr suggest that in the transition from time 1 to time 2, the forces operating are the net effects of positive and negative reinforcement and positive and negative diffusion. Rather than looking at the consequences of these assumptions for which nations are at war at a given time, I would like to look at the effects of these assumptions on the number of wars that occur at a given time and how the number of nations at war changes over time. I should note that this is a different problem from the one posed by Most and Starr.

Two further assumptions will be made. First, I assume that the net effect of positive and negative reinforcement and positive and negative spatial diffusion is stable over time. This assumption will be represented by treating them as constants. Second, I will assume that change in the population of nations, including growth in the number of nations, has no consequences for the operation of reinforcement and diffusion. This will be represented by working with proportions of nations rather than with the actual number of nations, which changes considerably over this period.

The appropriate formal language for this problem is not one like the propositional calculus, which is inherently static. Instead, one needs a language in which time is a central feature. I have chosen to use discrete time systems because the process is conceptualized as discrete with respect to time: time 1, time 2, and so on. Let:

W(t)	represent the proportion of nations at war at a given time;
W(t-1)	represent the proportion of nations at war at (t-1);
r	represent the net effect of reinforcement;
d	represent the net effect of diffusion; and
i	represent a nonzero initial condition.

Then:

$$W(t) = rW(t-1) + d[1 - W(t-1)] + i$$

The equation represents the proportion of nations at war at any time as equal to the proportion of nations that were at war last time on which reinforcement was operating plus diffusion operating on the nations not at war last time plus the nonzero initial condition. A couple of explanations are required. First about diffusion. Most and Starr show that diffusion works most strongly on those nations that were not at war last time. Since the variable W is measured in proportions, $1 - W(t-1)$ represents that proportion of nations that were not at war last time, and thus is multiplied by the constant d. Second, the nonzero input i combines the proportion of nations that were at war at time 1 and the kronecker delta sequence, which is 1 when t = 0 and 0 for all other t.

We want to know how many nations will be at war at a given time and how the number of nations at war changes over time if the assumptions on which this equation is based are true. This requires obtaining a solution to the above equation. Obtaining the solution is not particularly difficult (Boynton, 1980), but it does require more space to record than is appropriate here. Thus, the solution will be given without the proof.

$$W(t) = (i + [d(r - d)/(r - d) - 1])(r - d)^t + d/1 - (r - d) + i(r - d)^t$$

With this solution and values for r, d, and i, it is possible to compute the proportion of countries at war at any time (t).

Before introducing values for r, d, and i, it is possible to say several things about the solution. There are three terms on the right-hand side of the equation. The first term includes $(r-d)$ raised to the power of t; $(r-d)$ is squared when $t = 2$, cubed when $t = 3$, and so on. If the impact of reinforcement minus diffusion is greater than 1, this number will get larger over time. The system will be unstable; there will be no number larger than the proportion of nations at war at some future time. If this occurred one would conclude that this representation of the process was incorrect since proportions are bounded by 1, and even the number of nations is finite. The second term is a constant that will be positive if $(r-d)$ is less than 1 and negative if $(r-d)$ is greater than 1. If $(r-d)$ is less than 1, then the first term will decrease in size as time passes, and eventually the proportion of nations at war will be equal to the second term. Thus, it would be implausible for the second term to be negative. This analysis suggests two plausibility conditions that the equation must hurdle as actual values are given to r, d, and i if it is to be construed as a plausible representation of the process under investigation. The third term, $i(r-d)^t$ gives the initial condition since i is 0 for all t after $t = 0$.

Most and Starr report counts of wars from three separate studies of the same time period: the Correlates of War (COW) project, a combined Wright-Richardson list, and the Stockholm International Peace Research Institute—SIPRI (Most and Starr, 1980: 938). I computed the values of r, d, and i from the turnover tables presented by Most and Starr in the following way. The value of i is the proportion of nations at war for the first time period. The value of r is the proportion of nations at war in the first time period that were also at war in the second time period. The value of d was the proportion of nations not at war in the first time period that were at war in the second time period. The values are given below.

	r	d	i
COW	.21	.04	.29
Wright-Richardson	.27	.13	.33
SIPRI	.46	.22	.37

There is a considerable disparity in the results of the three studies. The SIPRI study found more wars than the other two studies. Thus, the values for r, d, and i are substantially greater for this study.

For these values of r, d, and i, the two plausibility conditions are successfully met. In each case $(r-d)$ is less than 1; thus the number of wars in the system does not increase indefinitely. Since $(r-d)$ is less than 1, the long-run value toward which the proportion of wars will go is positive.

Since the first term on the right-hand side of the solution goes to 0 as time passes, the proportion of nations at war at any time should approach $d/(1 - r + d)$. Based on the COW data, one would expect the number of wars to drop precipitously; within a few periods the proportion of nations engaged in war should approach .05. Based on the Wright-Richardson data, the proportion of nations engaged in war should drop to .15. Using the coefficients derived from the SIPRI data, the proportion of nations engaged in war will decrease to .29. The long-run differences suggested by the three studies are even greater than are the original counts. I do not know how to interpret this outcome except that to note that it suggests the need for some greater agreement on counting procedures in the study of war.

The point of this section is to suggest that it is possible and productive to examine a subject from a variety of perspectives. The principal thrust of the Most-Starr paper concerns the process by which nations at war (or not at war) at one time are or are not at war at a subsequent time. In this section I have approached the subject in a different way. I have asked how the proportion of nations engaged in war will change over time. Both seem reasonable questions, the answers to which can shed light on the same phenomenon. One by-product of this analysis is the point that formal languages are many and not one. Different formal languages are helpful for approaching problems in different ways, and, by virtue of their differences, shed somewhat different light on the problem.

Some Questions

I have made the rather strong claim that formal languages could help us develop a cumulative body of knowledge about political phenomena, that this would happen through an improved ability to join ideas and description, and that we would achieve a coherence in our empirical research that is now missing. A number of questions immediately pose themselves in the face of this claim, and I will ask and attempt to answer many of these questions in this section.

What exactly is there in formal languages that would lead one to make such a claim? Formal languages require a person to be quite explicit about the structure of the relationship between the variables that enter into the theory one is developing. "In return" for this explicit statement of structure, formal languages provide a set of rules by which propositions may be deduced from the structure. The deduced propositions flow from the basic statements of the theory in an explicitly rule-governed way. The deduced propositions are statements about the world that can be made on the basis of the basic statements of the theory, and they are statements that can be checked against empirical evidence. Thus, ideas and descriptions are joined in an explicit and rule-based fashion. The case study given in this chapter attempts to make this abstract statement concrete. In both the propositional calculus example and the discrete time analysis one starts with a set of statements about how the world is put together. These are then put explicitly into a formal language. Once that has been done one can make deductions, deductions about when a nation will or will not be at war in one case, and deductions about how many nations will be at war at some future point in the other case.

One part of the claim is that using formal languages will yield a more coherently related set of propositions. What is this coherence? Does it differ from coherence as the word is ordinarily used? Coherence is a word that is used very broadly in English. It does not stretch the word to speak of the coherence of a work of art or of the coherence of an argument. I do not intend to "take on" all uses of that word. The coherence that is the subject of this chapter is just the coherence noted in the above paragraph. Coherence means a way of explicitly (by rule) joining general statements with specific propositions. If one can show that a whole collection of empirical propositions can be joined through a set of more general statements, then one has coherence as I am using coherence in this chapter.

What are the properties of structures that lead to this coherence? A structure that explicitly lays out the relationships between the variables used in the development of a theory has the property that is being suggested. It is not enough to simply bring together ideas about how something happens. This is exactly what was done with the Most-Starr paper. They brought together a number of different ideas about how war or not-war at one point in time would lead to war or not-war at a later point in time. In my illustration I build a structure of relationships between those ideas.

Can one recognize some property or properties in a collection of ideas that leads to a formal statement of structure? There are two observations to be made in response to this question. First, in general more than one proposition is required for deductions. One cannot generate many deductions from a single proposition in the propositional calculus. And $y = a + bx$ does not lead to many deductions either. Second, "recognize" is probably not the correct characterization. A person who is attempting to formalize a collection of ideas would be more likely to say, "Ah, I see how to do it" than like "Ah, I see it." It is more a matter of figuring it out than recognizing it.

Am I just suggesting deductive theory as opposed to inductive theory? The distinction between deductive and inductive theory comes from one strand of philosophy of science. It is not really a description as philosophers of science do not describe. Their business is the reconstructing of the basis of sciences in order to ask the kinds of questions philosophers ask. Whatever one may think about that reconstruction of some sciences, it is not what I have in mind. A formal language is a tool that one uses in going about the business of giving a coherent explanation of some phenomenon. It is a tool that is used as much with information about what the world is like as it is used with abstract ideas. At least I have difficulty working with less than the full complement of ideas, description, and formal languages that help me put them together. It is the tool that lets me work back and forth between empirical research and ideas about the nature of the phenomenon being investigated. In the work, there is no distinction between deductive theory and inductive theory; inducing and deducing are going on more or less simultaneously.

How does one know that one has the correct formal language? I believe the best way to answer this question is to quote a distinguished mathematician, R. W. Hamming, from his paper "The Unreasonable Effectiveness of Mathematics" (1980: 89):

> Mathematics does not always work. When we found that scalars did not work for forces, we invented a new mathematics vectors. And going further we have invented tensors. In a book I have recently written conventional integers are used for labels, and real numbers are used for probabilities; but otherwise all the arithmetic and algebra that occurs in the book, and there is a lot of both, has the rule that
>
> $$1 + 1 = 0$$
>
> Thus my second explanation is that we select the mathematics to fit the situation, and it is simply not true that the same mathematics works every place.

It is a matter of working. There is no correct formal language—in principle. Political scientists have not busied themselves with inventing formal languages. I do not know anyone who is up to it. But it is a matter of selecting the language that works rather than discovering the correct one.

How do we know that formal languages that will work are available? We do not. Two options are available. We can work with the ones that are available, and that is a very big collection. We can invent new ones when we need them, but that requires more training than political scientists are likely to have for some time.

What are good examples of the use of mathematics in political science? A short bibliography is included in the References of this chapter that lists some of the most important work that has been done utilizing formal languages.

What Is the Point?

I began by noting a problem—perspectives are quite unrelated to research—which leads to a variety of inadequacies in our discipline. The chief inadequacy is the lack of intellectual coherence in our work. Then I reviewed Susanne Langer's characterization of theory and suggested that it could be subdivided into three parts: perspective, description, and structure.

What I have tried to show in the bulk of this chapter is that it is structure that joins perspective and description. Structure accomplishes two feats. It makes it possible to deduce hypotheses from a set of statements. This gives intellectual coherence; hypotheses and propositions no longer sit side by side. They are joined through their relationship to the initial assumptions. Structure opens up the kind of relationships we can look for. We need not be (more or less) limited to a single form.

Formal languages are important because they are already developed "empty" structures that are available for our use. Without this we are hard pressed to develop the structure of a theory with confidence. But there are many formal languages. Each has its own strengths and weaknesses. The propositional calculus is simple and melds nicely with certain problems in our discipline. But it would not work effectively if the process being investigated were a dynamic one, for this type of analysis needs another language such as discrete time systems. Formal languages are the tool of structure, but they are chosen because they are appropriate to one's problem.

I have argued that the problems we suffer in our discipline grow out of a missing element in our work. We are able to describe. We have perspectives. The missing element that joins the two is structure. A tool for working with structure is a formal language. But there is no magic here. I believe our work would be better if we were to incorporate this missing element into our armory of tools for understanding governing and politics. But it offers no simple solutions; we just should be able to get a little farther with the same amount of effort.

REFERENCES

BOYNTON, G. R. (1980) Mathematical Thinking About Politics: An Introduction to Discrete Time Systems. New York: Longman.

––– (1976) "Cumulativeness in international relations," in J. N. Rosenau (ed.) In Search of Global Patterns. New York: Macmillan.

BRAMS, S. (1975) Game Theory and Politics. New York: Macmillan.

CORTES, F., A. PRZEWORSKI, and J. SPRAGUE (1974) Systems Analysis for Social Scientists. New York: John Wiley.

DOWNS, A. (1957) An Economic Theory of Democracy. New York: Harper & Row.

GILLESPIE, J. and D. ZINNES (1977) Mathematical Systems in International Relations. New York: Praeger.

––– (1976) Mathematical Models in International Relations. New York: Praeger.

HAMMING, R. W. (1980) "The unreasonable effectiveness of mathematics." American Mathematical Monthly 87 (February): 89.

LANGER, S. K. (1967) An Introduction to Symbolic Logic. New York: Dover.

LUCE, R. D. and H. RAIFFA (1957) Games and Decision. New York: John Wiley.

MOST, G. A. and H. STARR (1980) "Diffusion, reinforcement, geopolitics, and the spread of war." American Political Science Review 74 (December): 932-946.

OLSON, M. (1975) The Logic of Collective Action. Cambridge: Harvard University Press.

RAPOPORT, A. (1960) Fights, Games and Debates. Ann Arbor: University of Michigan Press.

RICHARDSON, L. F. (1960) Arms and Insecurity. Pittsburgh: Boxwood.

RIKER, W. (1962) The Theory of Political Coalitions. New Haven, CT: Yale University Press.

SCHELLING, T. (1978) Micromotives and Macrobehavior. New York: W. W. Norton.

SIMON, H. (1957) Models of Man. New York: John Wiley.

ZINNES, D. (1976) Contemporary Research in International Relations. New York: Macmillan.

2

On the Concept of Threshold

BARBARA SALERT

The concept of a threshold has a long history in political analysis. Very loosely, the term refers to some point or set of points that marks a sudden and large change in a phenomenon—a change that is dramatic enough that the phenomenon may be said to have undergone a qualitative change. Marx used the concept in analyzing the dynamics of capitalism. The process, he argued, would result in predictable changes in the capitalist order until capitalism was sufficiently advanced that the social system would undergo a revolutionary change, resulting in a socialist order. More recently, the concept has been invoked in the analysis of such diverse phenomena as social movements (Granovetter, 1978), war (Holt, Job, and Markus, 1978), public opinion (Kernell and Hibbs, 1980), political violence (Koppstein, 1980), neighborhood integration (Schelling, 1978), public policy decisions (Schulman, 1975), and the survival of political parties (Sprague, 1980). While usage varies considerably, the common core seems to be that the concept of a threshold is invoked in situations where some behavior or pattern of behavior exhibits sudden, rapid, or discontinuous change in response to fairly smooth or relatively small changes in factors assumed to cause the behavior. In such situations the term threshold is used to mark the point or set of points at which the dramatic change occurs.

This definition, however, is vague: It could refer to virtually all relationships between variables that are not linear or approximately linear. In point of fact, the concept is generally not used and in any case should not be used as a substitute for "nonlinear relationships," if only because one hardly needs two terms for the same concept. The vagueness of the definition, I believe, stems from the fact that the concept is used in different ways and not from the fact that it is necessarily so broad as to encompass all nonlinear relationships.

The purpose of this chapter is to analyze the concept of a threshold and delineate some different meanings of the term. This analysis is not intended to be all-encompassing. It is quite possible that someone might wish to use the term in a way that is not covered here. The intent is merely to analyze some of the ways in which the concept of a threshold can be used in theoretical analysis and to examine the implications of these differing uses for the theoretical enterprise. The meanings of the term that are discussed below are ones that are or could readily be expressed in "formal languages." This does not mean that the term or any meaning that is considered is applicable only to quantitative analysis; however, it is easier to delineate meanings if formal languages are invoked.

Individual Decision Thresholds

The first meaning of "threshold" to be considered here arises in situations where people must choose among alternative discrete states of behavior and where the reasons for their choices are thought to lie in factors that change more or less continuously. To be more precise, the underlying factors may either change continuously or else in small enough steps that each alternative behavior state may be associated with a range of values in the underlying factors.[1] In either case, the underlying rationale is that discrete choices are imposed by the structure of the choice situation on a person whose preferences over the choice set may be expressed as a matter of degrees.

For the sake of simplicity let us assume that the choice set consists of only two alternatives for each person. The extension to more than two alternatives is straightforward, but the limitation to two allows for easier exposition. The concept of an individual decision threshold then rests on the following "ontology." A person can choose to be in one of two discrete states. That person has reasons for his or her choice or preferences over the choice set. These reasons or preferences, however, cannot be placed in a simple one-to-one mapping with elements of the choice set. Rather a range of values of underlying preferences correspond to each element of the choice set. The individual decision threshold specifies the appropriate range for each person. To put the point in ordinary language, the individual decision threshold marks the point where the person "jumps" from one choice to the other.

Examples of political phenomena that can be characterized in this fashion abound. Electoral behavior can easily fit into this framework. In the 1980 presidential election, for example, choices were largely limited to Carter and Reagan (or we could add the minor candidates and extend the argument). The preferences of the voters, however, were more complicated. A voter's ideal candidate might be someone very much like Carter, or someone very much like Reagan, or someone in between the two, or someone with some attributes of Carter and some of Reagan, or someone quite different from either of these two candidates. If preferences range over continuous dimensions of candidate evaluation (e.g., economic policies, foreign policy, leadership), then a threshold is needed to demarcate the subspace associated with a Carter vote from that associated with a Reagan vote.

Very diverse phenomena may fit into a similar structural choice situation. Decision thresholds have been used, for example, to model the choice faced by people who decide whether or not to join a social movement (Granovetter, 1978) and people who decide whether to stay or leave a neighborhood that is becoming integrated (Schelling, 1972, 1978). In the first instance, a person faces the choice of incurring some costs (e.g., time, money, risk of physical harm) by joining a social movement, or remaining outside the movement. This decision is presumably based on attitudes or preferences that may run over a number of dimensions, including the individual's valuation of the movement and its prospects for success, his or her assessment of the costs of participation, the extent to which social pressure is operative, and so on. As before, the decision to, say, join the movement may be associated with a range of values in the underlying attitudinal or preference variables, and a threshold is needed to separate the values associated with joining from those associated with nonparticipation. Entirely analogous arguments that will be considered in greater detail below apply to the choices faced by a person living in a neighborhood that is in the process of becoming integrated.

At this point the individual decision threshold is purely technical and serves merely to mark the place on an underlying preference dimension or dimensions where a person is induced to exit from one discrete choice and enter another. The very conceptualization of a choice problem in this way has theoretical consequences. First, appropriate techniques for estimating statistical parameters differ from those typically used in evaluating models with continuous dependent variables. Thus procedures used in estimating theoretical parameters and in evaluating the correspondence between theory and data will be partially determined by this conceptualization.

This consequence is hardly trivial, since our evaluation of theoretical assertions depends on the statistical techniques used in model evaluation (see, e.g., Kernell and Hibbs, 1980, for the implications of threshold models for appropriate statistical techniques and theoretical conclusions).

A second consequence that is probably more important in terms of analyzing the concept and its theoretical implications, is that the concept structures the theoretical enterprise. At minimum, one needs to know how the location of the threshold is determined by individuals in order to use the concept in the formulation of a theory of choice behavior. Different theories answer this question in different ways, and the different theoretical specifications of the location of the threshold can yield large differences in the analytic consequences of a theory.

Suppose we return to the electoral example and assume that people evaluate candidates along a unidimensional ideological factor. In particular we assume they have some "ideal point" on this ideological continuum and evaluate candidates according to their distance from this point. Hypothetical preference curves for five voters are illustrated in Figure 2.1.

As things now stand Voter 3 will vote for Candidate B since that candidate is closer to his or her ideal point. But if the preferences of this voter shift slightly to the left, Voter 3 will vote for Candidate A. And there things stop if we assume that preferences are exogenously determined. Any change in the preference of an individual due to exogenous factors affects the behavior only of that individual.

By contrast, an exogenous factor may have not only a direct impact on the individual but also an indirect or possible indirect impact on other people. If people evaluate candidates not only in terms of a unidimensional ideological factor but also in terms of the evaluations of their friends, then changes in exogenous factors may have widespread impact. In the voting example, if Voter 4 is a friend of Voter 3 and is convinced by his or her argument, Voter 4 may follow Voter 3 in a switch to candidate A. Since the indirect impact may extend a long way (as a person's decision affects the decisions of others which, in turn, affects the decisions of yet others, and so on), the possibility for large behavior changes accruing as a result of small changes in exogenous factors becomes very real indeed. In fact, this interdependence in the construction of individual decision thresholds provides a mechanism for the generation of the kind of aggregate outcome threshold discussed in the next section.

Thresholds Dividing Stable Equilibrium Outcomes

A second meaning of "threshold can be seen in macromodels of dynamic processes. In such models variables may move toward one or

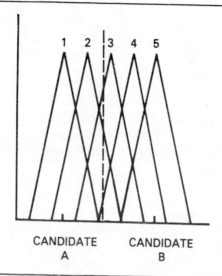

Figure 2.1 Preferences of Voters and Candidate Positions on a Unidimensional
Ideology Scale

more states known as stable equilibria. If two or more stable equilibria exist, then thresholds can be defined as boundaries between the regions surrounding the stable equilibria.

As an illustration, consider Sprague's (1980) model of third-party survival. The argument is reasonably complicated and need not be pursued in detail here; the conceptualization of a threshold, however, is very simple and can serve as a prototype of an aggregate outcome threshold.

Sprague is concerned with elucidating the mechanism that might generate the tendency of majority, single-ballot systems to favor a two-party system (the "law" is Duverger's [1963] and has received considerable empirical support). Put another way, the question becomes, "Why do third parties tend to die out in majority, single-member constituency systems?"

To answer this question, Sprague develops a model of the dynamics of party (electoral) support. The model incorporates assumptions about voter behavior as well as institutional arrangements of electoral processes. Specifically, Sprague assumes that (1) each party has a "natural" level of popular support—a level of support the party would receive if voters had perfect information and other political parties were not competing for votes; (2) people like to support winners; and (3) party systems are biased, i.e., the proportional allocation of legislative seats to some party does not, in general, equal the proportion of the vote received by that party.

The third assumption is particularly crucial for our purposes. Sprague defines the bias point as the proportion of the vote that for a particular class of electoral systems is exactly fair, i.e., will allocate the same proportion of legislative seats to a party. This bias point can be estimated and turns out to differ considerably for different electoral systems. In particular it is about .32 for plurality/majority systems and .12 for proportional representation systems.[2] Thus a third party in a plurality/ majority system must get one-third of the votes to get its "fair" share of elected representatives. A third party in a proportional representation system need only get slightly above one-tenth of the votes to get its fair share.

The three assumptions are formalized in a dynamic model of changing electoral support for particular parties. The formalization is complicated and need not concern us here. However, the qualitative behavior of the model, portrayed in Figure 2.2 illustrates the way in which the bias point (B) serves as an aggregate outcome threshold. The logic of electoral support exhibited in Figure 2.2 works as follows. If a party manages to capture a share of the popular vote exceeding the bias point of the electoral system under which it operates, the party will tend toward an equilibrium level equal to its natural level of support in the population (L). On the other hand, if the party fails to capture a proportion of the vote exceeding the bias point of the electoral system, it faces a trend toward an equilibrium level of extinction (0). The bias point, B, is the threshold that separates regions in which behavior tends toward one of two locally stable equilibria, i.e., L and O. Since B is high in majority systems, the likely fate of a third party becomes extinction.

Sprague's model illustrates the pattern of growth and decline of party support that can serve as a mechanism that explains why third parties do not survive well in majority electoral systems. The model yields an aggregate outcome threshold that distinguishes parties that will retain significant electoral support from those that will not.

The threshold in Sprague's model appears to be very different from the kind of threshold described in the previous section, that is, an individual decision threshold. Certainly, the two are different in terms of the technical definition. In dynamic systems a locally stable equilibrium is an equilibrium for which the following condition holds: if the system is perturbed from the equilibrium within a region of the equilibrium, the system will return to the equilibrium. In Figure 2.2 the relevant region for

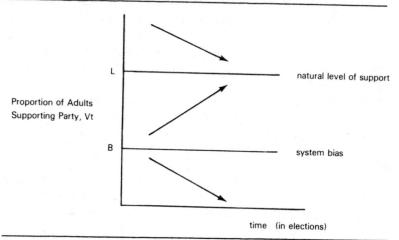

Figure 2.2 The Dynamics of Party Growth and Decay

L extends as far down as B; the region of O goes between O and B. The threshold B divides the relevant regions of the locally stable equilibria.

Individual decision thresholds are not structurally analogous. For one thing, the discrete choices do not constitute equilibrium points in the sense in which the term is used in dynamic systems, i.e., a state which, if reached, is perpetuated over time. For another, if we were to conceive of the discrete choices as equilibria, they would not be locally stable. In fact, the very notion of a threshold in this case is used to represent the idea that certain small deviations in underlying conditions cause a jump from one discrete state to another. The idea of an individual decision threshold is closer to a step function than it is to a threshold separating stable equilibria in dynamic models.

Why, then, do we use the same word for two different concepts? The issue need not be prejudged. Perhaps we should not. However, there are some links between the two. For one thing, there is a certain conceptual similarity. Both mark points (or regions) where something shifts or exhibits a trend that shifts from one state to another. A more important reason is that individual decision thresholds provide a mechanism for generating stable outcome thresholds at the aggregate level. To illustrate this, one of Schelling's models of neighborhood integration is developed in some detail.

The Integration of Micro and Macro Models

Schelling's model of neighborhood integration depicts the following situation: Both blacks and whites find a particular neighborhood desirable and want to live there so long as the racial composition of the neighborhood remains tolerable. Preferences about racial compositions vary across individuals but all get translated into individual decision thresholds on the maximum acceptable percentage of the other race that is tolerable. Thus, for example, a black might adopt a threshold rule to the effect that he or she chooses to live in the neighborhood so long as whites consititute no more than 70 percent of the population (i.e., blacks constitute at least 30 percent on the assumption that blacks and whites are the only relevant populations).

We may thus specify a frequency distribution of individual decision thresholds for different kinds of populations. It is important to note that these populations represent the *available* populations that would choose to live in the neighborhood if the racial composition is acceptable and not only those people currently living in the neighborhood. Two hypothetical frequency distributions for white populations are illustrated in Figure 2.3. The graphs represent the frequencies with which decision thresholds occur at specified percentages. For ease of graphic presentation, thresholds are translated into minimum percentages of whites tolerable, as opposed to maximum percentages of blacks tolerable. These graphs follow Schelling (1972). Note that there are two important differences between the two white populations: (1) Population B is more tolerant than Population A, in that the mean level of whites demanded is lower, and (2) Population B is bimodal, that is, there is a distinguishable group of whites who will live in the neighborhood so long as whites are not too small a minority and another group that demands that whites consitute a fairly sizable majority.

We may translate these frequency distributions for the two white populations into cumulative frequency distributions as in Figure 2.4. Now the vertical axis shows the percentage of the available population whose individual decision thresholds occur at no more than 30, 40, 75, 90, or any other specified white percentage demanded in the neighborhood. The 45°-angle line shows the actual racial combinations possible in the neighborhood. Note that at a point of 50 percent white population in the neighborhood (on the 45° line), the cumulative frequency distribution for available Population A lies under the 45° line. This means that the most tolerant 50 percent of the whites demands considerably more than a 50 percent white population in order to live in the neighborhood. In fact, the

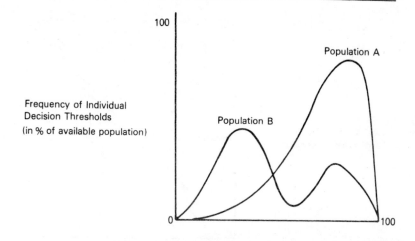

Figure 2.3   Frequency Distribution of Individual Decision Thresholds for Two
White Populations

Population A curve indicates that only about 10 percent of available whites would choose to live in a neighborhood that was 50 percent white and 50 percent black. Thus, if the neighborhood became 50 percent black, some whites would leave. In fact, some whites will be induced to leave whenever the cumulative frequency distribution falls below the 45° line.

On the other hand, suppose the actual distribution in the neighborhood were 95 percent white. The cumulative frequency distribution for Population A in this case lies above the 45° line, i.e., more than 95 percent of available whites have thresholds demanding a white population no greater than 95 percent white in order to live in the neighborhood. In fact, as the curve is drawn, about 99 percent of available whites would live in a neighborhood that was 95 percent white. There is no inducement for whites to leave. In general, if the cumulative frequency distribution for whites lies above the 45° line, whites choose to live in the neighborhood; if this distribution falls below the 45° line, some whites will move. At the point where the distribution crosses the 45° line, things are exactly balanced: There are as many (and no more) whites who demand that percentage white as there are whites in the neighborhood.

To get some idea of aggregate outcomes we need to introduce a cumulative frequency distribution of individual decision thresholds for the

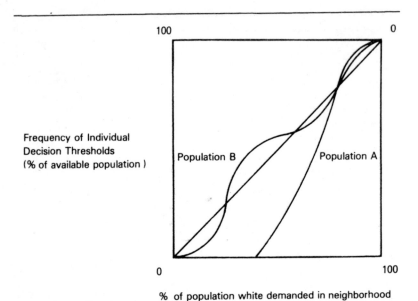

Figure 2.4   Cumulative Frequency Distributions for Populations A and B of Figure
           2.3

black population. This is done in Figure 2.5, where a hypothetical distribution for blacks is graphed along with the white distribution of Population
A from Figure 2.4. In order to put the black distribution on the same
graph we need to "invert" the plot. Thus minimal percentages of blacks
demanded can be read off the top scale, which measures percentage black
from right to left (corresponding to the horizontal axis on the bottom,
which measures percentage white from left to right). The cumulative
frequency for blacks is now measured downward. Looking at the graph
right side up, we can simply reverse the interpretation: If the black
cumulative frequency distribution lies above the 45° line, blacks will
choose not to live in the neighborhood; if this distribution lies below the
45° line blacks will choose to live in the neighborhood.

In Figure 2.5 white flight occurs whenever the white population drops
below T and black flight occurs whenever the white population exceeds U.
In the first instance the neighborhood becomes all black; in the second it
becomes all white. Both equilibria are locally stable. If the white population stays between T and U, both blacks and whites are content. There

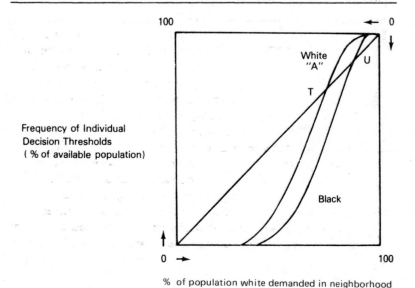

Figure 2.5 Superimposed Cumulative Frequency for Black and White Populations

may be a locally stable equilibirum in this region, but we would need a precise specification of moving rates for whites and blacks to find it. At any rate, T and U serve as thresholds delineating two and possibly three locally stable equilibrium outcomes. The situation may be translated into the graphic form used in Sprague's model of third-party survival, as in Figure 2.6.

The situation becomes more complex if we substitute the white Population B for the Population A of Figure 2.5. Then the superimposed cumulative frequency distribution appears as in Figure 2.7. As before, blacks will leave if the white population exceeds U and whites will leave if the white population drops below T. As before, there is also a region—between U and V—where both whites and blacks are content, but it is impossible to locate stable outcomes, if there are any, without precise specification of movement rates and absolute numbers for the two populations. But now there is another region to consider: white populations between T and V. Note that if the white population lies between W and V, some whites will leave, whereas blacks will find the neighborhood desirable. Thus the white percentage will decline. If, on the other hand, the

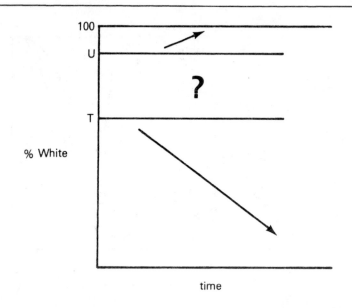

Figure 2.6 Dynamics of White Population Corresponding to Cumulative Frequency
Distributions in Figure 2.5

white population lies between T and W both whites and blacks want to live in the neighborhood and we need to know more about numbers and moving rates to determine outcomes.

For our purposes, the important point is that the stable outcome thresholds of Figures 2.5 and 2.7 (such as T and U) occur as a consequence of the model of individual decision thresholds discussed in the previous section. Substantively, this means that if individual whites base their decision to move on the racial composition of the neighborhood, then there may be one or more "tipping points" in a neighborhood at which white flight occurs. Note that this occurs as a consequence of the individual decision threshold model, i.e., without imposing additional assumptions on the aggregate problem. To be sure, the aggregate analysis cannot be completed without more specification. In particular, we cannot determine all of the locally stable equilibria without specifying how blacks and whites compete for housing when both groups find the neighborhood desirable. But we do know, even in the absence of such specification, that there are at least two locally stable equilibria at the ends of the 45° line separated by one or more thresholds.

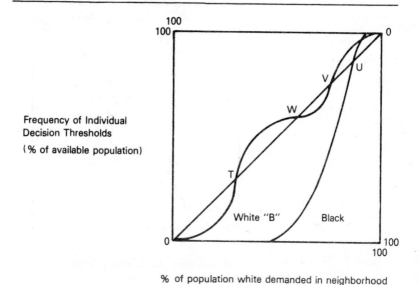

Frequency of Individual
Decision Thresholds
(% of available population)

% of population white demanded in neighborhood

Figure 2.7   Superimposed Cumulative Frequency Distributions for Black and White
Populations

As a further consequence, small changes in the distribution of white attitudes may result in large changes in the racial composition of a neighborhood. This is illustrated in Figure 2.8 for two hypothetical distributions of white individual decision thresholds. People in Population C are not much more intolerant of blacks than those of Population D; some, in fact, are considerably more tolerant. But white flight will occur at a much lower percentage of black residents in Population C than it would in Population D. The distribution of tolerances becomes crucial and relatively small changes in these distributions can have large changes in the likelihood that a stable integrated neighborhood will emerge.

This adds a possible third layer to the analysis. We started with the concept of an individual decision threshold as a point where a person decided to live outside rather than inside the neighborhood. As a consequence, we may generate a neighborhood tipping point or stable outcome threshold that marks the onset of white flight (and possibly several other thresholds as well). Finally, we may consider what happens as we vary the mean and variance of a particular class of frequency distributions (e.g., normal distributions) of individual decision thresholds. The example above

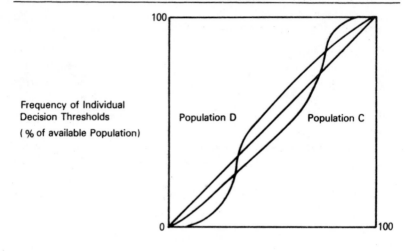

Figure 2.8   Stable Outcome Thresholds for Two White Populations

suggests that we may encounter a "superaggregate" threshold dividing integrated and segregated neighborhoods. In fact, recent work in the area indicates that varying the means and variances of normally distributed individual decision thresholds will yield elementary "catastrophes"—i.e., there will be a bifurcation between neighborhoods that "go black" and those that do not (see Koppstein, 1980). An examination of catastrophe theory and its links to individual decision threshold models extends far beyond the scope of this chapter.[3] For our purposes the important point is simply that while individual decision thresholds are conceptually distinct from aggregate and superaggregate thresholds separating regions of stable outcomes, the two concepts are linked by virtue of the fact that models of one generate models of the other.

The Use of Threshold Models in Political Analysis

For the most part, thresholds are used as constructs in particular theories on particular subjects. There is no, so to speak, "general theory" of thresholds. However, the kind of threshold used in Schelling's model—an individual decision threshold defined, partly, by the behavior of others—may be quite relevant for many political phenomena and may provide a conceptual tool for attacking phenomena that have posed difficult analytic problems.

Recall that any individual decision threshold presupposes a certain choice structure, namely, a choice among a few discrete states where each state is associated with a range of values in the variable underlying the choice. Many political phenomena—e.g., voting, participation in social movements, adoption of political attitudes regarding support of some issue—can be cast in terms of this kind of choice situation.

The crucial additional feature is that the threshold be defined in a way that makes two important assumptions about the behavior in question: (1) an individual's behavior is influenced by the behavior of others in ways that yield a tendency toward social conformity, and (2) this tendency varies across individuals. The first assumption means that the threshold will be defined in terms of the behavior of others regarding the choices at hand and the second means that there will be a distribution of thresholds thus defined within a population.

Both assumptions seem applicable to many choice situations, particularly those involving mass political behavior. The second is perhaps more obvious than the first as people's ideologies, social and economic positions, opportunities, and personalities vary, and hence their threshold points—which reflect these factors to some degree—might also be expected to vary. The first is less obvious and, in fact, has not been prominent in most of the literature focusing on individual choice behavior.

Nevertheless, the assumption of social influence seems highly relevant in many contexts. Consider, for example, a riot. We could argue that people have different grievances, beliefs about the legitimacy of violence, valuations of the costs of rioting, and so on that determine the probability that a given person will engage in riot behavior. This is undoubtedly true. One rarely finds a middle-class businessman who believes that the social order is essentially just and that he has means of political influence that are more efficacious and less costly than violence entering into a riot. Underlying grievances and beliefs no doubt generate probabilities of riot behavior and these probabilities differ across individuals.

But this is not the whole story. A riot, by definition, involves people *simultaneously* engaging in certain kinds of illegal actions. If these actions can be represented by a simple probability function whereby each person has some probability of rioting due to individual grievances and beliefs, we would expect riot behavior to occur almost randomly over time with certain areas (those with more people in the higher probability ranges) experiencing higher average riot behaviors than others. The first part of this scenario does not occur. The pattern of riots is that things are more or less quiet for a long time until some incident occurs, other people nearby join in, and the behavior spreads among some population for a relatively short time, i.e., one to seven days. Then the riot ends. Riot behavior, in short, is not randomly distributed over time but occurs as identifiable clusters of behaviors.

The fact that riots occur as relatively short flare-ups means that there are empirical reasons for supposing that a person's behavior is influenced by the behavior of others. That is, the probability of rioting depends not only on some underlying individual propensity due to personal beliefs and grievances, but also on the extent to which riot behavior is occurring in the relevant setting. People appear to be more likely to riot if others are rioting. If this is true, riot behavior should indeed occur in identifiable "clusters."

There are also theoretical reasons for supposing that a person is more likely to riot if others in the area are rioting. For one thing, as Granovetter (1978) points out, the costs of rioting may be a decreasing function of the number of rioters. An individual who breaks into a store in broad daylight and steals a television set may expect to have several policemen hunting him or her down in a number of minutes. If 3000 people are engaging in the same or similar activities police resources may be taxed. For another, the social costs associated with nonrioting may increase in a riot situation. If people see their friends attacked by the police a sense of solidarity may prompt them to defend their "brothers." Or, a person may feel like a traitor if he or she does not support (and hence participate in) the actions of "like-minded" people. Finally, beliefs may change during the course of a riot. A person who felt defiance was futile may, upon seeing angry crowds, eager newspaper reporters, and concerned politicians, change his or her mind.

The theoretical and empirical reasons supporting an assumption of social influence are not peculiar to riots. Similar reasons apply to many political phenomena. Individual decision threshold points defined in terms of the numbers of people who have chosen a particular form of behavior provide a possible representation for a choice situation that satisfies the structural constraints of discrete choice based on underlying continuous factors or factors that take on a wide range of discrete values, and also on the theoretical constraints that the choice reflects both differing individual propensities and social influence. Other possible representations—e.g., indifference curves or contextual models—can be used to represent some of these components. But they do not represent all of them.

Furthermore, the fact that individual decision threshold models will generate aggregate dynamic models containing thresholds separating locally stable equilibria indicates that such models may provide a handle for gaining insight into a type of problem that has thus far been difficult to analyze, namely, phenomena that may exhibit very rapid change apparently in response to small changes in underlying exogenous causes. Such phenomena may be represented in many alternative ways as well, e.g., a function with a nonconstant derivative. But nonlinear representations tell us nothing about mechanisms. If we know, for example, that riot dynamics could be represented (i.e., the function "fit" the data with remarkable accuracy) by some complex transcendental function, the interesting question would be, why? Ultimately, it is people who engage in political acts and in order to understand some aggregate outcome we need to understand how the outcome resulted from the behavior of those relevant to the outcome.

This last point would be trivial if aggregate outcomes were merely the sum or average of individual acts. But this may not be the case. The reader may easily verify, for example, that increasing the average tolerance of white residents in Schelling's model will not necessarily decrease the threshold governing the onset of white flight. Similarly, individuals trying to maximize their self-interest will not necessarily arrive at an outcome that maximizes the self-interest of individuals comprising the group.[4] Individuals act and aggregate outcomes result but the link between the two may be complicated. It is for this reason that explicit consideration of mechanisms becomes important in understanding some aggregate phenomenon.

Claims should not be exaggerated. Any theoretical construct, however useful, is only one component of a theory, and to say that a decision threshold that is defined in terms of the behavior of others is a useful concept is not to say that use of this concept will produce an immediate understanding of all political phenomena that have some social influence component. In fact, a variety of problems remain in the very development of a concept of individual decision thresholds that can serve as a theoretically useful construct. That is, Schelling's conceptualization may not be directly transferable to political phenomena that may be similar in some but not all respects to the neighborhood integration situation.

In Schelling's use, the individual decision threshold is defined in terms of the racial composition of the neighborhood, i.e., a characteristic of the group. This makes sense if we assume that (a) the relevant group can be identified, (b) people have preferences about the aggregate characteristic, and (c) they constitute a part of the aggregate characteristic. These assumptions seem reasonable for many, but not all, processes that might exhibit a social influence component. Suppose, for example, we are studying voting behavior and believe that a person's preferences and beliefs about candidates and issues are influenced by his or her friends. Since different people have different friends there is no single relevant group. We can either use the concept "as is" to study a particular social network, if a closed circle of overlapping friends can be found, or else we can find an alternative way of representing thresholds that allows for varying definitions of the relevant group. (A third option, of course, is to simply use the assumption of a single group as a crude approximation.)

A second possible avenue of modification concerns the definition of a threshold in terms of an aggregate characteristic. In Schelling's model the threshold takes the form of a decision rule to the effect of, say, "I will move if the black-white ratio is above 2:1." An alternative conceptualization would be that the racial composition of the neighborhood is an important consideration but there is a probability distribution governing moving that depends on the racial composition of the neighborhood. The threshold is still there but it is invoked only with a certain probability. Would this change the analysis and, if so, how? The answer is not known as the problem, to the best of my knowledge, has not been solved.

A third issue concerns thresholds that may change over time. If we return to the riot example, it appears that if people have entry thresholds, they also have exit thresholds, since riots end. The exit process may also involve social influence but it may be time-dependent as well, i.e., people may stop in part because they become tired. Similar arguments may apply to social movements that rise and fall and other arguments involving exit thresholds may be applicable to political phenomena that can shift from one state to another and then back again. The use of exit threshold is not crucial for all phenomena where choice is reversible—it is not, for example, in Schelling's model—but it may be important for phenomena where thresholds are expected to change over time. The problem of representing entry and exit thresholds that may be time-dependent (or vary systematically with some other variable) remains to be studied.

Concluding Remarks

The rather vague concept of a threshold as a point marking a sudden and large change in some phenomenon that occurs in response to small changes in underlying conditions covers a variety of more precise meanings. This chapter has analyzed two meanings of "threshold" and explored some of the links between the two in the Schelling Model. The two meanings are very different in the sense that they do not share a common theoretical or formal representation. Nevertheless, they are linked by virtue of the fact that a class of models based on one conception of "threshold" will yield a model that incorporates the second conception of "threshold."

Individual decision thresholds that are defined as a function of the behavior of others may prove to be a very important theoretical construct in political analysis. For one thing, an individual decision threshold appears applicable to a wide range of choice situations that arise in politics. Second, the concept incorporates a notion of social influence that appears to operate in the political realm but is difficult to incorporate into other theoretical constructs. Finally, aggregations of individual decision thresholds will yield dynamic models that specify distinct aggregate outcomes and can be used to analyze the mechanisms producing each outcome. A very simple model, in effect, may generate an analysis of individual decisions, resulting outcomes, and the links between the two. There are, to be sure, many problems—both in theoretical substance and in terms of formal representations—that remain to be solved if the concept is to be used fruitfully in particular theories. But the general construct provides a useful and promising tool for political analysis.

NOTES

1. The major use of this latter case occurs when the underlying factor is the number of people involved in some activity (see, e.g., the discussion on Schelling below).

2. Estimation is accomplished by regressing legislative seat shares, S (as a proportion of seats at risk) on proportionate vote shares, i.e., $S=m_0 + m_1 V$. At the point of no bias (the bias point) $S=V$; hence, the bias point will be the intersection of the two lines or $B=m_0/(1 - m_1)$.

3. The interested reader is referred to Holt, Job, and Markus (1978), Isnard and Zeeman (1976), Koppstein (1980), Sussmann and Zahler (1978), and Zeeman (1976) for a preliminary discussion of the uses and controversies surrounding catastrophe theory.

4. Pareto optimal outcomes may not be reached. A vivid example of this occurs in the Prisoner's Dilemma game (see, e.g., Rapoport and Chammah, 1965).

REFERENCES

DUVERGER, M. (1963) Political Parties: Their Organization and Activity in the Modern State (Barbara and Robert North, trans.). New York: John Wiley.

GRANOVETTER, M. (1978) "Threshold models of collective behavior." American Journal of Sociology 83: 1420-1433.

HIBBS, D. and H. FASSBENDER [eds.] (forthcoming) Contemporary Political Economy. Amsterdam: Elsevier-North Holland.

HOLT, T., L. JOB, and L. MARKUS (1978) "Catastrophe theory and the study of war." Journal of Conflict Resolution 22: 171-208.

ISNARD, C. A. and E. C. ZEEMAN (1976) "Some models from catastrophe theory in the social sciences," in Lyndhurst Collins (ed.) The Use of Models in the Social Sciences. Boulder, CO: Westview.

KERNELL, S. and D. A. HIBBS (1980) "A critical threshold model of presidential popularity," in D. Hibbs and H. Fassbender (eds.) Contemporary Political Economy. Amsterdam: Elsevier-North Holland.

KOPPSTEIN, P. (1980) "Cascades, decision-making and galvanization." New Haven, CT: Yale University.

RAPOPORT, A. and A. M. CHAMMAH (1965) A Prisoner's Dilemma: A Study of Conflict and Cooperation. Ann Arbor: University of Michigan Press.

SCHELLING, T. C. (1978) Micromotives and Macrobehavior. New York: W. W. Norton.

SCHELLING, T. C. (1972) "A process of residential segregation: neighborhood tipping," in A. H. Pascal (ed.) Racial Discrimination in Economic Life. Lexington, MA: D. C. Heath.

SCHULMAN, P. R. (1975) "Nonincremental policy making: notes toward an alternative paradigm." American Political Science Review 69: 1354-1370.

SPRAGUE, J. (1980) "On Duverger's sociological law: the connection between electoral laws and party systems." Political Science Paper No. 48. Washington University.

SUSSMANN, H. and R. ZAHLER (1978) "Catastrophe Theory as applied to the social and biological sciences: a critique." Synthese 37: 117-216.

ZEEMAN, E. C. (1976) "Catastrophe theory." Scientific American 234: 65-83.

Synthesis

The Benefits of Coherence and Precision

ELINOR OSTROM

The lack of coherence is our discipline may partially result from the domination of the languages of data analysis over the languages of theory construction. If so, this domination must be reversed so that the development of theory precedes the choice of appropriate methods to test a theory. Salert reminds us that the way a process is conceptualized affects the appropriate techniques that should be used to estimate statistical parameters in empirical models of a process.

This necessary relationship of theoretical and statistical languages was ignored in empirical studies that showed political structure does not matter. This conclusion was based on the fact that political variables accounted for a small proportion of the variance in government expenditure levels after economic and social variables had first been entered into a multiple regression model. Multiple regression techniques were first developed to examine the independent effect of land, labor, and fertilizer in agricultural productivity (see Ezekiel and Fox, 1959). Since the amounts of land, labor, and fertilizer are conceptualized as *independent* and their effect on productivity is *additive*, the theoretical model underlying multiple regression is the appropriate model for conceptualizing how these variables are related. The general linear model has proved to be a useful way to analyze many different phenomena, particularly how various inputs are converted into outputs. Political scientists need, however, to begin to explore other ways of thinking theoretically about complex sets of interrelated variables particularly when theorizing about the effect of political structure.

Almost all of the various general perspectives in political science see political variables as mechanisms that affect the way economic and social variables are transformed into policies. Institutional arrangements structure processes. They affect the way inputs are converted into outputs. As such they operate to constrain or enhance a conversion process. To continue with an agricultural analogy, institutional arrangements more closely resemble different types of production technologies such as horse-drawn plows or large gas-powered tractors than inputs such as land or labor. As such, they affect the proportioning of inputs rather than being added as an input.

Fortunately, Boynton, Salert and others in the discipline are taking major steps to reestablish the priority of theory over data collection and analysis. Theory has come to mean a set of logically connected statements without the requirement that assumptions used in a theory have themselves already been established as empirical laws. We are more able to draw on the theoretical insights of the earlier political theorists than we were a few decades ago. We need to formulate many of the insights of earlier theorists in more rigorous form, but as both Boynton and Salert point out, a variety of different conceptual languages is available for use in the effort to formalize our perspectives on diverse political processes.

One of the most difficult tasks we face is to find ways of modeling individual behavior within the context of social and economic processes as structured by institutional arrangements. The links between individual behavior and macrosocial behavior are not easy to discern. Simply "adding up" individual behavior does not account for observed system dynamics.

The recent paper by John Sprague (1980) briefly discussed by Salert is a major step toward conceptualizing complex micro- and macrointeractions and the effects of institutional variables, and toward providing the type of cumulation called for by Boynton. It is thus worthwhile to take a second look at this paper as a case study of how theory and research can be integrated to produce more coherence in political science.

Sprague's starting point is Duverger's empirical law that political institutions—electoral laws—affect the development of party systems. As Sprague points out, Duverger's law is simply a statement that electoral laws and the type of party system are related. Two-party systems are more likely to develop in single-member district systems while three- (or more) party systems tend to develop in proportional representation systems. Stating this relationship is *not* a theory. The relationship could, however, be a *derivation* from a theory. Since the relationship is empirically well supported, it is worthwhile to develop a theoretical explanation for how this empirical relationship could occur. In other words, what process would produce this relationship? Instead of starting with an empirical law and constructing a theory from this starting point, Sprague constructs a theory to explain the empirical law.

Sprague's theory begins with two unpretensious assumptions about individual preferences and institutional reward patterns.

"Voters like to win."

"Them that has, gets."

The first assumption animates his model. A voter who initially prefers a new third party will continue to vote for its candidates if sufficient numbers of them are elected so that the voter is not wasting a ballot on inevitable losers. The second proposition characterizes the biasing aspect of electoral systems. Parties obtaining a large proportion of the vote usually receive more than a proportionate share of legislative seats. This general institutional constraint is more pronounced in single-member district electoral systems than in proportional representation systems.

Sprague first develops a formal algebraic model of the electoral world prior to the inclusion of the two propositions stated above. Then, instead of *adding* these variables, they are integrated into the model in a multiplicative fashion. "It is the jointness, the interdependence, of electoral rules, mass behavior, and third-party management that makes the problem interesting, and the natural algebraic representation is as a product" (Sprague, 1980: 15). By stipulating some initial conditions and stimulating the behavior of the system, Sprague is able to identify the type of qualitative behavior that results over several election periods.

If a third party begins with a level of party support above that of the bias point of the electoral system, sufficient electoral seats will be obtained to reward the voters who like to win. The party should survive and eventually gain electoral support that represents its "natural" relative position in capturing voter preferences. However, if the bias point is higher than the initial vote achieved in the first election, a dramatically different equilibrium will be reached—that of extinction (see Figure 2.2 in Chapter 2).

The behavior of this model over a series of elections provides a coherent account for the cross-sectional data analysis that has frequently found more than two parties in proportional representation systems (characterized by low bias points) and few surviving third parties in single-member constituencies (characterized by high bias points). Sprague does not attempt to predict any *particular* elections but rather how an underlying process operates over time. To predict specific elections, he would need to add variables to the model for many of the time- and place-specific events that constitute the hurly-burly of everyday politics. The underlying institutional "rigging" of the electoral process would then be less obvious.

> In the real world of politics, however, each election is a new initial condition and these deterministic institutional biases are masked by the turbulence of politics as usual. Other short- or long-run conditions affect a party's prospects, and the effects of institutional arrangements are lost in the noise. But, and this is the main point, the institutional arrangements are always there underlying the hurly-burly of particular campaigns, and inexorably extracting their tax from small parties and distributing their rewards to large parties. "Them that has, gets" [Sprague, 1980: 18-19].

Not only does the Sprague work illustrate how to use formal languages effectively to achieve coherence and how to develop precise models of macroprocesses with thresholds dividing different equilibria—the two major themes of the chapters in Part I—the paper also provides an illustration of the type of work currently in progress that may produce a cumulative research program. Sprague's work draws inspiration from Duverger, who is a perceptive political analyst of an earlier era. Sprague attempts to develop a theory to explain empirical regularities for which there is considerable evidence. Institutional arrangements are a central concern. They are modeled as an interactive constraint on a process. Institutional arrangements channel the time path of electoral results toward one equilibrium rather than toward another. And finally, Sprague is extremely self-conscious of the language he uses in the development of his model. As he states:

> The argument combines a hypothesis concerning political institutional structure with a hypothesis concerning political behavior, a social psychological hypothesis, in the same algebraic entity. Their joint consequences are easily studied with the model because it combines these disparate theoretical considerations in the same linguistic form. The modelling process leads to the representation of mass behavior and institutional arrangements, widely different phenomena descriptively, in the same language [Sprague, 1980: 22-23].

Since science is a language-bound activity, this self-conscious awareness of the significance of the type of language used to model political process is an essential ingredient for any real theoretical development to take place and for genuine cumulation to continue the process once theoretical breakthroughs begin to occur. As one who has taught introductory methods courses to entering graduate students for some years, the course I will teach this fall looks quite different from those which I have offered in the past. The focus will be on theory development and theory cumulation rather than on diverse methods for data collection and analysis. It is my fondest hope that these students will become self-conscious of the theoretical languages they can use to think about how institutional arrangements structure political processes, and how they can draw on the work of many political scientists of all ages to increase the level of cumulation in the discipline.

REFERENCES

EZEKIEL, M. and K. A. FOX (1967) [1959] Methods of Correlation and Regression Analysis. New York: John Wiley.

SPRAGUE, J. (1980) On Duverger's Law: The Connection Between Electoral Laws and Party Systems. Department of Political Science Paper Number 48. St. Louis: Washington University.

PART II

Structure and Interaction in Dynamic Models

Introduction

Two Types of Dynamic Models

The two chapters in Part II, by Brito and Intriligator and Zinnes et al., are clearly representative of the scientific study of international relations. Both apply formal mathematical models and analyses to the study of international phenomena—arms races and crises, respectively. Zinnes and her co-authors go on to utilize econometric techniques to estimate best-fitting models of interstate interaction and to derive the attendant properties of these estimated models. Both authors reveal the impact of nonpolitical science theories and methods in their works. Brito and Intriligator, themselves economists, speak of utility functions, allocation of resources, and optimal control methodologies in their consideration of the behavioral and economic dimensions of arms races. Zinnes et al. see crises as dyadic interaction processes—an interpretation derived from various social psychological theories of perception and communication. Further indication of the interdisciplinary influences in their work can be seen in the use of the phrases "autoregressive" and "stimulus-response" to label two of their competing models. Finally, the two chapters are representative of current, and one hopes, future work in the "scientific" vein in that their authors demonstrate a clear interest in, and sensitivity to, the substantive implications of their at times highly technical analyses.

There are three important commonalities in the two chapters that follow. First, both focus on hostile and competitive interaction between states that occurs *prior* to the outbreak of overt physical violence between the actors. Acquisition of arms, especially in an accelerating, directly competitive fashion between two states, has long been viewed as a danger-ous phenomenon, if not one directly contributing to the outbreak of war. Even those scholars who view deterrence, i.e., massive accumulation of weapons, as a viable and safe posture in the superpower arms race are consistently concerned with the possibility that technical innovations, arms acquisitions, or perceptual shifts may destabilize the system.

Brito and Intriligator in their work take on the ambitious task of constructing an encompassing framework for the analysis of the U.S.-USSR arms race. Their model tries to account not only for the pattern of arms acquisition (in the tradition of L. F. Richardson and his successors) but also the bureaucratic process of domestic resource allocation (in the tradition of Allison, Halperin, and others). Zinnes et al., on the other hand, are concerned with instances termed "international crises," i.e., incidents characterized by mutually antagonistic interchange and decision making under what are perceived as threatening conditions. Many authors have hypothesized that the occurrence of such circumstances enhances the likelihood of war breaking out, and indeed, the end result of many crises has been overt conflict. However, the nexus between crises and war is not well understood. It is not known, for instance, if certain or all crises sequences exhibit common characteristics. Assuming for the moment that this might be true, could one utilize such information about the properties of war-resulting crises of the past to forecast or to provide warning in contemporary crisis-prone environments? Such questions are addressed by Zinnes and her co-authors.

Second, both sets of authors conceptualize interstate behavior as a dyadic, dynamic, interaction process—dyadic in that only two parties are involved, dynamic in that interaction (or interchange between the parties) is seen as a continuous, over-time phenomena, and a process in that the interaction is assumed to take on certain functional forms and to exhibit certain properties over time. The medium of the process obviously differs from one investigation to the other. For Zinnes et al., crises interactions are composed of sequences of directed behaviors and/or messages. For Brito and Intriligator, the arms race involves continuous defense expendi-tures and acquisitions of arms as well as the (hypothetical) reciprocal exchange of these weapons. The ideas pioneered by L. F. Richardson of interstate interaction as action/reaction processes are evident in the under-pinnings of each of the studies.

Third, following directly from the above, is the adoption in each chapter of formal mathematical models as vehicles to explore the inter-state interaction processes. To be more specific, both authors create sets of differential equation models in which the *rate* of interchange becomes the dependent variable to be explained. The use of these models forces the authors to make limited explicit sets of assumptions and in turn allows them to derive logically sets of deductions and implications about the properties of the processes and the behavior of the actors.

In as much as their work is typical of much of the formal mathematical-model-based work in international relations scholarship today, the work by Brito and Intriligator and Zinnes et al. presented here must be examined in light of two penetrating questions that critics raise about such exercises. These are

(1) How can international processes be most realistically modeled using dynamic systems (models)?
(2) What can we conclude about international processes from utilizing these dynamic models?

A model consists of a set of assumptions about behavior from which one may logically derive statements that describe the behavioral properties or outcomes to be expected as results of the process. In general, a model is said to succeed to the extent that its builder establishes a congruence between the properties of the model and relevant characteristics of the actual behavior process. (This property of a model is usually termed its isomorphism.) Thus, the modeling enterprise of Brito and Intriligator succeeds to the extent that their constructions capture the relevant aspects of the superpower arms race and weapons acquisition process. Put another way, Zinnes et al.'s models will prove unsatisfactory if crises interaction, in general, is not a dyadic process of interchange, and in particular, if it is not an autoregressive (model A), a stimulus/response (model B), or a combined, Richardson-like (model C) process. However, beyond the basic, and obvious, stipulation that the essential nature of the international process must be "built into" the model, there are other, more complex, evaluative judgments to make.

Consider, for instance, the various criteria implied by the phrase "realistically modeled." The model builder attempting to "realistically model" a phenomenon confronts a threefold tension between (a) parsimony and elegance, i.e., having as few assumptions and as uncomplicated a model as possible; (b) congruence with actual behavior, i.e., having a model with many and complex assumptions in order to reflect all of the various branches and decision points in an interaction process; and (c) goodness of fit between observed and predicted outcomes, i.e., having a model that charts the observed behavior pattern well but may not be parsimonious or highly congruent.

Zinnes et al. construct and work with a most simple set of assumptions in their models. They then proceed to evaluate, or choose between, competing models on the basis of their goodness of fit in describing observed crisis interaction. However, the utilization of very parsimonious models inevitably creates difficulties because the fit achieved by models with only a few variables would not be expected (usually) to be high.

Brito and Intriligator, on the other hand, formulate a large set of complex, interrelated assumptions attempting to reflect the decision points in a bureaucracy and the dynamics of a nuclear war. The tension that results in their work is between their desire to create as realistic as possible a model of the state's bureaucracy and strategy planning processes and at the same time to preserve a model that is internally consistent, readily manipulable to yield meaningful results, and ultimately estimable using available empirical data. At times concessions necessarily must be made on behalf of one or the other of these criteria. In the chapter by Brito and Intriligator, they are usually in favor of the second criteria (b) and at the expense of the other two.

If successful at creating a "realistic" model, there remains the question of what useful understandings may be derived from such constructions. Any such judgment must take into account the authors' intentions in each work. If their goal was to construct an abstract and refined representation, their model should yield statements highlighting the implications of major alterations in basic components of the process. If their goal was to construct a model that represented in a complete way all of the decision points in a process, the results should be statements indicating the sensitivity of outcomes to minor changes in the model assumptions and parameters. Finally, if their goal was to construct a model yielding the most accurate possible charting of the history of the interaction process, goodness of fit and robustness of statistical estimates become the appropriate criteria. If such models are constructed in order to forecast the future on the basis of past behaviors, a further test of adequacy becomes the accuracy of one's forecasts.

Thus, Zinnes et al., with their focus on forecasting, must be judged against different criteria than Brito and Intriligator, with their attempt to describe and to make policy prescriptions on the basis of their models. Brito and Intriligator attempt to construct a comprehensive model of the structure of decision making in arms races, which will help us to delineate an important missing element in many types of analyses. Zinnes et al. provide a parsimonious model focusing on another important missing element in dynamic models, the nature of dyadic interactions between units. Both make a contribution to the inquiry effort itself. The "meaningfulness" of their results cannot be separated from a consideration of their intentions.

3

Arms Races

Behavioral and Economic Dimensions

DAGOBERT L. BRITO and MICHAEL D. INTRILIGATOR

Arms races, the interactive acquisition of weapons by two or more nations, are recurrent phenomena of transcendent importance in world history. Since World War II the United States and the Soviet Union have been the major protagonists in the East-West arms race, a major aspect of postwar international relations. This arms race between the superpowers has been simultaneously both a consequence and a cause of East-West rivalry. It has involved an arms buildup that, because of technological advances, is unprecedented in terms of not only the potential destructiveness of the weapons but also of the economic cost and political consequences of their production and deployment.

The purpose of this chapter is to integrate our past research on the behavioral and economic foundations of arms races and to discuss some recent extensions of this research. Our past work has developed an overall framework for the analysis of arms races, consisting of two interactive components. The first component, discussed in the next section, is a *nuclear war component*. This component determines strategies and outcomes in a potential war. The second component, discussed in the following section, is an *allocative component*. This component determines choices between weapons acquisitions and consumption based on predic-

AUTHORS' NOTE: Support of the National Science Foundation under collaborative research grants is gratefully acknowledged. Both Judith A. Gillespie and Dina A. Zinnes provided valuable suggestions in revising this chapter for final publication.

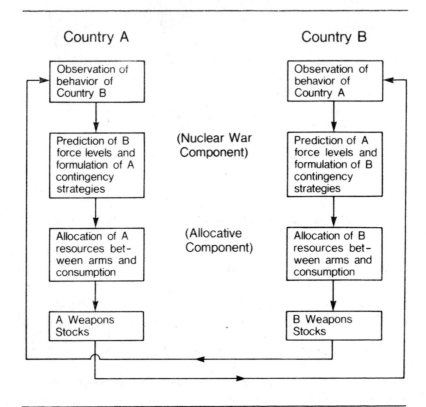

Figure 3.1   Interrelations Among the Components of the Overall Framework

tions of force levels and the formulation of contingency strategies. These two components of the overall framework are interactive in that the weapons stocks determined by the allocative component influence observations of behavior by the other country and thus affect the contingency strategies of the other country, as shown in Figure 3.1.

In Figure 3.1, each country observes the behavior of the other country, based, in part, on its weapons stocks. It then predicts force levels and formulates contingency strategies using the nuclear war component of the overall framework. These contingency strategies determine the allocation of resources to weapons according to the allocative component of the overall framework. The resulting stocks of weapons then influence the opponent, completing the interaction of this framework. Recent applications of this overall framework include strategic arms limitation agreements, nuclear proliferation, and the causes of arms acquisitions. They are discussed in the concluding section.

Nuclear War Component

The nuclear war component of the overall framework determines the outcome of an actual or potential nuclear war as a result of initial numbers of weapons, strategic decisions during the war, and certain technical and timing parameters (Intriligator, 1967, 1968, 1975; Saaty, 1968; Brito and Intriligator, 1973, 1974; Intriligator and Brito, 1976, 1977; for related developments see Kupperman and Smith, 1972, 1977). If the war occurs between countries A and B, each of which has a single homogeneous weapon, called a "missile," the nuclear war component can be expressed as the following system of differential equations and boundary conditions, which constitute a *dynamic model of a missile war:*

$$\dot{M}_A = -\alpha M_A - \beta'\beta M_B f_B \qquad\qquad M_A(0) = M_A^0 \qquad [1]$$

$$\dot{M}_B = -\beta M_B - \alpha'\alpha M_A f_A \qquad\qquad M_B(0) = M_B^0 \qquad [2]$$

$$\dot{C}_A = (1 - \beta)'\beta M_B v_B \qquad\qquad C_A(0) = 0 \qquad [3]$$

$$\dot{C}_B = (1 - \alpha')\alpha M_A v_A \qquad\qquad C_B(0) = 0 \qquad [4]$$

The variables $M_A(t)$, $M_B(t)$, $C_A(t)$, and $C_B(t)$ are the missiles in country A and B, respectively, at time t, and the casualties in country A and B, respectively, at time t. The war starts at time $t = 0$, at which point A has M_A^0 missiles, B has M_B^0 missiles, and there are no casualties on either side. Country A launches its missiles at rate $\alpha(t)$, so $-\alpha M_a$ in equation 1 represents the reduction in A missiles due to decisions by A to launch missiles. Similarly, $-\beta M_B$ in equation 2 represents the reduction in B missiles due to B launching its missiles at the rate $\beta(t)$. (The dependence of M_A, M_B, α, β, and other variables on time is omitted in equations 1-4 for convenience).

Missiles can be targeted counterforce at enemy missiles or countervalue at enemy cities. If A uses the counterforce proportion $\alpha'(t)$, of the αM_A missiles launched at time t, $\alpha'\alpha M_A$ are launched at B missiles while $(1 - \alpha')\alpha M_A$ are launched at B cities. If $f_A(t)$ is the counterforce effectiveness of A missiles, i.e., the number of B missiles destroyed per A counterforce missile, then $\alpha'\alpha M_A f_A$ represents the B missiles destroyed by A counterforce missiles, as shown in equation 2. Similarly, $\beta'\beta M_B f_B$ in equation 1 represents the A missiles destroyed by B counterforce missiles, where $f_B(t)$ is the counterforce effectiveness of B missiles. If $v_A(t)$ is the countervalue effectiveness of A missiles, i.e., the number of B casualties inflicted per A countervalue missile, then $(1-\alpha')\alpha M_A v_A$ represents the B casualties inflicted by A countervalue missiles, as shown in equation 4. Similarly, $(1 - \beta')\beta M_B v_B$ in equation 3 represents the A casualties inflicted by B countervalue missiles, where $v_B(t)$ is the countervalue effectiveness of B missiles.

The evolution of the war over time, as summarized by the dynamic model in equations 1-4, thus depends on initial levels of missiles M_A^0, M_B^0; strategic decisions regarding rates of fire, $\alpha(t)$, $\beta(t)$; strategic decisions regarding targeting $\alpha'(t)$, $\beta'(t)$; the effectiveness of missiles against enemy missiles, $f_A(t)$, $f_B(t)$; and the effectiveness of missiles against enemy cities, $v_A(t)$, $v_B(t)$.

From the viewpoint of either one of the countries, the problem of grand strategy is that of choosing both a rate of fire and a targeting strategy. For country A, the rate of fire α can range between zero and some maximum rate $\bar{\alpha}$ determined on the basis of technical characteristics of weapons. Similarly, the counterforce proportion α' can range between 0 and 1, where $\alpha' = 1$ is pure counterforce targeting (no cities) and $\alpha' = 0$ is pure countervalue targeting (only cities). Omitting intermediate values of both variables, the two extreme values for each of the two variables yield four alternatives for grand strategy shown as "stages" in Figure 3.2, which applies to country A (a similar figure applies to country B).

Stage 1, in which country A is firing missiles at the maximum rate at only enemy missiles is one of a First Strike, in which country A destroys as many enemy missiles as possible. Stage 2a, in which country A is firing missiles at the maximum rate at only enemy cities, is one of Massive Retaliation, in which country A inflicts as many enemy casualties as possible. Stage 2b, in which country A is firing missiles at the zero rate at only enemy missiles, is one of a Limited Strategic War, in which country A is limited both in terms of its rate of fire and the targets it chooses. In this stage missiles are held in reserve and used to threaten enemy missiles. Finally, Stage 3, in which country A is firing missiles at the zero rate at only enemy cities, is one of a War of Nerves. In this stage country A holds missiles in reserve and uses them to threaten enemy cities.

Assume that country A treats the country B strategy as fixed, rather than trying to influence it, and that A has the goal of maximizing a payoff function

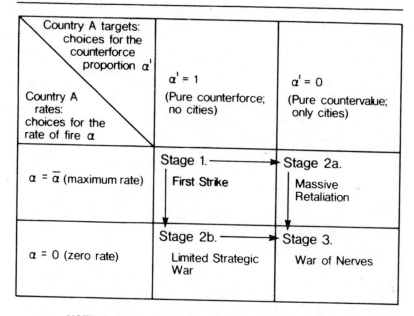

Country A targets: choices for the counterforce proportion α'	$\alpha' = 1$ (Pure counterforce; no cities)	$\alpha' = 0$ (Pure countervalue; only cities)
$\alpha = \bar{\alpha}$ (maximum rate)	Stage 1. ────────▶ First Strike	Stage 2a. Massive Retaliation
$\alpha = 0$ (zero rate)	Stage 2b. ────────▶ Limited Strategic War	Stage 3. War of Nerves

NOTE: Optimally country A starts the war using Stage 1, then proceeds through either Stage 2a or Stage 2b, and ends the war using Stage 3.

Figure 3.2   Alternative Grand Strategies for Targets and Rate of Fire for Country A

$$P_A = P_A [M_A(T), M_B(T), C_A(T), C_B(T)] \qquad [5]$$

which depends on missiles and casualties in both countries at the end of the war, time T. It has been shown (Intriligator, 1967) that country A will then select at any one time in the war t (where $0 < t < T$) one of the four grand strategies shown in Figure 3.2. In particular, it has been shown that while A could choose some rate of fire intermediate between 0 and $\bar{\alpha}$ it is optimal for it to choose only one of these extreme values, firing missiles at either the zero or the maximum rate. Similarly, it has been shown that while A could choose some counterforce proportion intermediate between 0 and 1, it is optimal for it to choose only one of these extreme values, firing missiles at only enemy cities or enemy missiles. Thus, A is confined to the four possibilities for grand strategy shown in Figure 3.2. Furthermore, given the payoff function in equation 5 and the differential equations and boundary conditions describing the evolution of the war in equations 1-4, it has been shown (Intriligator, 1967) that it is optimal for A to make a single switch in its rate of fire, namely, a switch from the maximum rate $\alpha = \bar{\alpha}$ to the zero rate $\alpha = 0$. Similarly, it has been shown that it is optimal for A to make a single switch in its targets, as summarized by the counterforce proportion, namely, a switch from pure counterforce targeting $\alpha' = 1$ to pure countervalue targeting $\alpha' = 0$.

If country A uses its optimal strategy the war therefore proceeds in three stages: Country A starts the war in Stage 1 in Figure 3.2, a First Strike, with $\alpha = \bar{\alpha}$ and $\alpha' = 1$, the situation in which A has not yet switched either strategic choice variable. Country A ends the war in Stage 3, a War of Nerves, with $\alpha = 0$ and $\alpha' = 0$, the situation in which it has switched both of the strategic choice variables. The middle stage of the war can be either Stage 2a, Massive Retaliation, with $\alpha = \bar{\alpha}$ and $\alpha' = 0$, if the switching time for targets precedes that for the rate, or it can be Stage 2b, Limited Strategic War, with $\alpha = 0$ and $\alpha' = 1$, if the switching time for the rate precedes that for targets. Country A thus optimally proceeds in three stages as shown in Figure 3.2, from Stage 1 to either Stage 2a or Stage 2b, and then, finally, to Stage 3.

The first stage of the war is optimally a First Strike (Stage 1), in which country A uses only counterforce targeting at the maximum rate of fire so as to destroy as many as possible of the enemy missiles. The second stage of the war is optimally one of two alternative possibilities. One, that of Massive Retaliation (Stage 2a), involves A continuing to fire its missiles at the maximum rate (as in Stage 1) but to target enemy cities rather than enemy missiles. The other, that of Limited Strategic War, (Stage 2b), involves A continuing to target its missiles at enemy missiles (as in Stage 1) but to fire its missiles at a zero rate. Which of these two alternatives will be optimally selected depends on the value to A of retaining a missile (for possible later use) relative to the value to A of inflicting casualties. These values, in turn, depend on the number of remaining missiles on both sides and the counterforce and countervalue effectiveness of these missiles. Finally, the third stage of the war is optimally a War of Nerves, (Stage 3), in which country A targets only enemy cities but chooses the zero rate of fire so as to threaten to inflict casualties on the enemy. It thus holds the enemy cities as hostages, placing itself in the best possible position for extracting concessions or a desired settlement of the war.

In proceeding optimally from the grand strategy in Stage 1 to either Stage 2a or Stage 2b and then finally to Stage 3, it should be noted that it is only in one of the two possible middle stages of the war, Stage 2a, the one in which the switch in the counterforce proportion precedes the switch in the rate of fire, that country A actually inflicts massive casualties in country B. In all other cases A has either selected only enemy missiles as targets, that is, a counterforce proportion of 1, as in Stages 1 and 2b, or it has chosen to hold its missiles in reserve, that is, a 0 rate of fire, as in Stage 2b and 3. It should also be noted, however, that either or both of the switching times could occur at the outset of the war (t = 0) or at the end of the war (t = T). If, for example, both switching times occur at t = T, then country A optimally uses its First Strike grand strategy throughout the war. On the other hand, if both switching times occur at t = 0, then country A optimally uses its War of Nerves grand strategy throughout the war. It is even possible for country A to use only its Massive Retaliation grand strategy (if the switching time for targets is at t = 0 but that for the rate of fire at t = T) or only its Limited Strategic War grand strategy (if the switching time for the rate of fire is t = 0 but that for the targets is at t = T). Thus there may be no switches in grand strategy over time, one switch, (e.g., from Stage 1 to 2a or from Stage 2b to 3 or from Stage 1 to 3), or, most generally, two switches in grand strategy during the war, the three stages of the war being those shown in Figure 3.2.

As already noted, this nuclear war component of the overall framework determines the outcome of an actual or potential nuclear war. The emphasis for purposes of analyzing arms races will be on a *potential* nuclear war, that is, a simulated or hypothetical war studied by defense planners in order to make decisions concerning acquisitions of missiles, rather than an actual war. Consider the situation in which country A is attempting to deter country B from initiating the war. Thus consider a simulated war in which B initiates the war as a First Strike, in which $\beta = \bar{\beta}, \beta' = 1$ (i.e., Stage 1 for country B) over the length of time θ_B, the length of time before A can retaliate. Country A responds with a Massive Retaliation strategy, $\alpha = \bar{\alpha}, \alpha' = 0$, as in Stage 2a in Figure 3.2, over the length of time ψ_A. If the time intervals are sufficiently small it can be reasonably assumed, for purposes of the war simulation, that the effectiveness ratios are constant. In particular, the B counterforce effectiveness ratio f_B over the initial First Strike interval is treated as constant, from time 0 to θ_B, while the A countervalue effectiveness ratio v_A is treated as constant over the subsequent Massive Retaliation interval, from time θ_B to $\theta_B + \psi_A$. The result of this simulated war is that at the end of the retaliatory interval the number of casualties in B is given as

$$C_B(\theta_B + \psi_A) = v_A(M_A^0 - f_B[1 - \exp(-\bar{\beta}\theta_B)] M_B^0)(1 - \exp(-\bar{\alpha}\psi_A)) \quad [6]$$

showing the dependence of the casualties A inflicts on B on the initial numbers of missiles M_A^0, M_B^0; the effectiveness of B missiles against A missiles f_B; the effectiveness of A missiles against B cities v_A; the maximum rates of fire $\bar{\alpha}$, $\bar{\beta}$; and the time intervals θ_B, ψ_A. This projected result of a simulated war will be used in the next section to study arms races in terms of the consequences of alternative stocks of missiles. It will also be used to study stability against war outbreak and alternative arms control initiatives.

Allocative Component

The allocative component of the overall model determines the allocation of resources to arms in the interaction between two opponents in an arms race (Brito, 1972; Intriligator, 1975). The availability of resources depends on bargaining and threats (see Brito and Intriligator, 1977b, 1978 for an application of bargaining to the allocation of international rights; on the bargaining problem see Brito, Buncristiani, and Intriligator, 1977, which generalizes the Nash, 1950, approach). This model allows behavioral elements to enter into the interactive acquisition of arms via choices as to weapons acquisitions, strategy, civil defense, missile defenses, and so forth. This model then determines choices between weapons acquisition and consumption (or capital formation). It builds indirectly upon the classic Richardson model (for presentations of the Richardson model, originally developed by Richardson in 1919, see Richardson, 1939, 1960; Rapoport, 1957, 1961; Montrol and Badger, 1974; Intriligator and Brito, 1976; for empirical studies, involving estimation of the Richardson model see Azar, 1970; Lambelet, 1971, 1973, 1975, 1976; Chatterjee, 1974; Luterbacher, 1975; Ruloff, 1975; Taagepera, Shiffler, Perkins, and Wagner, 1975; Rattinger, 1976; Ferejohn, 1976; Zinnes, Gillespie, and Schrodt, 1976; Hollist, 1977a, 1977b; McGuire, 1977; Schrodt, 1978).

Since Richardson, there have been several important developments in formal models of arms races. First, there have been attempts to justify and to interpret the coefficients of the differential equations of the Richardson model (Burns, 1959; Boulding, 1962; Abelson, 1963; Smoker, 1963a, 1963b, 1964, 1965, 1967a, 1967b; Intriligator, 1964, 1975; Caspary, 1967; Wolfson, 1968; Friberg and Jonsson, 1968; Chase, 1968, 1969; Alcock and Lowe, 1969; O'Neil, 1970; Zinnes and Gillespie, 1973; Ferejohn, 1976; Siljak, 1976, 1977; Busch, 1970; Sandberg, 1977; Intriligator and Brito, 1977). Second, there have been various studies of the political and strategic problems posed by technological developments (Brodie, 1959, 1966, 1973; Wohlstetter, 1959, 1974, 1975; Kahn, 1960, 1962, Szilard, 1964; Beaufre, 1965; Intriligator, 1968; Rathjens, 1969; Feld, 1971; Enthoven and Smith, 1971; Newhouse, 1973; Kupperman, Behr, and Jones, 1974; Carter, 1975; Nacht, 1975; Nitze, 1976). Third, there have been applications of economic theory and game theory to the problem of arms races (Morgenstern, 1959; Schelling, 1959, 1960, 1966; Ellsberg, 1961; McGuire, 1965; Saaty, 1968; Pitman, 1969; Blumberg, 1971; Brubaker, 1973; Brams, Davis, and Straffin, 1979). Fourth, there have been applications of control theory to the arms race (Brito, 1972; Gillespie and Zinnes, 1975; Simaan and Cruz, 1975a, 1975b, 1977; Gillespie, Zinnes, and Tahim, 1975, 1977; and Gillespie, Zinnes, Tahim, Schrodt, and Rubison, 1977). Fifth, there have been developments in strategic models with applications to arms races (Intriligator, 1967, 1975; Brito and Intriligator, 1973, 1974; Kupperman and Smith, 1972, 1977).

The allocative component of our overall framework builds primarily upon the last two developments, particularly Brito (1972) and Intriligator (1975). It treats arms races as the result of rational behavior of the actual agents involved, who evaluate weapons in terms of the potential outcomes of a simulated war. Thus both the role of weapons and the accumulation of weapons are endogenous in contrast to previous formal models. In Brito (1972) it was shown that, assuming agents do not overreact to predictions of what other agents are doing, the arms race is a dynamic process that is stable, converging to an equilibrium level of arms. In Intriligator (1975) it was shown that an arms race described by the Richardson model results from defense planners using a model of a nuclear war, where the coefficients of the Richardson model are explicit functions of the technical and timing parameters describing a potential war. It was also shown that the model leads to certain configurations of weapons that are stable against war outbreak and others that are not stable. The remainder of this section summarizes and integrates these results.

Control Theory

The application of control theory to the arms race to determine optimal rates of acquisition of new missiles is developed in Brito (1972). In this allocative model country A determines an index of defense D_A, a measure of its security at any time which depends on missile stocks in both countries

$$D_A = D_A(M_A, M_B) \qquad [7]$$

It is assumed that D_A increases (decreases) with $M_A(M_B)$ at a decreasing rate. The level of utility enjoyed by country A at any time t is given as

$$U_A(t) = U_A[C_A, D_A(M_A, M_B)] \qquad [8]$$

where C_A is here (unlike earlier) the level of consumption in country A. Thus, according to equation 8, the utility of country A depends (positively) on both the level of consumption and the index of defense. The objective of A is then that of maximizing welfare

$$W_A = \int_0^\infty e^{-rt} U_A[C_A, D_A(M_A(M_A, M_B)] dt \qquad [9]$$

given as the total contribution of utility at each instant of time, from time $t = 0$, discounted at the rate r. This welfare integral is maximized by choice of the acquisition of missiles Z_A, and the level of consumption C_A, where

$$\dot{M}_A = Z_A - \mu_A M_A \qquad [10]$$

$$Y_A = Z_A + C_A \qquad [11]$$

In equation 10, the net change in the level of A missiles is given as the acquisition of missiles Z_A less the resources needed to maintain and operate missiles, $\mu_A M_A$. In equation 11, the net national product Y_A, assumed given, is divided between the acquisition of missiles Z_A and consumption C_A, representing the choice between "guns" and "butter."

Under reasonable assumptions on the relevant functions (U_A, D_A) and parameters (r, μ_A) and comparable functions and parameters for country B, it was shown (Brito, 1972) using control theoretic methods that there exist functions F_A and F_B determining the arms race, where the rates of change of missiles are given by the differential equations[1]

$$\dot{M}_A = F_A(M_A, M_B) \qquad [12]$$

$$\dot{M}_B = F_B(M_A, M_B) \qquad [13]$$

Furthermore, it was shown that there exist equilibrium levels of missiles M_A^E and M_B^E for which there is no change in the levels of missile stocks in either country and thus satisfy

$$F_A(M_A^E, M_B^E) = F_B(M_A^E, M_B^E) = 0 \qquad [14]$$

Finally, it was shown that such equilibrium levels are stable if both countries act in a myopic manner, or if they do not overreact to new information, or if one or both attempts to behave as Stackelberg leaders (assuming the other acts as a "follower" in using its own reaction curve, as discussed in Intriligator, 1971).

An important special case of the differential equations (12 and 13) of an arms race is that in which both functions F_A and F_B are linear. This case is that of the *Richardson Model of An Arms Race,* in which equations 12 and 13 can be written

$$\dot{M}_A = a_1 M_B - a_2 M_A + a_3 \qquad\qquad (a_1, a_2 > 0) \qquad\qquad [15]$$

$$\dot{M}_B = b_1 M_A - b_2 M_B + b_3 \qquad\qquad (b_1, b_2 > 0) \qquad\qquad [16]$$

In this Richardson model the time rate of change of missile stocks in each country is a linear function of the stocks of missiles held by both countries. In both equations the rate of change of missiles depends linearly and positively on the opponent's missiles (the "defense" terms $a_1 M_B$ and $b_1 M_A$), linearly and negatively on own missiles (the "fatigue" terms $a_2 M_A$ and $b_2 M_B$), and on certain positive or negative constant terms (the "grievance" terms a_3 and b_3). In this case, setting $\dot{M}_A = \dot{M}_B = 0$, as in equation 14, the equilibrium levels of missile stocks satisfy the reaction functions

$$M_A = a_1' M_B + a_3', \qquad \text{where } a_1' = \frac{a_1}{a_2}, \ a_3' = \frac{a_3}{a_2} \qquad [17]$$

$$M_B = b_1' M_A + b_3', \qquad \text{where } b_1' = \frac{b_1}{b_2}, \ b_3' = \frac{b_3}{b_2} \qquad [18]$$

These are reaction functions in showing how A would react to B (equation 17) and how B would react to A (equation 18). The coefficients in these reaction functions are the normalized defense terms a_1' and b_1' and the normalized grievance terms a_3' and b_3', obtained by dividing a_1 and a_3 and b_1 and b_3, respectively, by the fatigue terms a_2 and b_2 (which are assumed to be positive). The resulting equilibrium levels, obtained by solving these equations simultaneously for M_A and M_B, are given by

$$M_A^E = \frac{a_1' b_3' + a_3'}{1 - a_1' b_1'} \quad \text{and} \quad M_B^E = \frac{b_1' a_3' + b_3'}{1 - a_1' b_1'} \qquad [19]$$

where it is assumed that both the grievance terms, a_3 and b_3 and the denominator $1 - a_1' b_1'$ are positive, the latter condition being the *stability condition*

$$a_1' b_1' < 1 \qquad [20]$$

Under these assumptions the equilibrium levels in equation 19 exist and the equilibrium is stable, small movements away from these levels generating forces that restore the equilibrium. Equations 19 give equilibrium levels of missiles in country A and country B as functions of the normalized defense and grievance terms.

The nuclear war component, as described in the previous section, in the case of a hypothetical war in which A attempts to deter B, is a special case of the control-theoretic model in which the index of defense is given by the number of casualties that would be inflicted in a retaliatory strike. Thus, from equation 6, replacing M_A^0 by M_A and M_B^0 by M_B, since war could begin at any time, the index of defense for country A can be written

$$D_A(M_A,M_B) = v_A [1 - \exp(-\bar{\alpha}\psi_A)] M_A -$$
$$v_A f_B [1 - \exp(-\bar{\beta}\theta_B)] \, [1 - \exp(-\bar{\alpha}\psi_A)] M_B \qquad [21]$$

Assuming A is attempting to deter B, the larger the number of casualties A inflicts on B in a retaliatory strike the larger is the defense index for A, given in equation 21 as the number of casualties in a retaliatory strike on B. In this case the defense index is linear in both M_A and M_B. The resulting arms race differential equations (12 and 13) are also linear, and they are thus of the same form as the Richardson model (equations 15 and 16), as shown in Intriligator (1975). The reaction function for A in equation 17 can be obtained by simply equating $D_A(M_A,M_B)$ in equation 21 with $\bar{C}_B$, the minimally acceptable level of B casualties that A believes it must be able to inflict in order to deter B. Solving the resulting equation for M_A gives the reaction function in equation 17, where the normalized defense and grievance terms are given as

$$a_1' = f_B [1 - \exp(-\bar{\beta}\theta_B)] \quad \text{and} \quad a_3' = \frac{\bar{C}_B}{v_A [1 - \exp(-\bar{\alpha}\psi_A)]} \qquad [22]$$

These results, and the corresponding results for b_1' and b_3', imply that the coefficients of the Richardson model can be expressed as specific and explicit functions of the technical and timing parameters of the simulated war, namely the maximum rates of fire $\bar{\alpha}, \bar{\beta}$; the initial counterforce effectiveness ratios f_A, f_B; the initial countervalue effectiveness ratios v_A, v_B; the time intervals for the simulated initial (First Strike) attack and retaliatory (Massive Retaliation) attack $\theta_A, \theta_B, \psi_A, \psi_B$; and the minimal unacceptable levels of casualties $\overline{C}_A, \overline{C}_B$. A stable equilibrium exists if the stability condition (equation 20) is met, which, in terms of the parameters of the simulated nuclear war requres that

$$a_1' b_1' = f_A f_B [1 - \exp(-\overline{\alpha}\theta_A)][1 - \exp(-\overline{\beta}\theta_B)] < 1 \qquad [23]$$

A sufficient (but not necessary) condition for (23) to be met is that f_A and f_B are each less than unity, i.e., it takes more than one missile to destroy an enemy missile.[2] If this condition is met, then the equilibrium levels of missiles for both A and B are stable and can be expressed as explicit functions of the parameters of the simulated nuclear war. To give a numerical example, if on both sides in the simulated nuclear war the maximum rate of fire is 10 percent per minute ($\overline{\alpha} = \overline{\beta} = 0.1$), it takes two missiles to destroy one enemy missile ($f_A = f_B = 0.5$); one countervalue missile inflicts 250,000 casualties ($v_A = v_B = 250,000$); the initial attack phase lasts 15 minutes ($\theta_A = \theta_B = 15$); the retaliatory attack phase lasts 10 minutes ($\psi_A = \psi_B = 10$); and the minimum number of casualties required for each side to deter the other is 40 million ($\overline{C}_A = \overline{C}_B = 40,000,000$), then the equilibrium level of missiles held by each side, which is stable, is approximately 414 missiles ($M_A^E = M_B^E = 414$). The sensitivity of the equilibrium levels of missiles to changes in these parameters in the simulated nuclear war is discussed in Intriligator (1975).

Figure 3.3 illustrates in the missile plane (M_A, M_B) the reaction curves for countries A and B, as given in equations 17 and 18, where the coefficients are explicit functions of the parameters of the simulated nuclear war.

In this figure, taken from Intriligator (1975), the two reaction curves are lines intersecting at the point E, which represents the equilibrium levels of missiles on both sides.[3] The reaction curve for A, marked "A deters," divides the plane into the region to the right of this line, in which A has enough missiles to deter B, from the region to the left, in which A does not have enough missiles to deter B. Thus $D_A(M_A, M_B)$ in equation 21 is more (less) than $\overline{C}_B$ to the right (left) of this reaction curve. Similarly, the reaction curve for B, marked "B deters," divides the plane into regions above and below this line that represent, respectively, situations in which

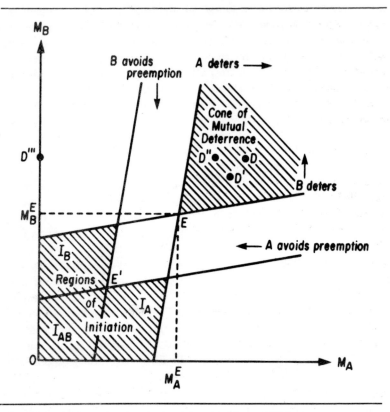

Figure 3.3 The Cone of Mutual Deterrence and Regions of Initiation

B does and does not have enough missiles to deter A. The upper shaded area is a *cone of mutual assured destruction,* in which each country deters the other. As long as the levels of missiles remain in this cone, the situation will be relatively stable against war outbreak. Arms control through arms limitation is feasible in this cone through either bilateral reductions, e.g., the movement from D to D′, or unilateral reductions, e.g., the movement from D to D″.

In addition to deterring the opponent, defense planners would want to ensure stability against war outbreak by avoiding situations in which it appears that they could carry out a successful preemptive strike. Having "too many" missiles relative to the other side could lead to fears of preemption, forcing the opponent to attack in order to take advantage of being the first to move, relying on the element of surprise. The other two lines in Figure 3.3, intersecting at E', are reaction curves for disarming first strikes. The line marked "A avoids preemption" divides the plane in that to the left of this line, A does not have enough missiles to destroy enough B missiles on a first strike so as to reduce the retaliatory strike to acceptable levels of A casualties. To the right of this line, A has enough missiles to disarm B and thus can attack B with some acceptable level of casualties. Similarly, below the line marked "B avoids preemption," B does not have enough missiles to attack A.[4]

The shaded regions of initiation are highly unstable against war outbreak. The most unstable is region I_{AB}, in which neither A nor B deters the other and neither avoids preemption in that both can successfully attack the other. The region I_A is one in which neither can deter the other and, while B avoids preemption, A has enough missiles to attack B with impunity. Thus A will be forced to attack or B will be forced to preempt, in either case leading to war. The region I_B is the symmetric case, in which either B attacks or A preempts.

Bilateral disarmament, interpreted geometrically as a movement to the origin, inevitably entails movement through the regions of initiation. The movement to the disarmed state may not lead to initiation, however, if it is accompanied by peaceful intentions. The movement from the disarmed state, however, may be highly explosive since, from it, either country could acquire a minimal level of missiles that would enable it to attack the other with impunity. In fact, the danger of war may be greatest if one side detected that the other was starting to rearm, since in such a case the missile levels move through regions of initiation in a crisis atmosphere.

Unilateral disarmament, interpreted geometrically as a movement by one country to zero levels of missiles, interestingly enough, may not lead to war outbreak provided the other side has enough missiles. For example, if B has enough missiles, then A could unilaterally disarm, say to D'''. At this point A avoids preemption; B deters A; and, while B does not avoid preemption, A has nothing to use for preemption. Of course at D''', country A does not deter B, so it would have to trust B's intentions. If B had a level of missiles significantly less than that at D''', then B would initiate.

This type of approach facilitates an analysis of bilateral and unilateral arms control and disarmament. In summary, either unilateral or bilateral arms control via arms limitation may be desirable, as long as the levels of missiles do not move outside the cone of mutual deterrence. Unilateral disarmament may also be desirable and not lead to war, provided the other country has enough missiles. Bilateral disarmament, however, leads to the greatest chance of war, either in the process of moving to a disarmed situation or, even more likely, in the process of rearming from the disarmed state.

Conclusions and Applications

The analysis of behavioral and economic aspects of arms races has resulted in an overall framework, consisting of a nuclear war component and an allocative component. (Another way of analyzing the allocative component is via a bureaucratic model, developed in Brito and Intriligator [1980]. See also Brito and Intriligator [1977a, 1979] for a related discussion of multiagent adaptive control.) This framework permits us to study several issues relating to arms races, including strategic arms limitation agreements, nuclear proliferation, and causes of arms acquisitions.

The application of the framework to strategic arms limitation agreements, such as the SALT treaties, suggests that such agreements can lead to new weapons development and a qualitative arms race (Brito and Intriligator, 1981; for previous studies of qualitative changes in weapons and qualitative arms races see Huntington, 1958; York, 1970; Bertram, 1978). The area of new weapons acquisition highlights the difficulties of arms control negotiations on the one hand and the nature of the arms race on the other. The development of new weapons carries its own momentum, and this momentum is very difficult to stop for various bureaucratic reasons, among them the difficulty of monitoring this area, the creation of pressure groups, and mistrust of the opponent's intentions. Indeed, qualitative changes in weapons can be even more important than quantitative changes, particularly when there are arms control agreements such as SALT that limit quantitative increases but cannot effectively limit qualitative changes. Such agreements can, in effect, spur a qualitative arms race as the superpowers compete to develop new weapons. In our analysis of quantitative arms limitation agreements, using the overall framework, we have shown that such agreements generally lead to research and development on new weapons, and that in some cases they lead to greater defense expenditures and lower levels of security. The behavioral assumptions that lead to these results are the inability of the government to control completely the budgets of the defense bureaus and the assumption that defense planners use worst-case analysis of unexplored weapons technologies.

A second application of the framework, to nuclear proliferation, leads to results concerning the effects of nuclear proliferation on stability (Brito and Intriligator, 1977c; Intriligator and Brito, 1978, 1981). Earlier studies of nuclear proliferation were primarily either case studies of particular nations or studies of technological issues (Gallois, 1961; Boskey and Willrich, 1970; Quester, 1973; Lawrence and Larus, 1974; Tullock, 1974; Dunn and Kahn, 1975; Maddox, 1975; Marwah and Schultz, 1975; Wohlstetter et al., 1976; Epstein, 1976; Greenwood, Feiveson, and Taylor, 1977). One of our previous papers (Brito and Intriligator, 1977c) concluded, on the basis of alliance structures, that there is a critical number of nuclear nations beyond which the international system becomes unstable in terms of additional weapons acquisitions. Later papers (Intriligator and Brito, 1978, 1981) concluded that nuclear proliferation might in certain situations increase stability against deliberate war, while, beyond a certain number, proliferation would reduce such stability. (Previous studies of the determinants of war outbreak include Gallois, 1961; Brodie, 1966; Lambelet, 1975; Wallace, 1979.)

A third application of the framework is to causes of arms acquisitions. In this framework the acquisition of arms depends on both the length of tenure of the government and the intensity and political power of its potential opposition. Thus the arms race is caused by internal factors, such as the self-interest of various power groups, domestic political and economic constraints, and bureaucratic momentum, as well as external factors, such as rival arms acquisitions, crises, and perceived external threats. Previous research suggests that in the short run, arms races are determined to a large degree internally on the basis of bureaucratic factors, while in the long run, they are determined on the basis of the competition between the nations.

While both internal and external factors can and probably do influence both superpowers in the East-West arms race, it is reasonable to presume, on the basis of postwar history, that certain stylized facts are probably true. First, the Soviet Union is relatively more influenced by internal factors, such as political and economic constraints and bureaucratic momentum, than by external factors, such as threats or crises. Perhaps the major exception to this general conclusion is the reaction of the Soviet Union to the Cuban missile crisis, which stimulated a major arms acquisition program after 1962. Indeed, much of observed Soviet arms acquisition in the last twenty years can be explained as a major commitment to build up weapons levels in both quantity and quality to match those of the United States as a result of the Cuban missile crisis, followed by a continuation of such a policy due to bureaucratic momentum. Soviet leaders could easily make the decision in the early 1960s to build up substantially their weapons levels in order to achieve parity with the United States. They have found it more difficult in recent years, however, to slow down this process, leading to Soviet arms, in certain respects, exceeding, rather than matching those of the United States. Thus bureaucratic inertia may have played a particularly important role on the Soviet side of the East-West arms race. (For previous studies of Soviet arms acquisitions, which are generally case studies not using a formal methodology, see Gallagher and Spielman, 1972; Spielman, 1978; Lee, 1978; Alexander, 1979.)

As to the United States, internal factors have played some role, particularly domestic political factors during election periods, but the United States appears to have been relatively more influenced by external factors, such as wars, crises, and perceptions of the opponent. One possible explanation for these stylized facts is that the leadership in the Soviet Union has been relatively more stable than that of the United States since 1963. Thus the various bureaucracies have had longer tenure, and vested interests are more entrenched. The bureaucratic arms race model we are developing is intended to explain these stylized facts; we hope that the model will lead to predictions that can be tested using more formal econometric techniques (as discussed in Intriligator, 1978).

NOTES

1. Both equations 12 and 13 and equations 1 and 2 are equations for $\dot{M}_A$ and $\dot{M}_B$. Equations 12 and 13 are the peacetime differential equations for an arms race, while equations 1 and 2 are the wartime differential equations for reductions in arms due to either their use in the war or their being destroyed by enemy missiles.

2. Even if f_A and f_B exceeded unity, condition 23 can be met if $\alpha\theta_A$ and/or $\beta\theta_B$ are large enough.

3. Figure 3.3 follows directly from the previous equations. The two reaction curves are the lines (equations 17 and 18) where the coefficients for equation 17 are given in equation 22, while those for equation 18 are given by comparable equations for b_1 and b_3, namely

$$b_1' = f_A[1 - \exp(-\bar{\alpha}\theta_A)] \quad \text{and} \quad b_3' = \frac{\bar{C}_A}{v_B[1 - \exp(-\bar{\beta}\psi_B)]} \qquad [22']$$

where θ_A is the length of time A can strike B before B can retaliate and ψ_B is the length of the B retaliatory strike. The slope of the reaction curve for A, obtained by solving equation 17 for M_B, is $1/a_1'$ or, using equation 22, $1/f_B[1 - \exp(-\bar{\beta}\theta_B)]$. The slope of the reaction curve for B is, from equation 18, b_1', given above as $f_A[1 - \exp(-\bar{\alpha}\theta_A)]$. The two lines intersect if the stability condition (equation 23) is met. They intersect at point E, which is (M_A^E, M_B^E), where M_A^E and M_B^E are given in equation 19, with a_1', a_3' as in equation 22 and b_1' and b_3' as above.

4. Note that the "A avoids preemption" line is parallel to the "B deters" line, the common slope being that of the reaction curve for B, as given in the previous footnote. Similarly, the "B avoids preemption" line is parallel to the "A deters" line, the common slope being that of the reaction curve for A, also given in the previous footnote. The reason why the slopes are identical is that the "A deters" line is obtained by equating $D_A(M_A, M_B)$ in equation 21 with $\bar{C}_B$ and solving for M_A, while the "B avoids preemption" line is obtained by equating the same $D_A(M_A, M_B)$ with $\hat{C}_B$, the maximum acceptable level of B casualties for which B will initiate the war (as perceived by A), and solving for M_B. Similarly, the "B deters" and "A avoids preemption" lines are obtained by equating $D_B(M_A, M_B)$, given as

$$D_B(M_A, M_B) = v_B[1 - \exp(-\bar{\beta}\psi_B)]M_B -$$

$$v_B f_A[1 - \exp(-\bar{\alpha}\theta_A)][1 - \exp(-\beta\psi_B)M_A \qquad [21']$$

with $\bar{C}_A$ and $\hat{C}_A$, respectively, and solving, respectively, for M_B and M_A.

REFERENCES

ABELSON, R. (1963) "A 'derivation' of Richardson's equations." Journal of Conflict Resolution 7: 13-15.

ALCOCK, N. Z. and K. W. LOWE (1969) "The Vietnam War as a Richardson process." Journal of Peace Research 6: 105-112.

ALEXANDER, A., Jr. (1979) Decision Making in Soviet Weapons Procurement. Adelphi Paper. London: International Institute for Strategic Studies.

AZAR, E. E. (1970) "The dimensionality of violent conflict: a quantitative analysis." Peace Research Society (International) Papers 15: 122-167.

BEAUFRE, A. (1965) Deterrence and Strategy (R. H. Barry, trans.). New York: Praeger.

BERTRAM, C. (1978) Arms Control and Technological Change: Elements of a New Approach. Adelphi Paper No. 146. London: International Institute for Strategic Studies.

BLUMBERG, A. A. (1971) "Model for a two-a $\gtrless$ sary arms race." Nature 234: 158.

BOSKEY, B. and M. WILLRICH [eds.] (1970) Nuclear Proliferation: Prospects for Control. New York: Dunnellen.

BOULDING, K. E. (1962) Conflict and Defense. New York: Harper & Row.

BRAMS, S. J., M. D. DAVIS, and P. D. STRAFFIN, Jr. (1979) "The geometry of the arms race." International Studies Quarterly 23: 567-588.

BRITO, D. L. (1972) "A dynamic model of an armaments race." International Economic Review 13: 359-375.

BRITO, D. L., A. M. BUONCRISTIANI, and M. D. INTRILIGATOR (1977) "A new approach to the Nash bargaining problem." Econometrica 45: 1163-1172.

BRITO, D. L. and M. D. INTRILIGATOR (1981) "Strategic arms limitation treaties and innovations in weapon technology." Public Choice 37: 41-59.

——— (1980) "A game theoretic approach to bureaucratic behavior," in P. T. Liu (ed.) Dynamic Optimization and Mathematical Economics. New York: Plenum.

——— (1979) "A multiagent approach to macroeconomic control." Policy Analysis and Information Systems 3: 1-9.

——— (1978) "International power and the distribution of world wealth," in Nake Kamrany (ed.) The New Economics of the Less Developed Countries: Changing Perceptions in the North-South Dialogue. Boulder, CO: Westview.

——— (1977a) "A fixed point approach to multiagent adaptive control." Annals of Economic and Social Measurement 6: 137-145.

——— (1977b) "Strategic nuclear weapons and the allocation of international rights," in J. V. Gillespie and D. A. Zinnes (eds.) Mathematical Systems in International Relations Research. New York: Praeger.

——— (1977c) "Nuclear proliferation and the armaments race." Journal of Peace Science 2: 231-238.

——— (1974) "Uncertainty and the stability of the armaments race." Annals of Economic and Social Measurement 3: 279-292.

——— (1973) "Some applications of the maximum principle to the problem of an armaments race." Modeling and Simulation 4: 140-144.

BRODIE, B. (1973) War and Politics. New York: Macmillan.

——— (1966) Escalation and the Nuclear Option. Princeton, NJ: Princeton University Press.

——— (1959) Strategy in the Missile Age. Princeton, NJ: Princeton University Press.

BRUBAKER, E. R. (1973) "Economic models of arms races: some reformulations and extensions." Journal of Conflict Resolution 17: 187-205.

BURNS, A. L. (1959) "A graphical approach to some problems of the arms race." Journal of Conflict Resolution 3: 326-342.

BUSCH, P. (1970) "Mathematical models of arms race," in B. Russett (ed.) What Price Vigilance? New Haven, CT: Yale University Press.

CASPARY, W. R. (1967) "Richardson's model of arms races: description, critique, and an alternative model." International Studies Quarterly 11: 63-88.

CARTER, L. J. (1975) "Strategic arms limitation (II): 'leveling VP' to symmetry." Science 187: 627-632.

CHASE, P. E. (1969) "Feedback control theory and arms races." General Systems 14: 137-149.

——— (1968) "The relevance of arms race theory to arms control." General Systems 13: 91-98.

CHATTERJEE, P. (1974) "The equilibrium theory of arms races: some extensions." Journal of Peace Research 11: 203-212.

DUNN, L. A. and H. KAHN (1975) Trends in Nuclear Proliferation, 1975-1995. Croton-on-Hudson, NY: Hudson Institute.

ELLSBERG, D. (1961) "Economics and national security: the crude analysis of strategic choices." American Economic Review 51: 472-478.

ENTHOVEN, A. C. and K. W. SMITH (1971) How Much Is Enough? Shaping the Defense Program, 1961-1969. New York: Harper & Row.

EPSTEIN, W. (1976) The Last Chance: Nuclear Proliferation and Arms Control. New York: Macmillan.

FELD, B. T. et al. [eds.] (1971) Impact of Technologies on the Arms Race. Cambridge: MIT Press.

FEREJOHN, J. (1976) "On the effects of aid to nations in an arms race," in D. A. Zinnes and J. V. Gillespie (eds.) Mathematical Models in International Relations. New York: Praeger.

FRIBERG, M. and D. JONSSON (1968) "A simple war and armament game." Journal of Peace Research 5: 233-247.

GALLAGHER, M. and K. SPIELMANN (1972) Soviet Decision-Making for Defense. New York: Praeger.

GALLOIS, P. (1961) The Balance of Terror. Boston: Houghton Mifflin.

GILLESPIE, J. V. and D. A. ZINNES [eds.] (1977) Mathematical Systems in International Relations Research. New York: Praeger.

——— (1975) "Progressions in mathematical models of international conflict." Synthese 31: 289-321.

——— and G. S. TAHIM (1977) "Deterrence as second attack capability: an optimal control model and differential game," in J. V. Gillespie and D. A. Zinnes (eds.) Mathematical Systems in International Relations Research. New York: Praeger.

——— (1975) "Foreign military assistance and the armaments race: a differential game model with control," Papers of the Peace Society (International) 25: 35-51.

——— P. A. SCHRODT, and R. M. RUBISON (1977) "An optimal control model of arms races." American Political Science Review 71: 226-244.

GREENWOOD, T., H. A. FEIVESON, and T. B. TAYLOR (1977) Nuclear Proliferation. 1980s Project/Council on Foreign Relations. New York: McGraw-Hill.

HOLLIST, W. L. (1977a) "Alternative explanation of competitive arms processes: tests on four pairs of nations." American Journal of Political Science 21: 313-340.

——— (1977b) "Analyses of arms processes in the United States and Soviet Union." International Studies Quarterly 21: 503-528.

HUNTINGTON, S. P. (1958) "Arms races: prerequisites and results." Public Policy 8: 41-86.

INTRILIGATOR, M. D. (1978) Econometric Models, Techniques, and Applications. Englewood Cliffs, NJ: Prentice-Hall.

——— (1975) "Strategic considerations in the Richardson model of arms races." Journal of Political Economy 83: 339-353.

——— (1971) Mathematical Optimization and Economic Theory. Englewood Cliffs, NJ: Prentice-Hall.

——— (1968) "The debate over missile strategy: targets and rates of fire." Orbis 11: 1138-1159.

——— (1967) Strategy in a Missile War: Targets and Rates of Fire. Security Studies Paper No. 10. Los Angeles: University of California.

——— (1964) "Some simple models of arms races." General Systems 9: 143-147.

——— and D. L. BRITO (1981) "Nuclear proliferation and the probability of nuclear war." Public Choice 37: 247-260.

——— (1978) "Nuclear proliferation and stability." Journal of Peace Science 3: 173-183.

——— (1977) "Strategy, arms races, and arms control," in J. V. Gillespie and D. A. Zinnes (eds.) Mathematical Systems in International Relations Research. New York: Praeger.

——— (1976) "Formal models of arms races." Journal of Peace Science 2: 77-88.

KAHN, H. (1962) Thinking about the Unthinkable. New York: Horizon.

——— (1960) On Thermonuclear War. Princeton, NJ: Princeton University Press.

KUPPERMAN, R. H., R. M. BEHR, and T. P. JONES, Jr. (1974) "The deterrence continuum." Orbis 18: 720-749.

KUPPERMAN, R. H. and H. A. SMITH (1972) "Strategies of mutual deterrence." Science 176 (April 7): 18-23.

——— (1977) "Deterrent stability and strategic warfare," in J. V. Gillespie and D. A. Zinnes (eds.) Mathematical Systems in International Relations Research. New York: Praeger.

LAMBELET, J. (1976) "A complementary analysis of the Anglo-German dreadnought race, 1905-1916." Papers of the Peace Science Society (International) 26: 219-266.

——— (1975) "Do arms races lead to war?" Journal of Peace Research 12: 123-128.

——— (1973) "Towards a dynamic two-theater model of the East-West arms race." Journal of Peace Science 1.

——— (1971) "A dynamic model of the arms race in the Middle East, 1953-1965." General Systems 16: 145-167.

LAWRENCE, R. M. and J. LARUS [Eds.] (1974) Nuclear Proliferation: Phase II. Lawrence: University Press of Kansas.

LEE, W. T. (1978) Soviet Defense Expenditures: An Unconventional Approach. New York: Praeger.

LUTERBACHER, U. (1975) "Arms race models: where do we stand?" European Journal of Political Research 3: 199-217.

MADDOX, J. (1975) Prospects for Nuclear Proliferation. Adelphi Paper No. 113. London: International Institute for Strategic Studies.

MARWAH, O. and A. SCHULTZ [Eds.] (1975) Nuclear Proliferation and the Near-Nuclear Countries. Cambridge, MA: Ballinger.

McGUIRE, M. C. (1977) "A quantitative study of the strategic arms race in the missile age." Review of Economics and Statistics 59: 328-339.

——— (1965) Secrecy and the Arms Race. Cambridge, MA: Harvard University Press.

MONTROL, E. W. and W. W. BADGER (1974) Introduction to Quantitative Aspects of Social Phenomena. New York: Gordon & Breach.

MORGENSTERN, O. (1959) The Question of National Defense. New York: Random House.

NACHT, M. L. (1975) "The delicate balance of error." Foreign Policy 19: 163-167.

NASH, J. F. (1960) "The bargaining problem." Econometrica 18: 155-162.

NEWHOUSE, J. (1973) Cold Dawn: The Story of SALT. New York: Holt, Rinehart & Winston.

NITZE, P. H. (1976) "Assuring strategic stability in an era of detente." Foreign Affairs 54: 207-232.

O'NEIL, B. (1970) "The pattern of instability among nations: a test of Richardson's theory." General Systems 15: 175-181.

PITMANN, G. R., Jr. (1969) Arms Races and Stable Deterrence. Security Studies Project. Los Angeles: University of California.

QUESTER, G. H. (1973) The Politics of Nuclear Proliferation, Baltimore: Johns Hopkins Press.

RAPOPORT, A. (1961) Fights, Games and Debates. Ann Arbor: University of Michigan Press.

——— (1957) "Lewis Fry Richardson's mathematical theory of war." Journal of Conflict Resolution 1: 249-304.

RATHJENS, G. W. (1969) "The dynamics of the arms race." Scientific American 220 (April): 15-25.

RATTINGER, H. (1976) "Econometrics and arms races: a critical review and some extensions." European Journal of Political Research 4: 421-436.

RICHARDSON, L. E. (1960) Arms and Insecurity. Pittsburgh: Boxwood.

——— (1939) "Generalized foreign politics." British Journal of Psychology Monographs Supplement 23.

RULOFF, D. (1975) "The dynamics of conflict and cooperation between nations: a computer simulation and some results." Journal of Peace Research 12: 109-121.

SAATY, T. L. (1968) Mathematical Models of Arms Control and Disarmament. New York: John Wiley.

SANDBERG, I. (1977) "Some qualitative properties of nonlinear Richardson-type arms race models," in J. V. Gillespie and D. A. Zinnes (eds.) Mathematical Systems in International Relations Research. New York: Praeger.

SCHELLING, T. C. (1966) Arms and Influence. New Haven, CT: Yale University Press.

——— (1960) The Strategy of Conflict. Cambridge, MA: Harvard University Press.

——— (1959) "Surprise attack and disarmament," in K. Knorr (ed.) NATO and American Security. Princeton, NJ: Princeton University Press.

SCHRODT, P. A. (1978) "Statistical problems associated with the Richardson arms race model." Journal of Peace Science 3: 159-172.

SILJAK, D. (1977) "On the stability of the arms race," in J. V. Gillespie and D. A. Zinnes (eds.) Mathematical Systems in International Relations Research. New York: Praeger.

——— (1976) "A competitive analysis of the arms race." Annals of Economic and Social Measurement 5: 283-295.

SIMAAN, M. and J. B. CRUZ, Jr. (1977) "Equilibrium concepts for arms race problems," in J. V. Gillespie and D. A. Zinnes (eds.) Mathematical Systems in International Relations Research. New York: Praeger.

——— (1975b) "Nash equilibrium strategies for the problem of armament race and control." Management Science 22: 96-105.

——— (1975a) "Formulation of Richardson's model of arms race from a differential game viewpoint." Review of Economic Studies 42: 67-77.

SMOKER, P. (1967a) "Nation state escalation and international integration." Journal of Peace Research 4: 61-75.

——— (1967b) "The arms race as an open and closed system." Peace Research Society Papers 7: 41-62.

——— (1965) "Trade, defense and the Richardson theory of arms races: a seven nation study." Journal of Peace Research 2: 161-176.

——— (1964) "Fear in the arms races: a mathematical study." Journal of Peace Research 1: 55-64.

——— (1963a) "A mathematical study of the present arms race." General Systems 8: 51-60.

——— (1963b) "A pilot study of the present arms race." General Systems 8: 61-76.

SPIELMANN, K. (1978) Analyzing Soviet Strategic Arms Decisions. Boulder, CO: Westview.

SZILARD, L. (1964) " 'Minimal deterrent' vs. saturation parity." Bulletin of the Atomic Scientists 20: 6-12.

TAAGEPERA, R., G. SHIFFLER, T. PERKINS, and D. WAGNER (1975) "Soviet-American and Israeli-Arab arms races and the Richardson model." General Systems 20: 151-152.

TULLOCK, G. (1974) The Social Dilemma. Blacksburg, VA: University Publications.

WALLACE, M. (1979) "Arms races and escalation." Journal of Conflict Resolution 23: 3-15.

WOHLSTETTER, A. (1975) "Optimal ways to confuse ourselves." Foreign Policy 20: 170-198.

——— (1974) "Is there a strategic arms race?" Foreign Policy 15, 16: 3-20, 48-81.

——— (1959) "The delicate balance of terror." Foreign Affairs 37: 211-234.

——— et al. (1976) Moving toward Life in a Nuclear Armed Crowd? Los Angeles: Panheuristics.

WOLFSON, M. (1968) "A mathematical model of the Cold War." Peace Research Society Papers 9: 107-123.

YORK, H. F. (1970) The Race to Oblivion. New York: Simon & Schuster.

ZINNES, D. A. and J. V. GILLESPIE [Eds.] (1976) Mathematical Models in International Relations. New York: Praeger.

——— (1973) "Analysis of arms race models: USA vs. USSR and NATO vs. WTO." Modeling and Simulation 4: 145-148.

——— and P. A. SCHRODT (1976) "The Arab-Israeli arms race: an empirical examination." Jerusalem Journal of International Relations 2: 28-62.

4

Modeling Precrisis Interactions

DINA A. ZINNES, BARBARA J. HILL,
DAVID L. JONES, and STEPHEN J. MAJESKI

Research on international crises has typically focused on developing a
workable definition of "crisis" or on identifying those events that take
place once a crisis, however defined, occurs. The analyses to be reported
here differ from these more standard approaches to the study of crisis. The
focus of this research is on *forecasting* international crises. The goal is to
find a set of conditions that always precede a crisis and then to use these
conditions to predict crises. Although our purpose is not to define "crisis,"
the search for conditions that signal an international crisis must be related
to those elements that define this concept. Thompson's (1979) recent
analysis of crisis definitions is a useful starting point.[1] Through an examination of various definitions, Thompson developed a set of criteria that
define "international crisis":

> An international political crisis situation encompasses a sequence of
> interactions between two or more actors (at least one of which must
> be a state) involved in an international dispute/conflict relationship
> and the realization of the following necessary and sufficient
> conditions:
>
> 1. At some point in the interaction sequence, actors on one or
>   more sides to the conflict must perceive their opponents as
>   communicating demands/challenges which are considered to

AUTHORS' NOTE: John Gillespie made important contributions to this research.
Although he did not see the final results reported here, he was deeply involved in the
development of the overall research design and in many of the details of the analysis.

be sufficiently threatening that they bring about a significant increase in the perceived probability of sustained, full scale violence between the disputants. This marks the beginning of the crisis if the following condition is also met.

2. At some subsequent point in the interaction sequence but prior to the actual outbreak of sustained, full scale violence, actors on one or more sides to the conflict must engage in non-routine decision-making which the decision-makers perceive (correctly or incorrectly) as a "fight or flee" decisional turning point in the conflict interaction sequence. A "fight or flee" decisional turning point involves attempting to choose a critical response to the opponent's demands/challenges which is designed to lead immediately to one of three outcomes: the outbreak of sustained, full scale violence, the capitulation of one side, or the implicit/explicit negotiation of compromise (a process which includes allowing the crisis to fade away) [Thompson, 1979: 30-32].

There are two components of this definition that are relevant for crisis forecasting. Note, first, that throughout the definition reference is made to "interaction sequences" that are conflictual or hostile. Thus, crises occur as a result of an unfolding series of hostile interactions; they are the endpoints of a set of "precrisis" events. Forecasting international crises requires that we examine the hostile interactions in periods that precede crises. The conditions that permit forecasting are embedded in the interaction sequence.

A second important component of this definition suggests that the hostile interaction sequence has critical cognitive/perceptual consequences for decision makers. Decision makers perceive threats that suggest a heightened probability of war, and they confront "fight-or-flee" decisional turning points. Unlike the "hostile interaction sequence," however, this component of the Thompson definition does not translate directly into forecasting conditions. First, it is not easy to observe the cognitive/perceptual states of mind of decision makers. But even more importantly, the definition implies that these cognitive/perceptual consequences are contemporaneous with the crisis itself. Consequently, they cannot be used directly for crisis forecasting.

Support for this research was granted by the Defense Advanced Research Projects Agency, Office of Army Research, under contract MDA-903-80-C-0149. This research benefited from the contributions of Su-Ik Hwang and Gregory S. Sanjian.

Nevertheless, this important ingredient of the definition can be used *indirectly*. We assume that the cognitive/perceptual states of mind occur as a consequence of an *unstable*, hostile interaction process. An unstable process is a process that is changing at such a rate that it will never "settle down" to a constant level. We are positing that in precrisis situations the hostile interactions are proceeding at such a rate that the interaction process is unstable, that is, the nations are interacting at an ever-increasing rate. Given such a situation, it is reasonable to assume that a decision maker would perceive a heightened probability of war and feel the necessity to make a fight-or-flee decision. Using the appropriate mathematics to model the dynamic interaction process, the concept of an unstable system can be given a very precise meaning.

Our analysis proceeds as follows. First, we select a set of previously defined international crises. For these crises, dynamic models are developed for the purpose of describing the activities of the nations in the period of time prior to the crisis. Because there are many different ways to describe the interactions of nations, three different dynamic models are developed. The model that best describes the behavioral interactions of the participant nations during the precrisis period is selected. The attributes of the best-fitting model can then be used to assess whether the precrisis period is unstable. If the underlying hypothesis of this research is correct, these periods should be unstable.

The Models

Three dynamic models were constructed to describe the behavior of nations in precrisis periods. Each model considers a pair of nations as the participants and describes the change in directed behavior of each nation toward the other. Directed behaviors have a source nation and a target nation. Nation X *directs* certain behaviors toward Y, both cooperative and conflictual, and the same is true for nation Y with respect to X. The models describe what factors affect the changes in one nation's behavior toward another. These models differ with respect to the variables that determine these changes.

Model I. The first model can be described using the following equations:

$$\dot{x}(t) = a_{11} x(t) + g \qquad [1]$$

$$\dot{y}(t) = a_{22} y(t) + h \qquad [2]$$

where

x(t) and y(t) are the amounts of hostility emitted by X and Y respectively at time t;

$\dot{x}(t) = dx/dt$ = the change in X's behavior toward Y;

$\dot{y}(t) = dy/dt$ = the change in Y's behavior toward X; and

g and h are relatively enduring levels of enmity or amity between X and Y.

Equations 1 and 2 describe two autoregressive processes. These two equations indicate that the change in each nation's directed behavior toward the other is a function only of its own directed behavior. Note that changes in the directed behaviors of X toward Y and Y toward X are not affected by the activities of the other nation.

Model II. A different representation of the directed behavior between X and Y in precrisis periods, however, is found in the second model:

$$\dot{x}(t) = a_{12} y(t) + g \tag{3}$$

$$\dot{y}(t) = a_{21} x(t) + h \tag{4}$$

This model proposes that the changes in the directed behavior of each nation are a function only of the directed behavior of the other nation. The model is a simple description of stimulus and response and postulates direct interaction between two nations.

Model III. A plausible argument can be made for consideration of yet a third model, a model that combines the ingredients of both Model I and Model II. Thus it is reasonable to postulate that changes in directed behavior are a function of both autoregressive and interactive factors. Using the same symbols defined previously, Model III can be written as:

$$\dot{x}(t) = a_{11} x(t) + a_{12} y(t) + g \tag{5}$$

$$\dot{y}(t) = a_{21} x(t) + a_{22} y(t) + h \tag{6}$$

It should be noted that no assumptions are made about the signs of the a_{ij} coefficients. It is equally plausible to argue that these coefficients are all positive—both types of factors increase a nation's emission of hostility— as it is to argue that some are positive and some are negative—e.g., the opponent's emission of hostility increases a nation's hostility while that nation's own hostility acts as a damper.

Operationalizing the Variables

The variables x and y in the above three models have been termed "directed behavior." While "directed" was defined previously, "behavior" still requires explication. The type of behavior most relevant to an international crisis is hostility. The best operationalization of these variables would therefore be the hostility inherent in the directed behaviors between pairs of nations, recorded at specified time points. An obvious data source for this purpose is the World Event Interaction Survey (WEIS).[2] This data set has coded every action directed by one nation toward another that was reported in the New York *Times.* Each action is coded into one of twelve hostile event types (Reject, Accuse, Protest, Deny, Demand, Warn, Threat, Demonstrate, Reduce, Expel, Seize, Force) or into one of ten cooperative event types (Yield, Comment, Consult, Approve, Promise, Grant, Reward, Agree, Request, Propose). The WEIS data set begins in 1966. Fortunately, it has been supplemented by another that covers the periods of time prior to World War II, the Cuban missile crisis, and the Korean War. This latter data set is known as the Maryland Special Data Set and uses the same categories and coding rules as employed in WEIS (see Hopple, Wilkenfeld, and Rossa, 1977). Thus, there are two event data sets that cover most of the major international crises since the onset of World War II.

Two measures are used to operationalize variables x and y in the above models. The first is a simple count, without reference to the type of hostile event, of the total number of hostile acts that one nation directs toward the other within a specified span of time. This is known as the *frequency* measure. The second measure incorporates cooperative as well as hostile events. This measure, known as *"net hostility,"* is constructed by counting the number of directed hostile acts and subtracting from this number the number of directed cooperative acts. The concept of "net" implies that the variable of relevance is a "residue" of hostility, the amount of hostility that is left after the amount of cooperation is taken into account.

The Selection of Crisis Events for Analysis

We examined the crisis lists in Moore (1975), Daly and Bell (1977), Hazlewood and Hayes (1976), Mahoney (1978), and Thompson (1979) and selected those crises that are included in a majority of these lists and

TABLE 4.1   International Crises

	Year	Conflict	Participants		
(1)	1941	Pearl Harbor	United States	vs	Japan
(2)	1950	North Korean invasion	North Korea, USSR, People's Republic of China	vs	United States, South Korea
(3)	1962	Cuban missile crisis	Cuba, USSR	vs	United States
(4)	1967	Sino-Soviet border conflict	USSR	vs	People's Republic of China
(5)	1967	Arab-Israeli Six-Day War	Egypt, Syria, Iraq, Jordan, Kuwait, PLO, Libya, Algeria, Saudi Arabia	vs	Israel, United States
(6)	1968	Societ intervention in Czechoslovakia	USSR	vs	Czechoslovakia
(7)	1969	Sino-Soviet border conflict	USSR	vs	People's Republic of China
(8)	1970	North Vietnamese invasion of Cambodia	North Vietnam	vs	Cambodia, South Vietnam
(9)	1970	Jordon-PLO conflict	Jordan, United States, Israel	vs	PLO, Iraq, Syria, Egypt
(10)	1970	First US-USSR Mideast crisis	USSR	vs	United States
(11)	1971	Indo-Pakistani War	India	vs	Pakistan
(12)	1973	Arab-Israeli October War	Egypt, Syria, Iraq, Jordan Saudi Arabia	vs	Israel, United States
(13)	1973	Second US-USSR Mideast crisis	USSR	vs	United States
(14)	1976	Syrian-Lebanese conflict	Lebanon, Syria, Egypt	vs	Israel

for which there were sufficient data in the two data sets. Fourteen crises were selected based on these criteria. These crises are listed in Table 4.1. The list contains most of the major crises of the past several decades. Note also that the crises reflect differences along several potentially important dimensions, e.g., types of participants—major/major, major/minor, and minor/minor powers—and geographical regions.

Fitting the Models to Precrisis Periods

Two decisions had to be made before the three models could be evaluated using WEIS data. The first decision concerned the period of time prior to the crisis event that should be analyzed: For how many weeks or months before the crisis should the directed events be monitored? Two time periods were selected: six months and twelve months. Two periods were used to determine if any differences could be found between longer or shorter precrisis time frames.

The second decision concerned the operational definition of t in x(t). Ideally t should be measured in daily units. Unfortunately, even in pre-crisis periods there are often many days during which neither nation directs any activity toward the other. For this reason it was necessary to aggregate the data over groups of days. For the six-month period, the data were aggregated over ten-day periods; for the twelve-month period, the data were aggregated over twenty-day periods. In each case, then, the number of data points for each crisis participant is eighteen. Since there are three models, two measurements (frequency and net hostility) for each variable, and two time frames, there are $3 \times 2 \times 2 = 12$ sets of analyses for each crisis.

The models were developed in terms of differential equations. This was done deliberately to reflect the underlying assumption that the process being examined is continuous. However, we can only observe a discrete sample from that process so that the statistical analysis of equation 5 is a regression of the form:

$$z(t) = x(t+1) - x(t) = a_{11}x(t) + a_{12}y(t) + g \qquad [5']$$

where

$$z(t) \cong \dot{x}(t)$$

The models are, of course, estimated through time. Thus it is necessary to test for autocorrelated error. This is done using the Durbin-Watson d statistic.[3] Furthermore, since the models contain different numbers of variables, comparisons across models require that the R^2s be adjusted to account for different numbers of independent variables.[4]

Research Design Overview

We have postulated three models of the behavior of nations in precrisis periods. The variables in those models have been operationalized in two ways using WEIS-coded data. Fourteen international crises have been identified. Using the dates on which these crises began as the endpoints for our analysis, data sets for six- and twelve-month precrisis periods were created for each of the fourteen crises. Thus we have now established the basis for the two principal stages of our analysis.

The first stage of the analysis involves consideration of the fit of the various model, measure, and time-frame combinations. Two approaches can be used. First, the best overall result can be selected *for each crisis.* This would mean that the best model, measure, or time frame for one crisis would not necessarily be the same as the best model, measure, or time frame for a different crisis. From this perspective, the goal is to obtain the best single description for each individual crisis. The second approach is to examine the fourteen crises as a total group and to select, *over all crises,* a model, measure, and time frame that on the average best represents the total set of crises. Using either approach, the result of this first stage is to provide the best-fitting regression model descriptions of the behavior of nations in precrisis periods.

The second stage of the analysis involves consideration of the stability of these models. The stability of a linear dynamic system is determined by the coefficients obtained from the regression analyses. In a later section, we will elaborate on the methodology we employed in this stage.

Evaluating the Three Models

Table 4.2 reports the adjusted R^2 results from these analyses. There are two major sections in this table, one for the six-month analyses, and another for the twelve-month analyses. Each section is further divided by model (I, II, or III) and then by measure (with F denoting frequency and NH denoting net hostility). Values are not reported for analyses with insufficient data. The last two rows of the table report the average adjusted R^2 values and their standard deviations for each column. If a case had insufficient data for the regression analysis, it was not included in the average.

Two conclusions can be drawn from Table 4.2. First, perhaps most surprising, Model II provides exceedingly poor fits for nearly all crisis cases. Since Model II is the stimulus-reponse interaction model, these results are indeed perplexing for a precrisis period, and warrant some further thought and attention.

The second conclusion to emerge from this table concerns the relative merits of Models I and III. Consider the average adjusted R^2 results in the next to last row of Table 4.2. For each measure and time frame, Model III is superior to Model I. Furthermore, a comparison of the standard deviations given in the last row of the table shows that the variability in the two distributions is not appreciably different. In fact, the variability for Model III in the net hostility data is somewhat less than the variability for the comparable data set under Model I. Model III would thus appear to be the best overall model. Furthermore, if we compare the frequency results with the net hostility analysis, it is also clear that the net hostility measure is superior. There appears, however, to be very little difference between the six- and twelve-month periods.

Although Model III combined with the net hostility measure provides the best *overall* results, this conclusion should not obscure the fact that this combination does not fit all cases equally well. Indeed, a careful examination of Table 4.2 shows several crisis and time-frame combinations for which Model III and the net hostility measure do extremely poorly. For these particular cases, can the results be *appreciably* improved by moving to another model or measure? In general, the answer is no. The appropriate comparisons reveal that in a majority of instances the potential improvements in adjusted R^2 are minimal. Thus, the approach of finding the best model and measure combination for each crisis and time-frame combination is not warranted.

The Concept of Stability in Dynamic Systems

Stability is a concept that has many meanings, particularly in the political science literature. In the present context, stability refers to a mathematical property of dynamic systems. This mathematical property corresponds to most intuitive interpretations of stability, but it has a very precise definition. To provide a basis for understanding fully the results of the second stage of the analysis, the following brief discussion of stability is provided.

The three pairs of equations (1 through 6) are systems of differential equations. Each model describes changes in the variables x and y and indicates whether the process is increasing or decreasing. To determine

TABLE 4.2 A Comparison Adjusted R^2 for Models I, II, and III over Fourteen Crises

| | | Six-Month Analysis | | | | | | Twelve-Month Analysis | | | | | |
| | | Model I | | Model II | | Model III | | Model I | | Model II | | Model III | |
Dyad	Nation	F	NH	F	NH	F	NH	F	NH	F	NH	F	NH
1	JA	.149	.330	−.067	−.044	.111	.381	−.040	.447	.055	−.005	−.096	.410
	US	.457	.367	−.059	---	.433	.335	.264	.337	−.062	−.026*	.542	.290
2	NK	.477	.453	.247	.345	.813*	.522	.458	.421	.014	.188	.615	.522
	SK	.580	.573	.062*	−.046*	.561	.551	.267	.642	−.032	−.058*	.429*	.616
3	CU	.432	.533	−.062*	−.056*	.470	.528	.204	.478	−.061*	.117*	.165	.442
	US	.294	.380	−.062	−.030	.338	.411	.024	.303	.153	−.037	.342	.427
4	SU	.458	.450	.035*	.022*	.464	.451	---	---	---	---	---	---
	PC	.250	.304	.026	.016	.198	.259	---	---	---	---	---	---
5	AR	−.060*	−.047*	−.038	−.003*	.162*	−.064*	−.060*	−.073*	.041	.104	.022*	.086*
	IS	.182	.572	.003	.216	.141	.556	.448	.674	.187	.190*	.409	.654
6	SU	.251	.892*	.009*	−.027*	.209	.900*	---	---	---	---	---	---
	CZ	.337	.318	.207*	.064*	.290	.282	---	---	---	---	---	---
7	SU	---	---	---	---	.735*	.779*	.735*	.779*	.132	−.008	.761*	.769*
	PC	---	---	---	---	.603	.593	.603	.593	.007*	−.066*	.575	.558

8	NV	.175	.171	.117	.072	.132	.157	.182	.249	.145	.099	.143	.334
	SV	.206	.165	.153	.107	.157	.111	.129	.147	.139	.182	1.93*	.124
9	JR	.431	.462	.383	.411	.397	.436	.357	.318	.251	.461	.312	.422
	PL	.516	.561	.304	.343	.518	.545	.398	.487	.287	.031*	.356	.543
10	SU	.533	.564	-.067*	.217*	.592	.587	.432	.604	.195*	-.066*	.684	.621
	US	.369	.598	-.057*	-.050*	.358	.649	.315	.304	.310*	.113*	.343	.256
11	IN	-.055	-.066	-.012	-.048	.024	.020	-.023	.034*	-.037	-.061	.057*	.124*
	PK	.017	.027	.062*	.030*	.334	.334	.086	.076	-.054	-.049	.279	.288*
12	AR	.162	.557	.474	.014*	.438	.565	.579	.446	-.063*	.030*	.654	.421
	IS	.570	.308	.105*	.019	.556	.269	.378	.365	.286	-.023	.615*	.438
13	SU	.410	.287	-.029*	.317	.558	.293	.283	.178	-.061	.205	.239	.303*
	US	.185	.345	-.047	.109	.127	.335	.004	.207	--	.006	-.026	.316*
14	SL	--	--	--	--	--	--	.471	.246	.005*	-.051	.448	.285
	IS	--	--	--	--	--	--	.430	.254	.155*	-.027	.389	.244
MEAN COL		.3053	.3793	.0703	.0832	.3492	.3922	.2885	.3544	.0830	.0520	.3521	.3955
STD D COL		.1848	.2184	.1493	.1417	.1936	.2096	.2140	.2074	.1228	.1237	.2306	.1727

*These adjusted R^2 values are based on a GLS estimation procedure.

how either variable fluctuates over time it is necessary to obtain solutions to these three systems of equations. These solutions can be somewhat complex, especially in the case of Model III. For expository purposes, however, consider only the simplest model, Model I. Furthermore, consider this model in its simplest variation, that is, in its homogeneous form in which g and h are equal to zero. Equation 1′ and 2′, then, specify the resulting Model I′:

$$\dot{x}(t) = a_{11}\, x(t) \tag{1′}$$
$$\dot{y}(t) = a_{22}\, y(t) \tag{2′}$$

It can be shown that the solution to this simplified system is:

$$x(t) = c_1 e^{\lambda_1 t} \tag{7}$$
$$y(t) = c_2 e^{\lambda_2 t} \tag{8}$$

The parameters λ_1 and λ_2 are functions of the coefficients a_{11} and a_{22}. Indeed, in this special case, $\lambda_1 = a_{11}$ and $\lambda_2 = a_{22}$. The c_1 and c_2 parameters, however, can be made specific only with information concerning solutions of equations 1′ and 2′ at some particular point in time; that is, c_1 and c_2 are specified by solving the "initial value problem" for Model I′.

The stability of a dynamic linear system refers to the behavior of its solutions as t goes to infinity. The critical ingredients in equations 7 and 8 are λ_1 and λ_2. In equation 7, for example, if λ_1 is greater than zero it is clear that as t increases $x(t)$ will increase without bound for positive c_1 or decrease without bound for negative c_1. Since $x(t)$ represents the number of hostile acts that X is directing toward Y, this suggests that, as the precrisis time period increases, X's hostility toward Y will grow constantly in either a positive or negative direction. Such a system is said to be unstable. It is unstable because $x(t)$ will never "settle down," that is, $x(t)$ will never converge to a finite level of hostility. Thus an unstable system is an explosive system. On the other hand, if λ_1 is less than zero, it is easy to see that as t increases $x(t)$ in the limit approaches zero. This is a stable system.

The critical quantities that determine the stability of dynamic systems are the λ_i parameters in the solution. These parameters are found by forming the characteristic equation of the system. First, equations 1 and 2 are rewritten in matrix notation form. That is,

$$\dot{x}(t) = a_{11} x(t) + g$$
$$\dot{y}(t) = a_{22} y(t) + h$$

may be written as:

$$\dot{z}(t) = Az(t) + v \qquad [13]$$

where

$$\dot{z}(t) = \begin{bmatrix} \dot{x}(t) \\ \dot{y}(t) \end{bmatrix} \quad \text{and} \quad A = \begin{bmatrix} a_{11} & 0 \\ 0 & a_{22} \end{bmatrix} \quad \text{and} \quad \begin{bmatrix} v = & g \\ & h \end{bmatrix}$$

The characteristic equation for the matrix A is defined as the determinant of the matrix $A - \lambda I$, where I is the identity matrix. Thus the characteristic equation for 13 is:

$$(a_{11} - \lambda)(a_{22} - \lambda) - 0 = 0$$

or,

$$\lambda^2 + (-a_{11} - a_{22})\lambda + (a_{11} a_{22}) = 0$$

It is easy to show that the roots of this system are:

$$\lambda_i = 1/2[(a_{11} + a_{22}) \pm \sqrt{(-a_{11} - a_{22})^2 - 4(a_{11} a_{22})}]$$

for i = 1,2.

Thus it is seen that the elements of A determine the λ_i parameters which in turn determine the stability of the system. In the very simple system of equations given by Model I, the a_{ii} parameters indicate how each nation's past behavior affects its subsequent behavior. If these parameters are positive, then the roots of the characteristic function are positive and, therefore, the system is unstable. In short, if the past behavior of either nation X or Y acts as a stimulant, the system is "explosive." Models II and

III are slightly more complicated; the relationship between the coefficients and the elements of A is not so direct. Nonetheless, the same general logic applies to the interpretation of the λ coefficients.

A stable system is a system that will converge. The point in the x-y plane to which the system converges or "settles" is the equilibrium point and can be precisely determined by setting the differential equations for that system equal to zero. For the nonhomogeneous system described by equations 1 and 2, the equilibrium point is found by solving the following two equations:

$$\dot{x}(t) = 0 = a_{11} x(t) + g \tag{9}$$
$$\dot{y}(t) = 0 = a_{22} y(t) + h \tag{10}$$

The resulting equilibrium point for Model I is given by:

$$x(t) = -g/a_{11} \tag{11}$$
$$y(t) = -h/a_{22} \tag{12}$$

In the simple homogeneous system defined by equations 1' and 2', where $g = h = 0$, it is clear that the equilibrium is given by:

$$x(t) = 0 \tag{11'}$$
$$y(t) = 0 \tag{12'}$$

The equilibrium indicates the amount of hostility that the two nations will be exchanging when the dynamic ceases. From that point forward, there are no *changes* in the emission of hostility by either nation (unless the system is disturbed by exogenous forces). Note that in the case of equations 11 and 12, if g, h, a_{11}, and a_{22} are all negative, then the dynamic will cease at two negative values, suggesting that the two nations are emitting negative hostility, that is, cooperation. Figure 4.1 illustrates both stable and unstable solutions for equation 7. Note that the stable solutions asymptotically approach the equilibrium value $x(t) = 0$, whereas the unstable solutions diverge from this value.

Evaluating the Stability of Model III, Net Hostility

Using Model III and the net hostility measure as the best description of precrisis behavior across the crises, the second step of the analysis involves the use of the estimated a_{ij} coefficients to assess the stability properties of

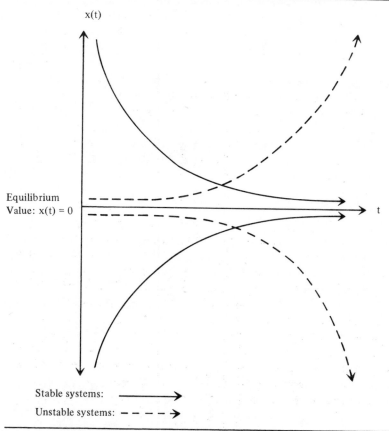

x(t)

Equilibrium
Value: x(t) = 0

t

Stable systems: ⟶

Unstable systems: – – – – →

Figure 4.1 Plots of Stable and Unstable Systems

these precrisis periods. The assessment of stability is based on the coefficients of both equations. Consequently, it makes sense to evaluate the stability of the model only in those cases where both equations provide adequate fits for the two participating nations. Two criteria were used to determine whether Model III fit both nations adequately: (1) the adjusted R^2 value for each crisis participant must be at least .25 and (2) across both crisis participants the average adjusted R^2 must be at least .36. Since no appreciable difference could be discerned between the fits for the six- and twelve-month periods, stability analyses are performed for both periods. Table 4.3 reports the individual adjusted R2 values, the average adjusted R^2 value across the two crisis participants, the λ_i roots of the character-

TABLE 4.3 Stability Analysis for Model III, Net Hostility

Dyad Nation	Six-Month Analysis					Twelve-Month Analysis				
	Individual Adjusted R^2	Average Adjusted R^2	λ_1	λ_2	Stable Unstable	Individual Adjusted R^2	Average Adjusted R^2	λ_1	λ_2	Stable Unstable
(1) JA-US	.381 .335	.358	−0.844*	−0.844*	(S)	.410 .290	.350	−0.962	−1.084	(S)
(2) NK-SK	.522 .551	.537	−0.950	−1.106	S	.522 .616	.569	−0.770	−1.396	S
(3) CU-US	.528 .411	.470	−0.704	−1.337	S	.442 .427	.435	−0.888	−1.215	S
(4) SU-PC	.451 .259	.355	−0.678	−1.201	(S)	—	—	—	—	—
(5) AR-IS	−.064 .556	.310	0.167	−1.299	(U)	.086 .654	.370	1.118	−1.776	(U)
(6) SU-CZ	.900 .282	.591	−0.807	−2.083	S	—	—	—	—	—

(7) SU-PC	—	—	—	—	—	.769 .558	.664	-1.134	-1.372	S
(8) NV-SV	.157 .111	.134	-0.382	-1.061	(S)	.334 .124	.229	- .554*	- .554*	(S)
(9) JR-PL	.436 .545	.491	-0.891	-1.311	S	.422 .543	.483	-0.608	-1.105	S
(10) SU-US	.587 .649	.618	-1.227*	-1.227*	S	.621 .256	.439	-0.690	-1.394	S
(11) IN-PK	.020 .334	.177	0.097	-0.953	(U)	.124 .288	.206	-0.381	-1.643	(S)
(12) AR-IS	.565 .269	.417	-0.685	-1.190	S	.421 .438	.430	1.298	0.738	U
(13) SU-US	.293 .335	.314	-0.690*	-0.690*	(S)	.303 .316	.310	-0.880*	-0.880*	(S)
(14) SL-IS	—	—	—	—	—	.285 .244	.265	-0.473	-1.138	(S)

* the real part of a complex root.

NOTE: Line across row indicates insufficient data for analysis; parentheses in last column indicate fit across both participants inadequate to draw conclusion on stability property.

istic equation, and the result of the stability analysis for both time periods. From this table it can be seen that there are six crises (NK/SK, CU/US, SU/CZ, JR/PL, SU/US [10], AR/IS [12]) with adequate data and sufficient fits for the six-month time frame to permit meaningful stability analysis. In these six crises the surprising result is that the systems are always stable, as evidenced by the fact that in each case both λ_i values are negative, or in the case of complex λ_i's, their real parts are negative.

With one exception, this startling result is also found for the twelve-month time period. For this set, six crises (NK/SK, CU/US, SU/PC [7], JR/PL, SU/US [10], AR/IS [12]) have adequate data and fits to permit stability analysis. The only unstable case among them is the Arab-Israeli crisis of 1973. Why this case becomes unstable only when a longer time frame is used is intriguing, but unclear.

The basic hypothesis underlying this research is not supported by this empirical analysis. Precrisis periods were found to be stable, not unstable. This surprising and counterintuitive finding is made even more puzzling by the fact that the results are so consistent over the crises. It is rare in research of this type to find such consistency; one might have anticipated that some precrises would be stable and some unstable. This overwhelming consistency led us to consider another possible interpretation of precrisis behavior.

Stability and Equilibrium

Recall that stable systems are converging toward a system equilibrium. The equilibrium point is strictly a function of the a_{ij}, g, and h values. Depending on the combination of positive and negative values of these parameters, the equilibrium point could be characterized by any combination of hostile and cooperative behavior. Thus an interesting hypothesis emerges. If the equilibrium point is a value for x and y such that *one or both* nations must emit hostility, then a possible explanation for the crisis is that the system dynamic, even though stable, is driving the two nations to a point where at least one must be emitting hostile behavior.

A simple initial test of this new interpretation of precrisis behavior is to calculate the equilibrium point for each of the stable precrisis systems, and to locate these points in the x-y space illustrated in Figure 4.2. Before doing so, however, it is important to recall the operationalization of the variables x and y in the stability analyses. The above results are based on net hostility, the frequency of hostile acts minus the frequency of coop-

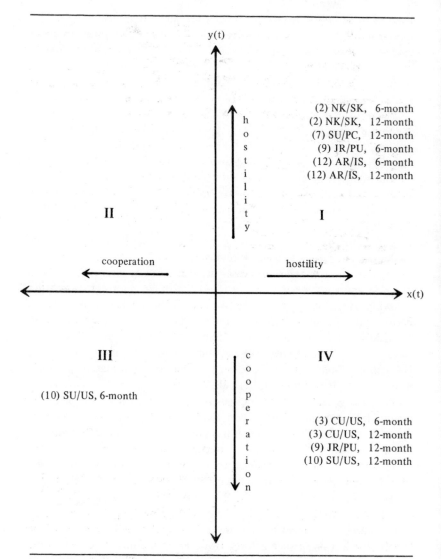

Figure 4.2 Quadrant Locations of Equilibria for Stable Systems that Passed Adequate Fit Criteria

erative acts. If the equilibrium point is positive for both nations, that is, if it is located in quadrant I in Figure 4.2, then the implication is that both nations are emitting more hostility than cooperation at equilibrium. If both of these values are negative so that the equilibrium point is located in quadrant III, the implication is that both nations must emit more cooperation than hostility at equilibrium. If the hypothesis is correct, the latter case should not occur. It is of course possible that one of the values could be positive and the other negative so that the equilibrium point would be located in either quadrant II or quadrant IV of Figure 4.2.

The locus of equilibrium for each of the eleven stable crises found in the stability analysis discussed above is reported in Figure 4.2. The results are essentially supportive of the hypothesis we have proposed. Six cases—North Korea/South Korea and Arabs/Israel, both crises for the six- and twelve-month time frames, USSR/PRC for the longer time frame, and finally Jordan/PLO for the shorter time frame—exhibit equilibria in quadrant I. Here both parties emit net hostile behavior; the stable relationships between these pairs involve mutual hostility. As might have been expected, each of these cases may be seen as a part of a larger protracted conflict characterized by periodic intense violence.

Four of the five remaining cases are located in quadrant III in which one side emits net hostile behavior and the other emits net cooperative behavior. Three of the four cases that involve superpower confrontation occur in this group: Cuba/US for the six- and twelve-month time frames and USSR/US for the longer time frame. Interestingly, in each of these cases it is the United States whose equilibrium net behavior is cooperative. No such consistency is seen in Soviet behavior at equilibrium; it appears in different cases in quadrants I, III, and IV.

Two cases remain to be discussed. First, Jordan/PLO appears in quadrant IV for the twelve-month time frame. For the six-month time frame, however, we have seen that this precrisis interval has an equilibrium in the first quadrant. A tentative explanation is suggested by the apparent evolution of this conflict. There is some evidence that in the earlier stages of this conflict there were uneven, but continuing efforts at accommodation and coexistence by the Palestinian guerilla groups and by Hussein and the Jordanian military. The twelve-month equilibrium result, which suggests a cooperative posture on the part of the PLO, may well be largely a reflection of such efforts. However, in the months closer to the open conflict that constitutes this crisis, the overall conflict seems to have been transformed into a more zero-sum form of conflict in which the Jordanian goal apparently became one of terminating PLO military power within Jordan. Thus, in the six-month time frame, a quadrant I equilibrium should not be unexpected.

The final case appears to be anomalous: The 1970 Soviet/American precrisis equation is located in quadrant III for the six-month time frame. This implies a mutually net cooperative interactive process at equilibrium. This result is not consistent with two related results discussed above. First, in the twelve-month time frame this equilibrium is located in quadrant IV. Second, this crisis was a derivative or spinoff of the Jordan/PLO crisis, whose precrisis equilibrium for the same time frame, we have already seen, is located in the "opposite" quadrant, quadrant I. There is evidence, however, of superpower cooperation to contain this crisis, a state of affairs that is of course consistent with the location of the equilibrium for this case in the cooperative-cooperative quadrant. Nonetheless, though ten of the eleven stable cases found are supportive of the hypothesis that stable precrisis processes are converging toward, or have equilibria in, regions entailing net hostile behavior, this case fails to support the proposed hypothesis.

Summary and Conclusions

The research reported here makes the assumption that an international crisis is the consequence of an unbounded buildup of hostile interactions between nations. We postulated that the directed hostile behaviors between nations may be modeled as dynamic processes, and we hypothesized that these processes are unstable in periods preceding crises. We proposed that if this hypothesis were substantiated, then instability in the interactions between nations might be a useful predictor of international crises.

Our investigation of these ideas proceeded through three stages. First, we examined a variety of models of directed behavior between nations, measures of hostility, and precrisis time intervals. We concluded that the most satisfactory model was Model III, which is described by equations 5 and 6, in which changes in the directed hostile behaviors of crisis participants are a function of both autoregressive and interactive components. In addition, we concluded that the preferred measure of hostility is net hostility, which we operationalized as the difference between the frequencies of hostile and cooperative behaviors. These choices were preferred in the sense that the corresponding regression model provided the best fits for the fourteen crises considered. These crises include most of the major crises of the post-World War II era. The appropriate data on precrisis interactions were extracted from the WEIS and Maryland international events data sets. Finally, we found that these results were essentially indifferent between a six-month and a twelve-month precrisis time frame. Hence, we proceeded to the second stage of our analysis entertaining both time frames.

The second stage consisted of stability analysis of Model III, net hostility results for both the six- and twelve-month precrisis time periods for those cases with sufficient data and adequate statistical fits. The results of this stage of analysis are nearly uniformly inconsistent with our hypothesis. In eleven of twelve cases that satisfied these data and statistical fit criteria, we found that precrisis periods were *stable* rather than unstable as hypothesized. Nonetheless, we continue to find the hypothesized connection between unstable interactions and crises to be compelling on substantive grounds. Therefore, rather than rejecting this proposition, we believe it first must be reconsidered under different conditions including additional crisis cases, shorter aggregation intervals, and different data sets.

Nonetheless, the unanticipated consistency of our results, though negative, required explanation. Consequently, we moved to a final stage in our analysis in which we observed that a stable system may be described by the equilibrium point to which it is converging. We thus examined the additional hypothesis that in precrisis periods stable processes will have equilibria characterized by net hostile behavior. That is, at equilibrium one or both actors will be engaged in net hostile behavior directed toward the opponent. In ten of the eleven cases, this hypothesis is supported. In six cases the equilibria are in regions in which both crisis participants emit net hostility, and in four other cases the equilbria are in regions in which one participant emits net hostility.

Our findings, then, tentatively suggest the following overall proposition for additional research. Precrisis dyadic interactions are unstable, that is, unbounded, or, if stable, have equilibria characterized by net hostile activity by one or both participants.

NOTES

1. Thompson's definition is the result of an exhaustive evaluation and critical analysis of 25 commonly used crisis definitions in international relations research.

2. The World Event Interaction Survey (WEIS) data collection project was begun in 1967 by Charles McClelland at the University of Southern California. A version of this data set is available through the Inter-University Consortium for Political and

Social Research. See Fitzsimmons et al. (1969) for an outline of WEIS data collection and coding procedures, and McClelland (1968) for a description of the theoretical assumptions of the data set.

3. It is well known that, in the presence of lagged endogenous variables, the Durbin-Watson d statistic is asymptotically biased toward acceptance of the null hypothesis of independence of the residuals. While there is no question that the d statistic is asymptotically biased, there is no clear consensus on the power of the statistic. Although Malinvaud (as cited in Johnston, 1972) "confirmed" its lack of power, Taylor and Wilson (1964) concluded that "the test on OLS residuals was quite powerful." We chose to use the d statistic, realizing its limitations, because the standard alternative, Durbin's h statistic, is a large-sample statistic that is biased toward rejecting the null hypothesis of serial independence of residuals for sample sizes comparable to those of this study (see Spencer, 1975).

4. We use the adjusted R^2 measure, denoted by $\overline{R}^2$, because we wish to compare the fits of models with different numbers of explanatory variables. R^2 is inappropriate for this purpose since it *cannot* decrease as the number of explanatory variables increases. The use of this unadjusted measure would introduce a bias in our work toward accepting Model III simply as an artifact of its larger number of explanatory variables. In contrast, $\overline{R}^2$ is explicitly adjusted for the number of explanatory variables k as well as for the sample size n. Its relationship to R^2 may be represented as:

$$\overline{R}^2 = \frac{1-k}{n-k} + \frac{n-1}{n-k} \, R^2$$

These and other issues are elaborated in Johnston (1972) and Theil (1971).

REFERENCES

DALY, J. A. and B. D. BELL (1977) Probability Tables. Early Warning and Monitoring Project Research Memorandum No. 14 (August). McLean, VA: Decisions and Designs, Inc.

FITZSIMMONS, B. A., G. A. HOGGARD, C. A. McCLELLAND, W. R. MARTIN and R. A. YOUNG (1969) World Event Interaction Survey Handbook and Codebook. Los Angeles: University of Southern California.

HAZLEWOOD, L. and J. J. HAYES (1976) Planning for Problems in Crisis Management. Arlington, VA: CACI.

HOPPLE, G. W., J. WILKENFELD, and P. J. ROSSA (1977) "WEIS crisis data set: documentation report." University of Maryland. (mimeo)

JOHNSTON, J. (1972) Econometric Methods. New York: McGraw-Hill.

MAHONEY, R. B., Jr. (1978) Analysis of the Soviet Crisis Management Experience. Interim Technical Report (May). Arlington, VA: CACI.

McCLELLAND, C. A. (1968) International Interaction Analysis: Basic Research and Some Practical Uses. Los Angeles: University of Southern California.

MOORE, J. A. (1975) Crisis Inventory. Arlington, VA: CACI.

SPENCER, B. G. (1975) "The small sample bias of Durbin's test for serial correlation when one of the regressors is the lagged dependent variable and the null hypothesis is true." Journal of Econometrics 3: 249-254.

TAYLOR, L. D. and T. A. WILSON (1964) "Three pass least squares: a method for estimating models with lagged dependent variables." Review of Economics and Statistics 46: 324-346.

THEIL, H. (1971) Principles of Econometrics. New York: John Wiley.

THOMPSON, W. R. (1979) Definitional and Dating Problems in the Analysis of International Crises. McLean, VA: International Public Policy Research Corporation.

Synthesis

Problems and Prospects in Dynamic Modeling

BRIAN L. JOB

By comparing and contrasting the previous two chapters, one can get a feel for the larger issues concerning the role of dynamic models in international relations research. It is with an eye to this sort of larger question that the following discussion is structured around three main themes. First is the issue of how the models reflect the structural characteristics and interactions of units in crises and arms race situations. Second is the issue of the information and insights that these models yield; and third is the matter of future refinements to enhance the utility of mathematical modeling in international relations.

Dynamic Models of Competitive Interstate Interaction

There are two common alternative conceptualizations of interstate behavior. One holds that a state's behavior toward a another state is the result of the internal dynamics and previous behaviors of the first state itself. The other alternative holds that, in competitive dyadic situations, the first state's behavior is a set of responses to the second state's behavior, and vice versa. These sterotypic conceptions are often called the "closed" and "open" models, respectively, with terms such as "internal" or "autoregressive" and "external" or "stimulus-response" also used as descriptors. Thus, regardless of whether one is examining foreign policy decision making (e.g., Allison, Kanter, Halperin, or Steinbruner), or crisis interaction (e.g., Hermann, Tanter, or Brecher), or arms racing (e.g., Zinnes and Gillespie, Ostrom, or Richardson), there will be debate over whether a state's actions are determined internally or are responses to external messages and behaviors.

Common sense tells us that the answers will not be this simple and clear cut—the utility of these theories is in their posing of extremes to serve as reference points in evaluating real-world behaviors. Interstate interaction, be it arms purchases or exchanges of diplomatic messages, is likely to be influenced by *both* each state's previous behavior and its opponent's behavior. Such a combination of effects may be represented by models as well.

The most prominent such "combined-effects" model was set forth by L. F. Richardson, who viewed a two-nation arms race as a dynamic system of interaction represented by a pair of differential equations. In his terms, the dependent variable, i.e., the rate of acquisition of arms by state A is determined by the level of state B's arms (a positive influence), the previous level of state A's arms (a negative influence), and the condition of enmity or cooperation between the states (called a grievance factor). While Richardson himself restricted the applicability of his model by envisioning only one configuration of the signs on the coefficients in the model, Zinnes and others have demonstrated the wider applicability of such combined-effects models if the direction of effects is not specified in advance.

Anyone currently setting out to model interstate interaction systems (a) has to confront the question of the relative effects of internal versus external determinants and (b) finds a tradition in the modeling literature built around two prototypic models—the open and the closed—and a variety of formulations attempting to capture the combined effects of these two sets of factors. These themes are present in both Zinnes et al. and Brito and Intriligator chapters. However, the authors go about constructing their dynamic systems models in quite different fashions.

Zinnes adopts the idea of using an autoregressive model, a stimulus-response model, and a combined-effects model, each in their most simple form, as a set of three competing formulations to find which one best describes the observed pattern of interstate interactions in international crises. Her logic is to reduce things to their bare bones, to find out if one prototypic behavior pattern predominates in observed crisis behaviors, to analyze the stability properties implicit in this particular formulation, and to see if such information will allow warning or forecasting in other precrisis situations. The focus in this chapter is on analyzing precrisis interaction sequences to see if they display the hypothesized formal characteristics of an unstable process. The medium of interchange between states is the gross, or net, volume of hostile messages directed from one state to another. The behaviors of all parties on each side of a conflict are aggregated together.

Despite the fact that there appears to be an intuitive fit between the theories of crisis behavior and the notions of dynamic systems models, few persons have attempted this sort of an analysis before. Therefore, Zinnes et al. are breaking new ground in this chapter, which provides an additional reason for the apparently simple and straightforward model constructions they employ. But as was pointed out (by Baugh, Simowitz, and Feste), the emphasis on simplicity in the formulation and operationalization of the three crisis models carries with it the danger of being overly simplistic. It was argued, for instance, that multiparty crises should have been disaggregated into dyadic confrontations, that imposing a 6- or 12-month time limit to precrisis interaction was arbitrary, and that the intensity of the hostility of the message traffic should have been considered.

There is a much greater tradition of modeling of arms races than of modeling crises—including in the former, of course, the works of Brito and Intriligator themselves and those of Gillespie and Zinnes. Thus, in their chapter, Brito and Intriligator set out to avoid the criticisms of simplicity and neglect of bureaucratic decision-making structures that have been leveled at various other arms race modelers by constructing a framework that ideally encompasses all domestic aspects of strategic planning, allocation of domestic resources, and arms acquisitions in arms races. Their approach to the construction of model is thus an almost opposite one to that taken by Zinnes et al. They devise a grand model consisting of two components—a nuclear war component and an allocative component.

Both components are important, yet the reader is left confused as to how levels and rates set or derived in one component are affected by, and affect, the levels and rates of the second component. For instance, how are rates of fire, targeting strategy, desired opponent casualty levels, and acceptable casualty losses for oneself—all central variables in the nuclear war component of the model—necessarily affected and altered by a decision taken in the allocative component of the model that the state cannot afford the level of missiles previously determined to be "optimal" (in the nuclear war component).

The Brito and Intriligator chapter, therefore, tends to demonstrate another side of the simplicity-versus-complexity issue in modeling. By opting for a most complete and intricate structure, one that in principle would take into account *all* external *and* internal determinants of arms races, Brito and Intriligator run the risks of being criticized on the one hand for being too complex to be comprehensible and tractible, and on the other for neglecting supposedly important additional decision mechanisms. That is, having implied that they are going to include most every factor in the arms race process, they leave themselves open to a series of claims that additional features must be built in. Given their current formulation, it appears fair to conclude that the different sectors of their model illustrate quite disparate levels of congruence and isomorphism to actual decision-making structures and interactive processes. It is also not clear exactly what is input into the models and what variables, decisions, or levels will be the outputs of the models.

The tradeoffs and choices that face Zinnes et al. and Brito and Intriligator are typical of those facing anyone trying to model an international interaction process. Brito and Intriligator provide insights into some factors that need to be considered in mapping the structural dimension of arms races, yet they leave out some crucial variables and relationships. While Zinnes contributes a way of modeling combined effects in interactions, she excludes some key considerations. Complexity in the formulation of assumptions and equations implies costs in terms of the ability of the modeler to manipulate and/or estimate his or her model. The advantages of simplicity, however, may be achieved only at the expense of a certain amoung of "realism."

The Results of the Modeling Enterprise

Most often, it is the property of stability, in conjunction with the existence of equilibrium points, that is of concern in models of international behavior. Particularly when considering possible preconflict interchanges such as arms races or crises, the prospect of knowing whether or not the processes of interstate behavior are "stable" takes on particular significance. However, an important qualification must be noted. The notions of stability in the formal terms derived from a mathematical model are often very different from those notions of stability relevant to the understanding of a particular international phenomenon. This warning applies to both the Zinnes et al. and Brito and Intriligator chapters. In the Brito and Intriligator study, stability refers to the characteristics of the process in the vicinity of certain equilibrium points, i.e., points where the rate of arms acquisition by both sides equals zero. If, upon disturbance from equilibrium, the process tends back toward this condition, it is regarded as stable. Brito and Intriligator come up with some fascinating, counterintuitive results concerning equilibrium and stability in the arms race. They demonstrate, for instance, that their model describes an interaction sequence with two equilibrium points—one at high levels of arms, the other at lower levels. Disturbances from the latter rather than the former tend toward instability! Furthermore, under certain circumstances, it is bilateral rather than unilateral disarmament that "leads to the greatest chance of war." Brito and Intriligator's study is highly instructive in this regard. It demonstrates the remarkable analytic tools available to the mathematical modeler, and at the same time, makes apparent the careful interpretations that must be given to properties defined in mathematical (rather than in substantive) terms.

In contrast, it is instability that is central to the Zinnes et al. investigation. They commence with the intuitive notion that major international crises are by their nature "unstable" and, thus, that precrisis interaction processes, in turn, should have inherently unstable properties when analyzed. The unwary reader may translate these ideas of stability and instability to correspond to the occurrence of peaceful or conflictual outcomes of crises, but this is *not* correct. In terms of the Zinnes et al. mathematical models, a stable process is one in which the rates of interaction by both parties operate so that their activity tends toward a certain interaction level. An unstable process is one where one or both state's rates of interaction do not result in convergence to any specified level but continue to increase or decrease in an explosive fashion (see Figure 3.1). In the "real world," therefore, a stable precrisis process would be one where the rates of interaction would (most likely) increase until at some point a sustained (high) level of (hostile) interchange would continue. Such a convergence would not occur in an unstable process. Upon investigation, Zinnes et al. discover that, of the precrisis incidents that adequately "fit" their model specifications, all are stable in this sense. This is, of course, contrary to the expectation stated in their initial hypothesis.

The question arises, however, as to whether or not confusion of the meanings of "formal stability" and "real-world stability" have not led Zinnes et al. to be surprised by results that, in fact, may tend to confirm rather than disconfirm common wisdom about crises. Previous research on crises suggests a typical pattern termed the "conflict spiral" manifests itself, that is, states interact with each other with increasing frequency and intensity until decision makers, usually unable to cope with these levels of stress and hostility, move accidentally or deliberately to war. If conceptualized as a process in the terms of Zinnes et al., especially in terms of volume and not intensity of messages, one can view the crisis spiral phenomenon as a formally stable process: Both parties increase their interchange to some level (probably to the information processing capacity of the system), at which point the intensity level of the messages may or may not increase—this is not stated in the Zinnes chapter—and war may result because of decision maker behavior in these circumstances. Looked at in this way, stability rather than instability may have been the anticipated result of this modeling enterprize.

In a larger sense what is important is not so much an argument that is alternative to that of Zinnes et al., but rather, recognition of the disjunctures in meaning that can occur when one tries to translate, or adopt, the terms of formal properties of mathematical models into discussions of real-world behaviors. What Zinnes et al. demonstrate is a most intriguing result that, while not meeting their expectations, does succeed in provoking further investigation about crisis processes.

Further Considerations in the Modeling of International Interaction

Having explored in some detail the Zinnes et al. and Brito and Intriligator chapters, we turn to a consideration of what such modeling efforts do not tell us about arms race and precrisis interaction. This discussion does not arise because of shortcomings in the chapters themselves, but because, after reading them, it is apparent that the types of models they utilize allow certain questions to be answered and leave others open. There are three matters worthy of consideration in future modeling efforts.

First, both chapters suggest that "realistic" models of international interaction have to contain factors reflecting *both* internal and external determinants of state behavior. This was seen in the demonstrated superiority of the combined-effects model in the Zinnes et al. study. It was also evident that Brito and Intriligator could not model the arms race without considering both domestic decision-making mechanisms and opponent force levels and strategies, i.e., internal and external factors, in the same model. The challenge, however, is to integrate the linkages and cross-influences between that two sets of variables in a single, coherent model. Brito and Intriligator offer some useful formulations and tentative steps in this direction.

What needs to be further explored are theories and models that allow the relative influence of external and internal factors to ebb and flow in different stages of the interaction process. The assumption of a constant dynamic in the models, in the sense that forces are presumed to exert a constant influence over time, is not a sound one. Brito and Intriligator clearly suggest this themselves in their discourse of stylized facts about the arms race. At certain times both the Soviet Union and the United States appear to have acquired arms as a reaction to the actions or acquisitions of each other. At other times, especially several years after these external shocks to the national systems, arms acquisitions continue unabated— apparently driven by a set of powerful internal forces. To adequately reflect this alteration or fluctuation in the over-time impact of variables, more sophisticated theories and models with "triggers" and decay functions will be necessary. Thinking about the arms race for a moment, one way of approaching this may be to view opponent behavior less as a regular, incremental influence and more as a series of irregular, exogenous shocks coincident with major strategy or budgetary decisions in the opponent's system. When these occur, they would disrupt the "normal," domestically determined acquisition process leading to the setting of new strategies and acquisition target levels and to a subsequent readjustment period in the domestic bureaucratic and allocative components.

A similar argument applies to modeling crisis interaction. The findings that neither autoregressive nor stimulus-response models do as well as a combined-effects model is not surprising but also not that satisfying. While the overall effects of external stimuli in a precrisis sequence may be slight (thus the poor performance of Model II), our understanding of crises suggests that at certain junctures direct action and reaction between states occurs and perhaps is critical to the pattern and outcome of the precrisis sequence. Again, what we might turn to are models that capture these bursts of stimulus-response interchange, which in turn trigger the internally driven, self-reinforcing hostility escalation mechanisms in each state. Such an interpretation is in line with the sociopsychological theories of crisis; it also implies that instead of arbitrarily choosing a 6- or 12-month lead time for a crisis, one could search precrisis behavior patterns for indications of bursts or pulses of exchanged (hostile) activity that mark the "actual" initiation points of the crisis interaction cycle.

Second is the matter of thresholds, ceilings, and constraints in international interaction processes. Their general importance to the study of political phenomena is explored by Salert (Chapter 2), and their relevance to the study of arms races and crises was pointed out by Simowitz, Baugh, and Feste. In crises situations, constraints certainly exist on the capacity of decision makers to handle message traffic or stress; constraints exist in arms race as the levels of defense expenditure and thus acquisition of arms that states can or will accept. While a constraint connotes a ceiling that cannot be exceeded, a threshold, on the other hand, refers to a juncture or a level that, if crossed, results in a sharp and sudden change in the form or type of the behavior process. There may well be, for instance, thresholds in precrisis processes in that there are points that, when exceeded, result in a dramatic change in the behavior of antagonists in terms of message hostility or volume. (In fact, Feste pointed out the very notion of crisis implies the existence of one or possibly two threshold points—the first separating normal from precrisis behavior, the second precrisis from crisis behavior, with the latter usually implying a move to overt hostility.) Within arms races there may be technological innovations, or strategy changes, or turnovers in bureaucratic decision makers that operate as thresholds in determining acquisition rates. The problem is that thresholds and/or constraints suggest discontinuities, limits, and shifts in what are otherwise continuous, dynamic processes. For the modeler, whose first and major goal is to capture the functional form of the continuous aspects of the process, accounting for these phenomena is very difficult.

However, if mathematical models are to be "realistic" and are to play a larger role in policy and prescription and forecasting, steps to include constraints and thresholds must be taken. Brito and Intriligator and other arms race modelers will have to build economic constraints, public demand for consumer goods, and bureaucratic and executive decision changes into their models in a more explicit fashion. Current experience in both the United States and the U.S.S.R. suggests this necessity, albeit for differing reasons in each country (a remark that, in itself, suggests the need for separate models for the two superpowers with their widely divergent economic and political structures). To be specific, one of the problems with the current Brito and Intriligator formulation is its lack of exploration of the impact of financial constraints, resulting in the acquisition of suboptimal levels of arms, on the nuclear strategizing component of the model. In the Zinnes et al. work and subsequent models of crises and precrisis, we would look to see attempts to model notions of communication overload, hostility level thresholds, and threat points.

The third and concluding matter that needs to be considered about the models presented by Zinnes et al. and Brito and Intriligator is that by modeling the systems of interaction and interchange between states, these authors capture the overt or most accessible aspects of these processes. As both sets of authors (would) admit, what is left out is the consideration of the perceptions and the psychological dispositions of the decision makers. This is not an argument against the implicit "rationality" of dynamic interaction models. It is a argument (a) that modelers need at times to be more cognizant of the reality of the impact of decision makers' perceptions, and (b) that there may well be some ways, within the context of the current models, to include better or broader treatment of such factors. The first point is especially directed at Brito and Intriligator and at modeling within this tradition. Brito and Intriligator state, for example, that "assuming agents do not overreact to predictions of what other agents are doing, the arms race is a dynamic process that is stable." However, history and scholarship suggest the overreaction is almost an inherent feature of arms racing. If nations reacted "reasonably" one would probably find fewer circumstances where arms races broke out in the first place and fewer instances where they escalated drastically or resulted in conflict.

If the formal modeler is going to reach and convince the skeptics in both the scholarly and policymaking communities, allowance for perceptions and perceptual "error" are going to have to be included in international interaction models. This can be done; for instance, in Brito and Intriligator's chapter, the analysis of the differentials between arms levels necessary to deter and to preempt (Figure 4.2) could be cast within the context of decision makers' perceptions and calculations of uncertainty and margin of error. In work on crises, such as might follow Zinnes et al., there could be more direct consideration of the volumes of message traffic or of the intensity of hostility of interchange, which constitute constraints on the capacity of decision makers to react or operate as thresholds in terms of their willingness to resort to overt violence.

In sum, Brito and Intriligator and Zinnes et al. provide us with two quite different views from within the same perspective of the study of competitive interaction processes in international relations. The contributions of their work to this study are important, as are the implications of their findings and methodologies to the further study of political processes utilizing mathematical models of dynamic systems. They help us to explore several missing elements in polical inquiry that will improve our logic and help us to delineate important questions of interactions among units of analysis.

PART III

Aggregation and Sequence in Linkage Models

Introduction

Choosing a Unit of Analysis

CHARLES F. HERMANN

Basic inquiry questions of sequence and aggregation find a natural laboratory in the study of cross-national politics. The primary question linking both sequence and aggregation is one of the unit of analysis. At the core of cross-national research is the assumption that the nation is a meaningful unit of analysis. It is assumed that nations have certain shared characteristics that distinguish them from other kinds of political units, that they have other differentiating attributes in varying degrees, and that they have authoritative actors whose behavior can be said to be undertaken on behalf of the entire nation. Given these assumptions, the individual engaged in cross-national research seeks to discover generalizations about all or a subset of these national units by comparing their attributes and their actors' behaviors.

These assumptions underlying cross-national research have never been universally accepted. In the eighth decade of the twentieth century, political scientists and others concerned with comparative analysis remain divided over the basic question: Can the nation-state be a meaningful unit of analysis in the construction of political theories and the research intended to investigate those theories empirically?

"It is with the claim to be using legitimate *comparative* methods which could enable us to advance and to test genuine law-like *cross-cultural* generalizations that I shall initially be concerned" (MacIntyre, 1973: 172). With these words, MacIntyre begins an essay in which he challenges whether the meanings of political attitudes and the functions of political institutions can be regarded as comparable in different cultures. Others have expressed similar concerns about the impact of cultural and societal differences that mask what might appear superficially as similarities.

It can be asked if nations actually have any shared defining characteristics. What are the common properties when the concept of nation-state embraces entities ranging from the Soviet Union and the United States to microstates such as Bahrain, Grenada, Maldives, Nauru, and Seychelles (each with less than 400,000 population and fewer than 300 square miles of territory)? Economically, a number of multinational corporations have more wealth than many nation-states and they exercise influence over more people under their jurisidiction and beyond. Consider some of the traditional defining characteristics. Today it would be difficult to argue that the governments of all nations exercise complete sovereignty over their citizens or territory, have exclusive control over the legitimate use of force, or constitute the ultimate legitimate political authority over their populations.

Anytime one utilizes a unit such as the nation-state that is so heterogeneous as to include individuals, government bodies, and nongovernmental organizations such as multinational corporations, aggregation is a principal problem. Basic questions arise as to whether or not it makes sense to say, for example, what the United States does or how it behaves, let alone to say what Western nations do, or to go further to say what transnational behaviors can be mapped in the global arena. Problems of aggregation, then, are deeply tied to the question of units of analysis; these problems are nowhere better illustrated than in the field of cross-national politics.

Data problems also can be used to challenge the feasibility of cross-national research. It can be argued that critical data on many nations are completely unavailable or are of questionable validity. Governments may consciously bias data; even conscientiously collected information can yield grossly misleading indicators when comparing nations.

Finally, one must confront the insensitivity that any generalist may inevitably manifest in comparing 40, 80, or 120 nations about most of which he or she can have only quite limited knowledge. An able scholar can spend an entire life time learning the language, culture, history, and politics of a single country. Therefore, is it not extremely presumptious to assume that one person, or a small research team, can know enough to construct meaningful generalizations that may apply to more than 140 separate national entities?

These and similar challenges can be introduced for one of two purposes. They can be advanced as serious inquiries that do not presuppose an answer. Alternatively, they can be asked rhetorically on the assumption that the answers are self-evident. In the latter case, the questions become the basis for articles of faith that enable the believer to dismiss cross-national research efforts of the past, present, and future. By contrast, questions posed as open-ended inquiries can be powerful critiques against which to evaluate past cross-national efforts and in many cases can provide the incentives for the design of new efforts. Often the further attempts will not fully overcome the noted difficulty or will create new ones, but when compared to previous research efforts they may suggest some progress in reducing the gap between the preferred form of research and what had previously been achieved in cross-national undertakings. Whether such gaps can ever be adequately closed may not be knowable at present. Designing and executing cross-national studies, however, that attempt to respond to these basic questions can be an exhilarating challenge itself.

Current efforts at cross-national research deal with aspects of these basic questions. The chapters in this section illustrate how important issues are being addressed in continuing explorations. For example, behaviors have been an elusive set of concepts in cross-national research. Until recently, more attention had been given to various types of national attributes than to behaviors. Unless there is clear conceptual development of behaviors, it becomes impossible to determine whether actions by actors in different nations (i.e., those with different attributes) might reasonably be regarded as comparable. The ensuing articles develop such behavioral concepts as political conflict, state coercion, international interdependence, and citizen orientations.

Suggestions that cross-national research has tended to be overly simplistic may in part be seen as a concern generated by the tendency to confine explanations of national behavior to variation in aggregate national attributes. Many observers have long speculated that complex interactions of variables at multiple levels of analysis, rather than national attributes alone can plausibly be hypothesized to influence national governmental behavior. The following chapters deal with this challenge. National behavior is seen as a function of individual and transnational as well as national phenomena. Cross-level as well as cross-national explanations and research are advanced.

In reading the next two chapters, the reader should be encouraged to consider how they deal with change. Again, the distinctive treatments of the authors can be viewed as an effort to respond to the concern that cross-national research has been too simple by ignoring historical developments and by neglecting the more general issue concerning the treatment of time and the movement from static to dynamic analysis. Rosenau's treatment of the effects of recent changes in the international environment on domestic politics and Nesvold's search for lag-functions and conditioning variables can both be viewed as early attempts to come to grips with these issues in cross-national research.

Both chapters in this section focus on cross-national research, yet the problems that are confronted are those that researchers share in common across fields in the discipline. Aggregation will be a problem any time a researcher deals with a heterogeneous unit of analysis. The problem of sequence is part of the study of a process that is essential to any model of change. These problems are both ones of logic and levels of analysis. As you read, you will see the specific problems confronted by the authors and be able to make generalizations across many fields in the discipline.

5

The Civic Self in Transnational Perspective

JAMES N. ROSENAU

Important as it is, knowledge of the Iranian crop picker or the Polish coal miner is surely no more valuable than an understanding of the Western person-in-the-street. However, while social scientists have theorized at length about the impact of industrialization on the peasants of the Third World and the workers of the Second World, the literature is scant when it comes to theory about the impact of mounting global interdependence on the citizens of the First World. It is a central thesis of the ensuing analysis that this theoretical gap needs to be filled, that the consequences of an increasingly interdependent world for citizens of industrial democracies constitute a variable of crucial importance to the future strength and vitality of open, dynamic, and flexible polities. Mounting interdependence has heightened both the salience and the involvement of citizens in politics, enlarging the realm of activities in which their compliance or noncompliance is politically consequential and thereby heightening the relevance of how they order their priorities and rank their loyalties.

Stated differently, political scientists have long treated citizenship as a set of obligations and responsibilities that individuals assume on behalf of autonomous states, whereas today the state is increasingly less autonomous. A dynamic technology and a steady depletion of resources have

AUTHOR'S NOTE: I am grateful to Craig Etcheson for his help in preparing this chapter and to the Institute for Transnational Studies for its support. I am also greatly indebted to Harry C. Bredemeier for his crafting of the formulations set forth in the third and fourth sections of this chapter, all of which are drawn from an elaborate inquiry into the civic self that we are jointly developing. For this particular chapter, however, I alone am responsible.

greatly reduced the physical, social, economic, and political distances between communities and nations, with the result that the state is more dependent and less autonomous, more vulnerable and less competent, more complex and less unified, than ever before. Presumably, such changes can have profound consequences for individuals and the ways in which they handle the conflicting loyalties, competing legitimacies, and contradictory demands for compliance to which they are exposed. Presumably, too, such changes pose the need for political scientists to think afresh about the conceptual equipment appropriate to comprehending citizenship in an era of mounting interdependence. Such is the purpose of this chapter.

Seven Organizing Premises[1]

To facilitate thinking afresh we shall assume that the following dynamics are presently at work on a global scale:

(1) The centuries-long trend toward substantial annual increases in economic growth is in a process of reversal as the world's resources are being depleted and as demands upon them are growing.

The short- and long-term consequences of this reversal are numerous. They include the process whereby long-standing distributive issues are being recast as redistributive conflicts as well as the breakdown of society-wide consensuses around economic growth as the highest priority for the future.[2] The recent polarization of the Labor party in Great Britain and similar, though less pronounced, tendencies among both Republicans and Democrats in the United States are illustrative of these processes. The advent of endemic resource scarcities also means that national economies are increasingly dependent on foreign supplies and, accordingly, increasingly vulnerable to fluctuating political and economic trends abroad.

(2) States and their governments are less and less capable of resolving domestic problems since so many of the problems (most notably, inflation) are substantially conditioned by external factors over which they have no control.

It must be stressed that this assumption does not posit states as becoming weaker in their ability to maintain control over their citizens. Rather, it presumes that because the course of events derives as much from external as from internal sources, states are less and less able to devise and implement policies that are effective, that relieve the strains occasioned by resource scarcities, and that improve the quality of community and national life. This growing policy ineffectiveness may, in fact, encourage the use of repressive measures and the capacity to employ them, thus resulting in the paradox of states becoming more powerful as they become more ineffective. How long such a contradiction can persist in the context of democratic institutions is, of course, a question of overriding significance, but for analytic purposes we shall here assume that it will endure throughout the foreseeable future.

    (3) Individuals and groups are increasingly aware of the growing ineffectiveness of their own governments and have begun to look elsewhere for entities that will serve their expressive needs and advance their material interests.

Whether the entities to which citizens turn work through or outside the institutions of the state, the result is a lessening of the state's legitimacy and authority and a narrowing of the issues around which it can evoke the loyalties of citizens. Thus nationalism has begun to give way to what I have elsewhere called "subgroupism" (Rosenau, 1980: 87), a process that further undermines the competence and unity of the state. While the stiffening resistance of Alberta as well as Quebec to Ottawa may not portend the breakdown of the Canadian system, it certainly exemplifies this process, just as the hardening of battle lines in the U.S. Congress between the Snow Belt and the Sun Belt would appear to be another, less mature instance of it. Stated differently, no longer capable of keeping the world at a distance and sustained by a government whose effectiveness has been lessened by mounting interdependence, any nation-state appears destined to lose some of its competitive advantage as a focus of loyalty. The professional societies, ethnic subgroups, taxpayers associations, and many other organizations at home to which individuals have been more securely linked as interdependence grows, not to mention the proliferating entities abroad to which their fates may seem increasingly tied, lay strong claims to the allegiance and emotional involvements of citizens.

    (4) Partly in response to the mushrooming need of individuals for more effective entities with which to become affiliated, but also as a result of the deepening complexity and widening division of labor through which the world is becoming ever more interdependent, the salience, number, and variety of subgroups competing for the support of individuals is growing at a pace consistent with the declining competence of states and their governments.

Whether they be new associations, splinter factions, or established ethnic, linguistic, racial, professional, occupational, or political organizations, the nongovernmental subgroups to which individuals are turning offer viable alternatives, to an alienated, anomic response to mounting global interdependence. The expectation (Kornhauser, 1959) that people in mass industrialized societies would feel increasingly remote from the centers of decision and therefore become increasingly apathetic toward public affairs is proving to be unfounded. On the contrary, there are good reasons to believe that greater numbers of citizens are more politically involved than ever (Rosenau, 1974: 21-88) as they shift the objects of their legitimacy sentiments[3] and loyalties away from the national government. The growth of single-issue groups in the United States exemplifies the extent to which activation toward, rather than alienation from, public affairs has marked the politics of mass societies.

(5) As technology and resource depletion shrinks the world and renders what happens in one part of it increasingly relevant to and dependent on what happens in other parts of it, the realm of public affairs is widening and that of private affairs is narrowing.

Interdependence, in other words, is rendering remote events into close-at-hand experiences and expanding national and international agendas with new political issues that heretofore had either not been sources of conflict or had been handled through nonpolitical mechanisms. Currency crises, oil prices, food shortages, air pollutants, refugees, terrorists, and a host of life-style norms are among the new, interdependence-induced issues that now intrude upon the daily lives of citizens and burden the political institutions of societies.

(6) As individuals become increasingly aware of the expansion of the realm of public affairs and their governments' declining competence to manage it, they also become increasingly sensitive to the world's mounting interdependence and the various ways it impacts upon them.

Virtually by definition the expansion of public affairs at the expense of the private sector is confronting individuals with new and difficult choices in areas of their lives that had previously been free of political considerations. Which values are their highest priority, what groups of unknown others should be the focus of their loyalties, to what organizations should they attach legitimacy, how much and to what extent do they comply with governmental policies designed to conserve resources—questions such as these are now posed in the private household even as they dominate maintenance of the public household.[4]

(7) The greater awareness of mounting interdependence can result in alternative responses on the part of citizens, with some making choices that form a resistant response pattern while others compile an accommodative response pattern.

While a shrinking of the resource pie and a reslicing of its pieces surely heightens the self-interestedness of individuals, the forms their self-interests will take and the response patterns they will follow are still subject to variability, depending on the nature of each resource crunch, the quality of the leadership that emerges to handle it, and the extent to which the burdens of interdependence are shared. Indeed, the question of whether accommodative or resistant responses are to predominate among citizens or whether they are sensitive to the widening ramifications of their actions or actively contest, passively ignore, or otherwise offset their links to an increasingly interdependent world, constitute the most significant variables on the world scene today and serve to justify extensive, new efforts to reformulate the concept of citizenship.

The Need for a Reformulation

If the foregoing assumptions are sound, it seems clear that political scientists are ill-equipped to analyze the dynamics of citizenship, political efficacy, and public awareness in the polities of the present and the politics of the future. To be sure, we have come a long way in comprehending the processes of political socialization (Renshon, 1977), the underpinnings of political culture (Almond and Verba, 1963), and the varieties of political participation (Verba, Nie, and Kim, 1978). Recent years have also witnessed a renewed interest in clarifying the concept of political obligation on the part of political philosophers (Walzer, 1971) and in updating, elaborating, and utilizing the concepts of support (Trilling and Lindquist, 1975; Muller, 1977), alienation (Gilmour and Lamb, 1975), authority (Eckstein and Gurr, 1975), legitimacy (Lowenthal, 1976; Rothschild, 1977), and compliance (Young, 1979) on the part of empirical theorists. Nor has the concept of citizenship itself been ignored. Such diverse observers as Bell (1976), Berger (1974), and Kelly (1979), all seemingly stimulated by the Cold War, the Vietnam conflict, terrorism, and the many other recent issues wherein legitimacy and compliance appear to be at stake, have undertaken to rethink what it means to be a citizen of an open, democratic polity.

None of these formulations, however, allows, for the political conditions set forth above as presently evolving on a global scale. The socialization literature concentrates primarily on loyalties and orientations toward states and their governments and is virtually barren with respect to other political entities as a focus of the socializing process.[5] Much of the same can be said of the political culture and participation literature, albeit Inglehart (1977) and Almond and Verba (1963) do identify and explore a wide range of attitudes, activities, subgroups, and (in Ingelhart's case) supranational institutions through which citizens are linked to governments. Likewise, the dynamics of support, alienation, authority, legitimacy, and compliance are developed largely in the context of a world of sovereign states, with little attention paid to the transformations occurring in that world. One analyst (Eckstein, 1973: 1158) even conceded that his attempts to "squeeze" many international phenomena under the concept of authority have been fruitless, that such formulations could not be developed "without procrustean distortion."

This is not to imply, however, that the present writer perceives a need for reconceptualization not discerned by others. Notwithstanding its shortcomings, the literature does contain traces of discomfort over the growing gap between the changing nature of political structures and the analytic equipment available to comprehend it. "How new is the agenda for the study of the state today," one analyst observed, seemingly aghast at the rapidity of the change and the widening of the analytic gap. "How utterly different it is from any that was thought of as recently as a few decades ago" (Graubard, 1979: viii).

Traces of discomfort with traditional conceptions of citizenship go as far back as the early postwar decades when the international system was structured along bipolar lines and seemed to confront citizens with a dichotomous choice between "we" and "they." Propelled by the challenges of McCarthyism in the 1950s and the onset of the Vietnam War in the mid-1960s that raised questions as to what constituted appropriate attitudes and behaviors for citizens, several social scientists sought to clarify the nature of national loyalties and to emphasize that these could take several forms (Guetzkow, 1955; Grodzins, 1956; Schaar, 1957; Wilson and Banfield, 1964; Kelman, 1969).

If the studies of citizenship in the 1950s and 1960s were stimulated by a concern that the Cold War had unduly tipped the balance in the state's favor, requiring citizens to adhere to a narrow conception of loyalty, those since the early 1970s have been of quite the opposite character. Now the discomfort over the adequacy of the citizenship concept focuses on the breakdown of "civility" and the seeming deterioration of citizenship in general and loyalty in particular. As Bell succinctly states it, "The major consequence of this crisis [of belief] is the loss of *civitas,* that spontaneous willingness to obey the law, to respect the rights of others, to forego the temptations of private enrichment at the expense of the public weal" (1976: 244-245). Similarly, Kelly discerns that "citizenship has been buffeted by a crisis of allegiance" (1979: 34) and Berger is concerned about "the denigration of patriotism in important milieus of American intellectual and academic life" (1974: 24). In a like manner, Walzer seeks to explore (and, ultimately, rejects) the implications of the widely held view "that the commitment [of citizens] to the political community is less profound than it was, that there has been a decline of civic virtue and even of ordinary civility, and erosion of the moral and political qualities that make a good citizen" (1980: 55).

However, except for David Riesman, who has clearly acknowledged that his conceptualization of the other-directed citizen in the early 1950s has little relevance for citizens of the 1980s because world affairs have changed,[6] none of those who consider the nature and requirements of modern citizenship take explicit account of the ways in which a shrinking world is impacting on individuals. Stated differently, in none of the analyses of the breakdown of civility is interdependence cited as a causal source. Perhaps they imply as much by including resource scarcities, inflation, and terrorism among the factors that are undermining the way people relate to the community. But, clearly, these analyses lack an explicit recognition that global changes are having consequences for citizens.

This failure to trace the breakdown of civility to global factors is important because it leads to confusion as to where obligations as a private individual end and responsibilities as a public citizen begin. An awareness of mounting interdependence as a source of change leads directly to the view that the latter have been enlarged at the expense of the former (see assumption 5 above). Considered in a strictly domestic context, however, the boundary between an individual's private and public lives is annoyingly obscure.

I do not mean to suggest that mounting interdependence is the only source of the shifting nature of citizenship and the legitimacy sentiments it evokes. There are doubtless a variety of specific historical episodes and/or strictly domestic developments within each of the industrial democracies that have hastened the denigration of patriotism and a decline in the spontaneity with which people are ready to comply with governmental policies. Elazar (1979: 93-94) argues that domestic factors have contributed to the deterioration of national loyalties, noting that there is a close connection between this deterioration and the centralizing tendencies in American federalism that have shifted governmental functions away from local communities to Washington:

> I think that it is not unfair to say that most people develop national loyalties by projecting the satisfactions gained from their personal connections to the most immediate surroundings onto the larger whole. To Americans of generations past, "America" was family, church and local community writ large. When they were called upon to make sacrifices for the country, they did so because of their ties on this immediate personal level. They simply projected their particular local version of the American way of life onto the national scene. This meant, among other things, that a broad range of variations in that way of life, each rooted in a particular locality, could exist without damaging (and even enhancing) the overall American consensus. When the nature of those local and personal attachments is changed, corresponding changes occur, as has been seen in recent years.

While Elazar's analysis highlights the presence of domestic factors as sources of citizenship practices, it also underscores my central point that mounting interdependence has undermined the ties that link citizens to the state. If centralized government has lessened national loyalties, surely the transnationalization of many public issues has further confounded the capacity of citizens to project "the satisfactions gained from their personal connections to the most immediate surroundings onto the larger whole."

If this brief review of the literature is accurate, and if the foregoing seven assumptions describing political dynamics presently at work in the world are sound, clearly a gap exists between our capacity to understand individuals as citizens and the circumstances under which they must perform their citizenship roles. For all the analytic progress that has marked the discipline in the last two decades, clearly the changing structure of global politics and the advent of complex interdependence necessitates a new generation of conceptual tools—not as a substitute for our present analytic equipment, but as a supplement to it. Legitimacy, authority, support, compliance, loyalty, and citizenship need to be recast in a new context, one that allows for the emerging bases of public affairs set forth above. While it may be the case that the construction of "a theory of citizenship ... cannot be done under the present conditions" (Kelly, 1979: 35), surely some initial efforts to facilitate theorizing along these lines are both feasible and imperative. I hope that the ensuing effort to delineate new conceptual equipment will be a useful step in this direction.

Filling the Gap: Toward a New Generation of Conceptual Tools

The emergent structure of global politics suggests the need for two sets of analytic tools that are not now available in our conceptual storehouse. One involves a specification of the orientations through which citizens differentiate among and attach priority to the diverse collectives competing for their loyalty, legitimacy, sentiments, support, and compliance. The second need is for a conceptualization of various types of interdependence that will enable us to probe the diverse ways in which citizens can experience a shrinking world in which their lives are ever more closely tied to the course of public affairs.

Any attempt to specify the orientations on which the responses of citizens are founded must be both general enough to allow for the continuous expansion of the public realm into private affairs and detailed enough to permit differentiation among the various subgroups and supranational institutions that now rival the state as a focus of citizen loyalties and legitimacy sentiments. Four concepts are set forth here to meet this dual need: *unknown others* are posited as the boundary between the public and private realms; the individual's *systems concept* refers to the way in which he or she breaks down and ranks unknown others into concrete groups that seek his or her support and compliance as a citizen; the *civic self* is conceived as the overarching phenomenon that encompasses the feelings of affection for, dependence on, and responsibility toward both the unknown others and the systems that are salient in a citizen's life at any moment in time; and a series of *systems orientations* are enumerated to facilitate grasp of the different ways citizens may be inclined to give hierarchical structure to their systems concepts. The first two of these concepts are relatively self-evident, but the last two can usefully be elaborated.

The Civic Self

It follows that if the nation-state tops the hierarchy of a person's systems concept, that person's status as a citizen will be unambiguous and free of conflict. For by definition the status of citizen refers to formal membership in a nation-state and all the rights and obligations that it comprises. A systems concept that gives precedence to these rights and obligations readily allows citizens to feel patriotic, compile an accurate tax return, drive at the designated speed limit, enter the armed forces when drafted, and freely comply with the many other demands made upon them by their nation-states.

However, as unknown others and their subgroups have come to rival the state for the support of citizens, and as mounting interdependence has extended the public realm into issues not coterminous with the activities of the state, a person's sense of citizenship may be modified, subsumed, replaced, or otherwise confounded by another status. It is a status that may not involve a formal membership, but that may nevertheless consist of informal expectations and responsibilities no less binding than the formal obligations inherent in citizenship. It is a status that seems best labeled as the civic self, by which is meant the feelings of loyalty, dependence, and responsibility that individuals maintain with respect to unknown others not delineated by the state in their systems concept. The unknown others may be an organized collectivity (such as a labor union, an ethnic association, a corporation, or a church) or they may simply be an unspecified, generalized entity (such as the neighborhood, the species, or humanity), but in either event they can be a focus of affection, legitimacy sentiments, and compliance mechanisms, not to mention voluntary actions that spring from the conscience rather than from prior requests for support. To go out of one's way to dispose of trash in a litter basket or recycle newspapers, for example, is to express one's civic self. So is the act of ignoring a solicitation from Amnesty International, or buying a gas guzzler, or regularly sprinkling the lawn during energy or water shortages.

These examples are intended to suggest further dimensions of our civic selves. One is that the civic self is a neutral analytic concept. It encompasses those who ignore the needs of unknown others as well as those who take into account the welfare of the community. While an increasingly interdependent world would seem to require a more selfless, compassionate, and understanding civic self if its problems are to be surmounted and collective progress achieved, conceptual room must be left for the empirical possibility that many individuals will respond by turning inward and greatly narrowing the scope of their civic selves. This point is elaborated below in the outline of various systems orientations that can be associated with the civic self.

Second, it should be stressed that our citizen statuses and our civic selves may or may not be mutually exclusive. On the one hand, the interaction between them may be marked by tension, even antagonism, to the extent that our loyalties or self-serving actions alter our lawabidingness or redirect our legitimacy sentiments. Acts of civil disobedience are extreme instances of such tension, but there are numerous less clear-cut examples that could be cited. Executives of multinational corporations who put their company's profits ahead of their nation's foreign policies when making commitments in the Third World also exemplify situations where the two statuses are at odds. So do acts of labor officials and businessmen that knowingly add to inflation or of individuals who chose not to report all their income in order to limit their tax bill; and so on.[7]

On the other hand, there are a number of ways in which our civic selves and our citizenship statuses may be mutually reinforcing. To help Amnesty International or to conserve energy, for example, is certainly not to act against the interests of the state even as it advances the welfare of unknown others, and in all likelihood the state would actually benefit from such practices. Furthermore, as Wilson and Banfield (1964: 885) have empirically demonstrated, the cultures of different subgroups can vary substantially in terms of their stress on "how much a citizen ought to sacrifice for the sake of the community as well as of what the welfare of the community is constituted."

In sum, the civic self is not conceived as an analytic replacement for the citizen status. Membership in and commitment to the state is, in effect, considered to be only one aspect of our civic selves. We feel loyal to the history, symbols, procedures, and aspirations of the national community because the collectivity of unknown others for whom it acts protects and enhances our physical and emotional being. But it is only one collectivity of unknown others to whom we may be linked, and it is a central dimension of mounting interdependence that other such collectivities and the processes of aggregation that sustain them become increasingly salient—perhaps enlarging the civic self, perhaps constricting it, but in any event rendering it more complex.

Systems Orientations

How individuals cope with competing demands on their loyalties and resolve potential tensions between their civic selves and their citizen statuses depends crucially on the degree of hierarchical orderliness in their systems concepts. If they have an orderly concept in which the world of unknown others is neatly and harmoniously arrayed in such a way that its various systems are not perceived as mutually exclusive and competitive, then the necessity of choosing among systems does not arise and citizens so oriented can see themselves as simultaneously maximizing their skin-bound selves, their families, their organizations, their communities, their nation-states, and all of humanity when they undertake actions toward unknown others. I shall call this a *linear* orientation toward the public realm inasmuch as it allows individuals to extend their loyalties continuously along one dimension without disruption or conflict.[8] On the other hand, if the world of unknown others is experienced as disorderly and thus as a source of competing demands from conflictual systems, choices do have to be made and such citizens have to maintain a more elaborate orientation to guide them in assessing how to maximize benefits and minimize costs. I shall label this more elaborate response as a *discontinuous* orientation toward the public realm.

In preinterdependence days, most citizens had little difficulty maintaining a linear systems orientation in which cost-benefit decisions could easily be made. The nation-state was clearly located at the top of the hierarchy and maximizing its welfare seemed bound to also maximize the welfare of all other systems even if some of the latter made seemingly conflicting demands. As a former secretary of defense once observed, in what may be a quintessential expression of a linear systems concept, "What [is] good for the country [is] good for General Motors and vice-versa." However, as implied above in assumptions 3 and 4, the clarity of the systems concept may undergo considerable reorganization as interdependence mounts and newly salient subgroups compete with the state for the loyalties and legitimacy sentiments of citizens. Under these circumstances the citizen may be continuously faced with having to "choose sides," figure out "what really counts," and decide "whose side I'm on"—calculations that underlie and reflect a discontinuous systems orientation.

But, obviously, more conceptual refinement is needed than simply to dichotomize systems orientations toward the world of unknown others in terms of whether it is hierarchically or discontinuously organized. The way in which individuals are interdependently linked to that world and its importance relative to their private realms also seem crucial to the kind of systems orientations that comprise their civic selves. Allowance for these two variables can be made by conceiving of three basic types of interdependence and delineating three forms of balance between the public and private realms, a formulation that yields nine additional systems orientations.

The three forms of balance derive from whether citizens seek to maximize only their welfare at the expense of unknown others (a *selfish* systems orientation); whether they seek to maximize the unknown others at the expense of themselves (an *altruistic* systems orientation); or whether they seek to maximize the welfare of both themselves and at least some systems of unknown others (a *cooperative* systems orientation). Stated differently, a selfish orientation treats the private realm as superior to the public realm; an altruistic orientation posits the latter realm as superior to the former; and a cooperative orientation conceives of both realms as equally important rather than as hierarchically arrayed.

The three different types of interdependence between individuals and unknown others arise from the pattern of *their interests in third things* (or persons) and not from the nature of their interests in *each other*. The relations of people to each other are marked by independence or dependence, but when the third things (called X here) come between them, such as resources, products, or support, their relationships become interdependent in the sense that the outcome of their interactions over any X has consequences that extend beyond their relationship. For example, people may be independent of many unknown others until an oil shortage occurs, at which point the way in which they handle their common interest in access to gas pumps can have wide ramifications for the tensions and resources of the community. Viewed as interaction over Xs, three mutually exclusive types of interdependence between individuals and unknown others can be logically derived:[9] they can have *identical* interests in some x, *complementary* interests, and/or *divergent* interests.

Identical interdependencies arise (a) when citizens and unknown others all seek to obtain, avoid, produce, or retain the same X, (b) when there is a limited and finite amount of X available, and (c) when all concerned become conscious of each other's identical interest in X. Jockeying for position in a gas line during an oil shortage is a clear-cut illustration of situations in which the civic self becomes part of an identical interdependency. Complementary interdependencies arise in trading or bargaining relations, i.e., when citizens seek an X that unknown others offer or when they offer an X that unknown others seek. The gas line during an oil shortage again provides an incisive example: While individuals have an identical interest with the others in the line, they also have a complementary interest with the gas station attendants. Divergent interdependencies arise most notably in conflict situations, i.e., when citizens seek an X that unknown others want to keep or when they retain an X unknown others desire. Citizens and gas station attendants experience this kind of interdependency when the former seek to fill up at stations where the latter are saving their limited supply for their best customers.

In any concrete situation, of course, citizens may be linked to unknown others through all three types of interdependence. As would-be consumers of gasoline, they have identical interests with all other potential consumers, perhaps most vividly with all the others in the gas line at their particular gas station at that particular time, but also with all other gas consumers all over the world over an indefinite future time period. At the same time, they have two kinds of complementary interests with suppliers of gasoline, probably most vividly with the gas station attendant but also with the oil companies behind them and OPEC behind them. One kind of complementary interest with suppliers is that the citizens want the gas and the suppliers want to provide it—more or less. The second kind is that the suppliers want their money and the citizens want the suppliers to accept the money—more or less. As the "more or less" reminds us, they also have divergent interests with suppliers involving the *terms* of exchange. Citizens want from suppliers (all consumers want from producers) maximum output at minimum price, maximumly efficient and effective service, dedication to their interests, minimum complaints about working conditions and other problems, and many alternative sources of supply (maximum competition among producers). The suppliers want (all producers want in relation to consumers) minimum strain on themselves, maximum prices, maximum respect from citizens for the importance and difficulty of their producer roles, admiration—preferably awe—for the skill and courage with which they are coping with the difficulties, great patience and humility, many alternative consumers (maximum competition among consumers) and minimum competition among themselves.

Let us now consider how the three types of interdependence can interact with the selfish, altruistic, and cooperative orientations toward the public realm. The entries in the nine cells of Table 5.1 summarize the qualities that can be expected to characterize behavior under each condition. The implications of these qualities for the loyalties and compliance behavior of citizens are further clarified if one posits three hypothetical situations in which they might be evoked. Suppose, for example, interdependence was perceived in a situation involving motorists and government rationing of gasoline, that complementary interdependence was attributed by vacationers to a situation wherein the government has sought to protect the currency through exchange controls, and that divergent interdependence was ascribed by athletes to a situation in which the government banned participation in the Olympics. Under these circumstances one can readily imagine very different forms of compliance marking the responses of the relevant citizens in each of the nine interaction settings.

Possible Meanings of Mounting Interdependence

The foregoing formulation suffers from being too static. It allows for various types of interdependence, but it does not build in the dynamics of *mounting* interdependence. The systematic inclusion of this dynamic suggests that an increasingly interdependent world can have several meanings for citizens. It can mean greater dependence on, greater responsibility toward, and/or greater opportunities with respect to unknown others. The derivation of these differential impacts is best revealed by treating any status as consisting of two major components, that of producer-supplier and that of consumer-recipient. As a potential producer-supplier of things in any status, one's interest may lie either in *disposing* of them or in not doing so, that is, in *retaining* them. As a potential consumer-recipient of things, one's interests may lie either in obtaining them or avoiding them.

TABLE 5.1   How Different Types of Interdependence Might Evoke
Different Behavioral Characteristics on the Part of Citizens
Differently Oriented Toward the Public Realm

Orientations Toward the Public Realm	Identical	Complementary	Divergent
Selfish	resentful	exploitative	hostile
Altruistic	abnegative	devoted	paternalistic
Cooperative	fraternal	egalitarian	respectful

It must be reiterated that the terms "producer" and "consumer" are used more exclusively than in a narrow economic sense. Citizens, for example, are producers of loyalty, taxes, political support, and interest demands; and they are consumers of rights, duties, liberties, and exposures. Parents are producers of children and child care; parishioners are consumers of sermons; researchers are producers of knowledge; and so on.

To be increasingly interdependent with unknown others means, for one thing, to be more dependent on more others in both the consumer and producer aspects of one's statuses. It means to be less self-sufficient, less able to meet one's needs without the (more or less willing) help of unknown others. It is to be exposed to more competition for scarce resources and to be more likely to have inflicted on oneself things one would rather avoid. It is to be less able to escape others' presence and their outputs. In short, to be increasingly dependent in one's consumer-recipient roles is to be increasingly vulnerable to the frustration of *deprivation* by unknown others if they do not or cannot supply as much as one wishes; and to the frustration of *surfeit* if they supply more of something than one wants (including themselves on the crowded beach or highway, for example).

In the producer-supplier aspects of one's statuses, to be increasingly dependent is to be increasingly vulnerable to the frustration of *strain* if others demand more than one is mobilized to produce; and to the frustration of *slack* if they reject what one wants to produce (most, conspicuously, for example, one's labor services). It is to be faced with a wider range of others who might make demands on one, and with more information about more needy others. It is also to be more dependent for one's career opportunities not only on what others want, but also on others who are competing with one to meet these wants (Goode, 1960; Zetterberg, 1962).

The other side of interdependence is that more unknown others are more dependent on one. This side of increasing interdependence raises the salience of the question, "[To what extent] am I my brother's keeper?" (The first side, increasing dependence, raises the question, "Who is my keeper; what do others owe me?") In the consuming aspects of a status, increasing interdependence increases the possibility of victimizing others by demanding too much from them (straining them); and of hurting them by refusing to accept their offerings (slacking them, as by refusing to "buy American," for example), and even of hurting third parties or the nation by refusing, say, to allow the nuclear reactor in one's community. In the producer-supplier aspect of a status, having more unknown others more dependent on one means that one is more likely to surfeit them with one's own effluvia, or to deprive them by refusing to make available to them what they need (to deny equality of opportunity to minorities, for example; or to refuse to recycle one's newspapers or containers).

Increasing interdependence also may mean greater opportunity for people in any of their statuses. This is the much-celebrated functionality of a division of labor. In the consumer-recipient aspect of their statuses, citizens may benefit from the greater quantity and quality of goods, services, and information that can result from specialization. In the producer-supplier aspects of their statuses, people may benefit from the dependence of and competition among consumers, and from the greater array of specializations in which they develop proficiencies.

In brief, the meanings to citizens of growing interdependence amount to growing potential vulnerabilities, potential responsibilities, and potential opportunities with respect to each of which people must make new adjustments. When these possible changes are considered in the context of the global dynamics cited at the outset, it seems clear that the civic self is being subjected to enormous pressures, forcing an awareness of a shrinking world where disinterest and inertia may have once prevailed.

Conclusion

While there are doubtless other conceptual tools that should be fashioned to facilitate the analysis of citizenship in a shrinking world, it seems to me that there is one area where political scientists can be effective in the long run. It involves the development of a new perspective that is appropriate to the dynamics of a shrinking world and that leaders and publics can endorse as a criterion of citizenship to be stressed in the home, in school curricula, in organizational life, and in the many other places where the civic self is formed. At the heart of such a perspective is the concept of aggregation and the notion that interdependence, whatever its type, grows through a three-step process whereby the actions (or non-actions) of individuals are recognized, aggregated, and articulated by leaders as they address, contest, and/or resolve public issues. Say, for example, motorists alter their driving patterns and thereby reduce gasoline consumption. Such actions form part of a statistical pattern recognized by journalists and government agencies that are then praised or condemned by politicians seeking to promote or prevent the adoption of a particular energy policy. In a like manner one's readiness to strike or to go on "sick outs" is part of the aggregative process whereby those who preside over unions or professional associations are encouraged or hesitant to press demands. One's adherence to subcultural norms is part of the aggregative process whereby those who speak for ethnic minorities resist or acquiesce to the requirements of an industrial order. One's purchase of a foreign-made good is part of the aggregative process whereby those who conduct international affairs are confronted with alterations in the patterns of world trade and monetary exchange. One's readiness to attend parades for released hostages is part of the aggregative process whereby foreign policy officials are strengthened in their resolve by feeling the support of a national community.

It seems eminently reasonable to hypothesize that the more individuals appreciate the extent to which mounting interdependence is rendering them participants in an ever greater number of relevant aggregative processes, the more is an accommodative response pattern likely to pervade their civic selves. For to see public affairs as dynamic processes that transform private actions into public aggregations is to perceive one's fate as linked to unknown others and thus to encourage the formation of cooperative systems orientations and a greater sense of responsibility for the course of events. If this is so, political scientists need to highlight the virtues of training future citizens accordingly, which means maximizing the analytic capacity of young students to trace the multiplicity of aggregative processes that inextricably link them to the multiplicity of remote worlds in orbit around their private realms.

Such an enlarged view of the tasks of political socialization may be more easily accomplished than it seems. We may have more going for us than we realize. Not only does mounting interdependence bring the present into the private realm, but it also projects the future more obviously into our daily lives. Trend lines into the twenty-first century seem as much a part of current politics as the pressing situations of the moment. The bankruptcy of the social security system, the consequences of population shifts, the availability of oil, the erosion of forests and grazing lands, the undermining effects of prolonged inflation, the changes of increased atmospheric temperatures melting ice flows—such trend lines into the coming decades are very much a part of today's political dialogues and, as such, they seem bound to facilitate the effectiveness of a political socialization that treats citizenship as participation in aggregative processes.

Furthermore, unbeknownst to our students, they have had considerable experience in participating in aggregative processes, experience that we can build upon in our teaching. From the chain letters they are asked to perpetuate as children to the traffic jams in which they are caught as young adults, from the boycotts they may be asked to join to the water shortages they are asked to alleviate, our students have had ample first-hand exposure to the links between individual and collective behavior. Whatever they may do, they have learned that the traffic jam is worsened rather than improved when in their franticness not to be late they move forward at every opportunity and their car is forced to stop in a north/ south cross street, blocking traffic going east and west. So they basically know that individual actions can culminate in aggregate outcomes, and our task is to extend this analytic capacity into new domains, heightening their sensitivity to the flow of cause and effect and refining their ability to distinguish between the manifest and the latent, the intentional and the unintentional, the impulsive and the reflective, the continuity and the discontinuity. If we can foster talents of this kind, surely we will have laid the foundations for a civic self that can thrive in a shrinking world and that can allow the democratic polity to adjust creatively to the onrush of global interdependencies.

NOTES

1. An elaboration of these premises and the grounds for proceeding from them are set forth in several of my prior essays (Rosenau, 1980, 1981).

2. A cogent analysis of how and why the growth consensus has disintegrated in the United States can be found in Yankelovich (1980).

3. The term is Harry Eckstein's (1973: 1154).

4. The concept of the "public household" has been systematically elaborated by Daniel Bell (1976).

5. For exceptions in which political socialization is probed in the context of global entities and processes, see Alger (1977), Becker (1979), Oppenheim and Torney (1974), and Tolley (1973).

6. Riesman was recently quoted as finding his earlier formulations "totally irrelevant" today. "He further said about *The Lonely Crowd:* 'It was entirely an

intra-American book, written as if this country were alone in the world. One could not conceivably write such a book today. One must take account of the spaceship Earth' " (Robertson, 1980: 38).

7. For an enumeration of other examples that can lead to tensions between the two statuses, see Rosenau (1980: 28).

8. Of course, what persons with a linear orientation regard as action loyal to all salient systems may be regarded by one or more of the systems in the linear array as disloyal, with the result that their lives may be filled with commotion even though their systems concept is orderly. Many of those who engaged in nonviolent protests against U.S. actions in Vietnam, for example, saw their resistance as expressive of loyalty to American society even though the country's authorities came to a contrary conclusion. A succinct insight into a linear system orientation that can lead to a disruptive personal life is readily evident in this recent reaction of Daniel Berrigan to the prospect of going to jail as a result of an act of civil disobedience that failed: "We have to let go of the idea of its having an effect. We don't need to dwell on results—just that it's a good thing, and let it go after that. Something had to be done, and we couldn't live with doing nothing. . . . To be going to jail is to be going where we ought to be" (New Yorker, 1981: 31).

9. The derivation of the three types are reductions of a logically exhaustive attribute space based on the combination of any two persons' interest in something else developed by Lazarsfeld and Barton (1955).

REFERENCES

ALGER, C. F. (1977) "Foreign policies of U.S. publics." International Studies Quarterly 21 (June): 277-319.

ALMOND, G. A. and S. VERBA (1963) The Civic Culture: Political Attitudes and Democracy in Five Nations. Princeton, NJ: Princeton University Press.

BECKER, J. M. [ed.] (1979) Schooling for a Global Age. New York: McGraw-Hill.

BELL, D. (1976) The Cultural Contradictions of Capitalism. New York: Basic Books.

BERGER, P. L. (1974) "Reflections on patriotism." Worldview (July): 19-25.

ECKSTEIN, H. (1973) "Authority patterns: a structural basis for political inquiry." American Political Science Review 67 (December): 1142-1161.

——— and T. R. GURR (1975) Patterns of Authority: A Structural Basis for Political Inquiry. New York: John Wiley.

ELAZAR, D. J. (1979) "Constitutionalism, federalism, and the post-industrial American polity," pp. 79-107 in S. M. Lipset (ed.) The Third Century: America as a Post-industrial Society. Chicago: University of Chicago Press.

GILMOUR, R. S. and R. B. LAMB (1975) Political Alienation in Contemporary America. New York: St. Martin's.

GOODE, W. J. (1960) "A theory of role strain." American Sociological Review 25: 483-496.

GRAUBARD, S. R. (1979) "Preface to the issue, 'The State.' " Daedalus 108 (Fall): v-xix.

GRODZINS, M. (1956) The Loyal and the Disloyal: Social Boundaries of Patriotism and Treason. Chicago: University of Chicago Press.

GUETZKOW, H. S. (1955) Multiple Loyalties: Theoretical Approaches to a Problem in International Organization. Princeton, NJ: Princeton University Press.

INGLEHART, R. (1977) The Silent Revolution: Changing Values and Political Styles Among Western Publics. Princeton, NJ: Princeton University Press.

KELLY, G. A. (1979) "Who needs a theory of citizenship?" Daedalus 108 (Fall): 21-36.

KELMAN, H. C. (1969) "Patterns of personal involvement in the national system: a social-psychological analysis of political legitimacy," pp. 276-288 in J. N. Rosenau (ed.) International Politics and Foreign Policy. New York: Free Press.

KORNHAUSER, W. (1959) The Politics of Mass Society. New York: Free Press.

LAZARSFELD, P. F. and A. H. BARTON (1955) "Some general principles of questionnaire classification," pp. 83-93 in P. F. Lazarsfeld and M. Rosenberg (eds.) The Language of Social Research. New York: Free Press.

LOWENTHAL, R. (1976) "Social transformation and democratic legitimacy." Social Research 43 (Summer): 246-275.

MULLER, E. N. (1977) "Behavioral Correlates of Political Support." American Political Science Review 71 (June): 454-467.

New Yorker (1981) "The talk of the town." (January 19): 29-31.

OPPENHEIM, A. N. and J. TORNEY (1974) The Measurement of Children's Civic Attitudes in Different Nations. New York: John Wiley.

RENSHON, S. A. (1977) Handbook of Political Socialization. New York: Free Press.

ROBERTSON, N. (1980) "A sociologist 'emeritus' who is far from retired." New York Times (December 14).

ROSENAU, J. N. (1981) The Study of Political Adaptation. New York: Nichols.

――― (1980) The Study of Global Interdependence: Essays on the Transnationalization of World Affairs. New York: Nichols.

――― (1974) Citizenship Between Elections: An Inquiry into the Mobilizable American. New York: Free Press.

ROTHSCHILD, J. (1977) "Observations on political legitimacy in contemporary Europe." Political Science Quarterly 92 (Fall): 487-501.

SCHAAR, J. H. (1957) Loyalty in America. Berkeley: University of California Press.

TOLLEY, H. Jr. (1973) Children and War: Political Socialization to International Conflict. New York: Teachers College Press.

TRILLING, R. J. and D. P. LINDQUIST (1975) "Effective support: an empirical examination." Comparative Political Studies 7: 395-429.

VERBA, S., N. H. NIE, and J. KIM (1978) Participation and Political Equality: A Seven-nation Comparison. New York: Cambridge University Press.

WALZER, M. (1980) Radical Principles: Reflections of an Unreconstructed Democrat. New York: Basic Books.

WALZER, M. (1971) Obligations: Essays on Disobedience, War, and Citizenship. New York: Simon & Schuster.

WILSON, J. Q. and E. C. Banfield (1964) "Public-Regardingness as a value premise in voting behavior." American Political Science Review 58 (December): 876-887.

YANKELOVICH, D. (1980) "Economic policy and the question of political will," pp. 9-33 in W. E. Hoadley (ed.) The Economy and the President: 1980 and Beyond. Englewood Cliffs, NJ: Prentice-Hall.

YOUNG, O. R. (1979) Compliance and Public Authority: A Theory With International Applications. Baltimore: Johns Hopkins University Press.

ZETTERBERG, H. (1962) On Theory and Verification in Sociology. New York: Bedminster.

6

Stages of Political Conflict

BETTY A. NESVOLD

Interest in the problem of political conflict is as old as recorded history. Riots and rebellions threaten the stability of communities, disrupt the lives of those involved, overturn governments, and impede international trans- actions. These phenomena have engaged the attention of virtually all the major philosophers and have been a central focus of modern scholarly analysis. Despite extensive study of these acts and their destructiveness to the community, they remain a pervasive problem in most nations of the world today.

While the study of political conflict has its roots in antiquity, the analysis in this volume is distinctly modern. It utilizes the tools of systematic, scientific analysis to develop understanding of these persistent phenomena. Ted Gurr, a distinguished scholar in this field, has observed:[1]

> The distinctive characteristic of research on conflict in twentieth-century social science is the use of systematic methods of observation and comparative, usually quantitative analysis to develop and test generalizations. ... Some ... are descriptive ones, indicating how conflict phenomena are distributed among people or across time and space. Others are causal: they stipulate the antecedents or consequences of conflict phenomena. The general method of empirical research on conflict is always comparative; either there are simultaneous observations of a set of people, systems, or events (the cross-sectional approach) or there are multiple observations of one or several individuals, groups, or systems across time (the longitudinal approach). ... Probably the most visible of the distinguishing traits of contemporary conflict research is the widespread reliance on quantification [Gurr, 1980: 4].

The key problem in all scientific research is the development of valid, reliable measures of theoretical variables.[2] Much of the work in the early 1960s addressed this issue. Rummel (1966) and Tanter (1966), for example, collected data on domestic political conflicts occurring in 77 nations for two consecutive three-year periods. They subjected their data to factor analysis and identified three dimensions of conflict: Turmoil, Revolution and Subversion. The Turmoil Dimension included general strikes, major government crises, riots, and antigovernment demonstrations. The Revolution Dimension included purges, revolutions, and the number of persons killed in all conflict events. The Subversion Dimension included assassinations and guerrilla warfare. This early work made no attempt to develop or test hypotheses on causes or correlates of each of these dimensions, but it did provide a sophisticated, quantified measure of the concept of domestic political conflict. Similarly, Russett (1964) and Banks and Textor (1963) collected data on characteristics of nations, as well as on conflict, and did cross-national statistical analyses of the patterning among variables.

Theoretical development paralleled the inductive work cited above. Scholars of comparative politics were adapting social psychological models in cross-national analyses of political phenomena. Lerner (1958) based much of his theory of modernization on the concept of perceived deprivation, and he utilized aggregate statistical data to operationalize this variable. One can similarly cite the works of Apter (1965), Deutsch (1961), Russett (1964), Davies (1962), and Midlarsky and Tanter (1967). This research all had the following characteristics: It was based on a well-developed theoretical framework, variables were quantified, and hypotheses were developed and tested across a large number of nations. The 1960s thus saw the establishment of a new and rapidly growing body of scholarship in empirical and theoretical cross-national research.[3]

Turning more directly to political conflict, one important line of inquiry utilized frustration-aggression theory. This was initially developed in psychology as a theory of individual behavior, and it was developed into a model of social behavior. Succinctly stated, political conflict, the dependent variable, was conceptualized as aggressive behavior. The basic postulate of the theory is that frustration causes individuals to engage in aggressive behaviors. The task of the researchers was to develop indicators of social conditions that were presumed to be frustrating and to test the data to determine how frequently these conditions were associated with social conflict. The Feierabends (1971, 1966) conceptualized their independent variable as systemic frustration, while Gurr (1970) operationalized it as perceived relative deprivation. Most of their work relied on cross-sectional analysis. That is, all of the data for each nation were aggregated for a designated time period, and hypotheses were tested across all countries for that time period. Characteristically, the independent variable was operationalized by using data that indicated national levels of wealth, health care, mass media distribution, and the like.

The role of theory was crucial in the formulation of hypotheses. It was hypothesized that in very poor nations, expectations are so low that little frustration or deprivation is experienced. As nations engage in economic development, aspirations and expectations are raised, which, if not satisfied, lead to feelings of frustration and deprivation. It is only when full economic development is achieved that individuals in society have realistic opportunities to satisfy expectations. Thus it is hypothesized that riots and rebellions will be endemic at middle levels of development. It should be pointed out that this hypothesis runs counter to the prevailing assumption that economic development is the panacea that would resolve the social and political conditions that appear to underlie much of the conflict in society. Quite the contrary, empirical analysis supports the hypothesis that economic development stimulates aspirations and expectations more rapidly than they can be satisfied, creating widespread frustrations among the participants, and leading to frequent acts of political aggression.

The above description of one of the findings of this body of research demonstrates the major strength of cross-national research. It can uncover regular and recurrent tendencies that might be overlooked in detailed analyses of phenomena in single countries. The testing of hypotheses across a large and diverse group of nations can be expected to uncover broad patterns, but one must expect a fair amount of unexplained variance. Cross-national research thus provides a base on which to assess the in-depth analysis of phenomena in single countries.

Methodological Issues in the Role of Theory

The fundamental requisite in analyzing any topic is the selection of a fruitful theoretical approach. One's theory guides the formation of hypotheses, the empirical definition of key variables, and the design of the analysis itself. In the study of political conflict, for example, the selection of frustration-aggression theory, or one of its variants, leads to very different hypotheses than would, say, neo-Marxist theory. In the case of the latter, one would expect that increasing industrialization would lead to increasing concentrations of wealth, which inevitably lead to uprisings by the exploited working-class population. This linear relation between industrialization and political conflict is in direct contrast to the curvilinear relationship postulated by relative deprivation theory.

In any case, whatever theory one selects, it should generate a series of testable hypotheses, or, to state it differently, one's theory should provide the guidelines one needs to analyze the phenomenon of interest. It should be no disaster to select the "wrong" theory in which the propositions are not verified, so long as it generates a set of testable hypotheses. That, in itself, is a contribution to the state of knowledge. The methodological requirement is that the theoretical terms are amenable to empirical definition, and that the theory provide a parsimonious guide to analyzing the topic.

The development of valid, reliable empirical definitions of theoretical terms constitutes the most difficult task faced in the scientific study of social phenomena. The problems we are studying typically have a long history of philosophical analysis, of artistic discourse, and of journalistic attention. This rich verbal heritage complicates the task of selecting empirical indicators of key concepts. Returning to frustration-aggression theory for an example, it is a difficult task to operationalize the concept of systemic frustration. The difficulties stem from the fact that there is no conventionally accepted definition, and frustration is a state of mind. One must infer the state of frustration from observable conditions that are hypothesized instigators. The task is further complicated by the need to identify *societal* conditions likely to produce frustration in a large portion of *individual* members of society. Even if one does this successfully, no cross-national study of conflict has been able to determine whether participants in acts of political conflict were the individuals who suffered from frustrating conditions in their society.

One has reservations in pursuing the above discussion much further. The theory was fruitful, by any reasonable definition. It provided insights and guidelines for developing testable hypotheses. Subsequent studies produced findings that brought new knowledge about the cross-national patterning of political conflict. However, as research proceeded and attempts were made to reduce unexplained variance, the theory led to such complicated research designs that it may have begun to lose its explanatory power. As Eckstein put it, "The resulting 'modeled' world appears about as complex (and thus as mystifying) as the concrete world it models. . . . We find no illuminating simplification; we find only a complex world of variables, vertiginous with arrows and proportions. The artfulness of nature wins out over that of theory because, *contra* Bacon, nature is not 'put to the test' " (Eckstein, 1980: 162).[4] In other words, the goal of scientific research is to abstract phenomena from their empirical complexities and to isolate properties that demonstrate recurring associations.

Conflict Breeds Conflict

In the analysis that follows, an extremely parsimonious theoretical model is utilized. It has been borrowed directly from the Lichback and Gurr research (1981: 3-4), which is summarized in the following paragraphs:

> [We] specify and test with cross-national data the common-sense argument that *conflict breeds conflict*. The underlying assumptions are that societies and social groups have characteristic patterns of conflict behavior which exist in complex interaction with one another and that these patterns tend to persist over time. Hence, the conflict process is endemic to society, follows its own internal logic, and is largely self-contained and self-generative.
>
> This argument is a parsimonious alternative to theories which attribute properties of conflict to more "remote" variables such as international dependency, social structure, popular discontent, or group resources. Most global quantitative studies of conflict within nations have given little attention to relations among aspects of the conflict process itself.... Here we take the opposite tack: given information on the actors, forms, and properties of conflict over time, we propose a model of the conflict process. The results of this analysis will provide a baseline against which to judge the results of models which incorporate more "fundamental" causal variables.

Lichback and Gurr divided their data on political conflict into four components: the *extent* and *intensity* of *protest* and *rebellion*. They analyzed their data to determine whether the extent of protest was associated with the intensity of protest and did a similar analysis of the two dimensions of rebellion. They also examined the impact of protest and rebellion on each other. In their broader design they attempted to uncover characteristic patterning of conflict in a polity. They concluded that this self-generative model provided a less-than-sufficient explanation of variations in internal conflict. Despite their conclusion, this type of model might be very useful to understanding conflict behavior using some different central variables.

In the study that follows, only two dimensions of conflict are identified. Actions by the state are called *coercion,* and they include: martial law, political arrests, purges, executions, and any other acts directed at containing dissident behavior. The term *conflict* is reserved for acts challenging the regime or its policy. These include: riots, demonstrations, terrorist action, revolts, and so forth. The data were coded from the daily issues of the New York *Times* for the years 1955-1964. These were supplemented with data from *Facts on File* and the New York *Times* Index. In raw form, they contain some 50,000 events.[5] This large number of events over a ten-year time period should provide the kind of data base needed to isolate patterns and to trace relationships between the two kinds of conflict.

In Table 6.1 the frequency of coercion and conflict for the entire time period is reported. For convenience of examination, countries are grouped regionally. One notes, for example, that among the Western European nations, France experienced more conflict and more coercion than any other nation in this region. There were 1183 separate conflict events, 508 acts of coercion. Italy, the Western European nation with the next highest amount of conflict, experienced 532 acts, less than half the number in France, and it had only 71 coercive actions.

As one can note, Western nations tend to have less conflict and less coercion than is found in other regions of the world, but the range of scores among these nations is quite large. Similarly, African nations tend to have relatively low scores with only a few nations experiencing high levels of recorded acts of political conflict. With respect to these African nations, the data were collected during the period (1955-1964) in which most of them gained their independence from colonial control. The coercion and conflict indicated by these scores reflects the level of conflict that occurred during this time and the efforts of the colonial nation to contain it. This relationship may be characteristically different from that where both coercion and conflict are instigated by indigenous groups. These and other cases where foreign intervention was a significant identifiable component of conflict or coercion require separate analysis, and for that reason will not be included in some of the subsequent data analysis.

In addition to listing the scores on conflict and coercion, a ratio between them is calculated. In a later analysis, we examine the relationship between these variables as it varies from year to year in each nation. This ratio provides a baseline from which one can isolate unusually high levels of police control (coercion) vis-à-vis the level of conflict. Surely no government can survive that allows high levels of conflict to persist, and while our theoretical model postulates that conflict breeds conflict, we are

TABLE 6.1   Levels of Conflict and Coercion, 1955-1964

Country	Conflict	Coercion	Ratio
Western European Nations (n = 21)			
France	1183	508	.43
Italy	532	71	.13
United Kingdom	466	121	.26
West Germany	271	350	1.29
Spain	240	286	1.19
Belgium	208	24	.12
Portugal	162	87	.54
Canada	155	41	.26
North Ireland	148	33	.22
Greece	136	84	.62
Finland	67	13	.19
Austria	65	28	.43
Australia	45	13	.31
Denmark	42	13	.31
Ireland	33	20	.61
Netherlands	26	8	.31
Norway	21	6	.29
Switzerland	18	12	.67
Iceland	14	0	0.00
Sweden	6	15	2.50
New Zealand	2	0	0.00
$\overline{M}$ scores	183	83	.45
Middle Eastern Nations (n = 17)			
Algeria	4728	789	.16
Cyprus	2128	673	.32
Morocco	789	260	.33
Lebanon	472	154	.33
Iraq	448	367	.82
Yemen	303	75	.25
Syria	226	262	1.16
Turkey	214	365	1.71
Israel	193	81	.42
Iran	181	168	.93
Tunisia	173	93	.54
Sudan	162	111	.69
Jordan	156	207	1.33
Egypt	63	237	3.76
Libya	46	20	.43
Saudi Arabia	28	10	.36
Kuwait	18	1	.06
$\overline{M}$ scores	608	228	.38

(continued)

TABLE 6.1 (Continued)

Country	Conflict	Coercion	Ratio
Latin American Nations (n = 19)			
Cuba	2878	1655	.58
Argentina	1168	764	.65
Brazil	502	312	.62
Dominican Republic	468	347	.53
Bolivia	429	119	.28
Columbia	364	142	.39
Haiti	348	306	.88
Guatemala	320	179	.56
Peru	286	109	.38
Mexico	173	39	.23
Ecuador	169	68	.40
Panama	160	70	.44
Nicaragua	159	85	.53
Chile	156	64	.41
Honduras	139	64	.46
Paraguay	139	99	.71
Costa Rica	113	30	.27
Uruguay	99	16	.16
El Salvador	92	44	.48
$\overline{M}$ scores	430	232	.54
Asian Nations (n = 19)			
South Vietnam	3276	579	.18
Laos	1435	154	.11
India	1055	349	.33
Indonesia	739	544	.74
China	529	409	.77
South Korea	396	346	.87
Burma	380	112	.29
Pakistan	335	181	.54
Japan	302	39	.13
Ceylon	229	139	.61
Nepal	212	107	.50
Philippines	147	54	.37
Malaysia	116	65	.56
Cambodia	76	38	.50
Thailand	72	85	1.18
Taiwan	49	56	1.14
Afghanistan	38	11	.29
North Vietnam	25	49	1.96
North Korea	13	6	.46
$\overline{M}$ scores	496	175	.35

TABLE 6.1 (Continued)

Country	Conflict	Coercion	Ratio
African Nations (n = 24)			
Congo-Kinshasa	2096	685	.33
South Africa	490	596	1.22
Rhodesia	323	224	.69
Angola	316	106	.34
Kenya	300	170	.57
Zambia	276	62	.22
Malawi	168	128	.76
Ghana	127	166	1.31
Cameroun	114	32	.28
Uganda	112	71	.63
Nigeria	87	41	.47
Congo-Brazzaville	62	41	.66
Mozambique	53	34	.64
Ethiopia	52	26	.50
Dahomey	50	23	.46
Tanzania	41	53	1.29
Sierra Leone	33	12	.36
Togoland	33	8	.24
Somalia	32	11	.34
Senegal	30	28	.93
Liberia	27	15	.56
Guinea	15	16	1.07
Mali	11	7	.64
Mauritania	7	15	2.14
$\overline{\text{M}}$ scores	201	107	.52
Eastern European Nations (n = 9)			
East Germany	569	276	.48
Hungary	434	450	1.04
U.S.S.R.	267	485	1.82
Poland	262	280	1.07
Czechoslovakia	98	166	1.69
Yugoslavia	80	105	1.31
Rumania	50	30	.60
Bulgaria	40	90	2.25
Albania	10	26	2.60
$\overline{\text{M}}$ scores	201	212	1.05

aware that this is a great simplification of reality. All nations exercise police powers to contain disruptions. This is a normal, legitimate state activity. Particular practices, however, vary widely from nation to nation. It is this "normal" pattern of each individual country that we seek to operationalize with our ratio. In France one sees that acts of coercion occur 43 percent as frequently as acts of conflict, while in Italy they occur 13 percent as frequently. The global ratio is close to 50 percent. With this ratio we are identifying a pattern that existed for a ten-year time span and that is uniquely associated with each individual country. In a later analysis, the methodological assumption is made that this represents the normal (perhaps legitimate) amount of police control exercised in the containment of conflict.

Figure 6.1 arrays these data graphically. The regression line represents the global mean of about .50. Nations departing very far from this norm are identified, with those experiencing very high levels of coercion to the right of the line and those with very low levels to the left. Most of the nations cluster very closely to this line. Of those to the right, with high levels of coercion, the West German case is atypical compared to the activities in other nations. What made it coercion score very high was the large number of political trials that were being conducted in this time period—the arrests and trials of former Nazis. Thus, it does not reflect an attempt at controlling any conflict of that time period, but, instead, the meting out of punishment for offenses committed in the 1940s. South Vietnam, Laos, Cyprus, and Algeria are not included in Figure 6.1, nor were African nations, because their pattern appeared to be the result of war in which foreign powers were involved.

Many of the nations falling to the right of the line in Figure 6.1 are Eastern European ones. Despite tightly controlled polities, high levels of press censorship, and relatively low levels of conflict, police activity is highly visible. They are not the exclusive occupants of this area. One notes nations from all regions, with the exception of Latin America, that conform very closely to the global norm. Countries to the left of the line exercised very minimal coercion and may not be managing conflict effectively.

Hypothesis Testing

Before proceeding with the examination of these ratios between conflict and coercion, we tested their covariance within a shorter time period.

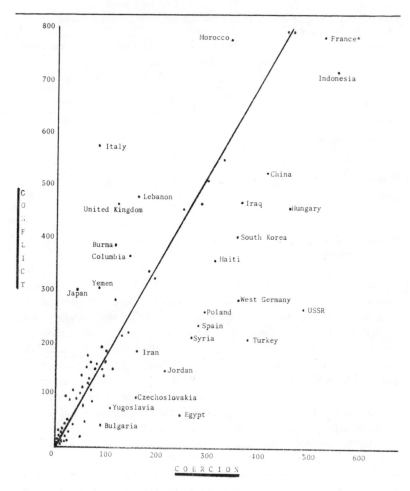

*France is actually at a point much higher (1183) on the conflict scale.

Figure 6.1 Levels of Conflict and Coercion, 1955-1964

Following the theoretical postulate that conflict breeds conflict, it was hypothesized that in any given year, the higher the level of acts challenging the government or its policy (conflict), the higher would be the level of police activity (coercion)—two forms of conflict behavior. Thus, the frequency of conflict was correlated with the frequency of coercion for *each* year for *each* nation. The results are presented in Table 6.2. As one can

TABLE 6.2   Regional Patterns of the Association Between Coercion
and Conflict

Region	Same Time Period	Coercion One Year, Coercion the Next	Conflict One Year, Conflict the Next
Western (n = 21)*	.75	.53	.53
Latin America (n = 20)	.91	.69	.83
Eastern Europe (n = 9)	.57	.39	.45
Asia (n = 20)	.69	.47	.65
Middle East (n = 17)	.68	.33	.41
Africa (n = 24)	.86	.66	.62
World Total (n = 117)	.72	.49	.57

*Correlation coefficients are calculated based on paired frequency distributions of
conflict and coercion for each year for each country.

see, the overall association is very strong ($r = .72$) when all 117 nations are
included. A new correlation coefficient was then calculated for nations
grouped by region. Again, the frequency of conflict was correlated with
the frequency of coercion for each year for each nation. In the Western
region, for example, the correlation for 21 nations of .75 was calculated
based of frequency pairings of conflict and coercion for each year for each
nation (210 data points for conflict and 210 data points for coercion). The
correlation by region is strongest in Latin America and weakest in Eastern
Europe. In the latter region, exercise of authoritarian control may be so
pervasive that it is relative independent of conflict activity.

It would be within the logic of our theoretical framework that high
levels of conflict in a given year would be *followed* by high levels of
coercion in the succeeding year. There may be a lag between the time
turmoil disrupts a nation and the time governmental forces can be mobilized to contain it effectively. Should that be a typical case, one might
identify it by correlating conflict levels one year with coercive levels the
following year. Such a hypothesis would be verified if the coefficients
were higher when the time lag is used than they would be when these
levels for the same year are correlated.

In contrast, it could be hypothesized that higher-than-normal levels of
coercive action call forth questions of legitimacy. Should this be the case,
dissident groups may be stimulated to organize and increase their attacks
on the regime. Should this latter hypothesis accurately identify a prevail-

ing pattern, then high levels of coercion in one year would be *followed* by high levels of conflict in the next year. In this case the correlation coefficient should be highest when this second type of time lag is introduced.

As one can see in Table 6.2, neither time lag demonstrates as strong an association between conflict and coercion as the analysis of the association during the same year, and neither of the former hypotheses is verified. We may have set too arbitrary a time period with the one-year lag. One may need to conduct an analysis that is sensitive to variations among nations. We shall return to this issue in a later section with an examination of patterning in select countries.

Before proceeding to individual country examinations, we felt it would be useful to control for structural coerciveness, as well as for industrial development, as we controlled for geographic region in Table 6.2. Since these variables have been used in other cross-national studies of conflict, we wanted to examine any impact they may have on conflict and conflict management.

For both structural coerciveness and industrial development, we trichotomized the control variables into high, medium, and low rankings. We operationalized coercion by using a measure that had been developed by the Feierabend research team and reported in Feierabend, Nesvold, and Feierabend (1970). For this measure, regime structures in each nation were analyzed and rated on a 6-point ordinal scale based on the concept "permissiveness-coerciveness." These ratings were then averaged to create a score of coerciveness. Industrial development was operationalized simply and conventionally be using data on energy consumption per capita, rank ordering the nations on this value and empirically trichotemizing the list.

Having grouped the nations in this way, we finished with six categories of nations, three categories for each of the structural coerciveness and the industrial development concepts. We then calculated correlation coefficients based on the paired frequency distributions for conflict and coercion for each year in each country in each category. The results are arrayed in Table 6.3. The correlation of .79 for the 24 countries in the low structural coerciveness category, for example, was calculated by using 240 paired data points for conflict and coercion.

The patterning is even more stable than it was in the regional groups. There is no identifiable group in which it is especially weak or where it is noticeably stronger than in nations of the world as a whole. One might add that correlation coefficients were reduced when time lags were introduced.

TABLE 6.3   Relationship Between Conflict and Coercion Using
             Selected Controls

Control	
Structural Coerciveness	
Low (n = 24)*	.79
Medium (n = 28)	.62
High (n = 29)	.72
Industrial Development	
High (n = 39)	.73
Medium (n = 39)	.68
Low (n = 35)	.79

*As in Table 6.2, the number of cases indicates the number of countries in the group.

The analysis is next conducted within each individual country rather than across all or subgroups of nations. We were interested in examining closely the patterning of conflict and coercion in countries that experienced a fair amount of conflict. Obviously, there is nothing much to look at in the very peaceful nations. As mentioned above, it was also decided not to include nations under colonial rule for five or more years of this ten-year period. The national norms and the legitimacy accorded to governmental actions should be significantly different under the colonial arrangement than under an indigenous government rule. Finally, we removed those nations where domestic conflict was contaminated with foreign intervention. The reamining 80 nations were rank ordered on their conflict score, operationally judging the lowest 20 percent (n = 17) as the peaceful nations. We then analyzed the 63 countries constituting the upper 80 percent of this group. The conflict scores in these nations ranged from a low of 49 to a high of 2128.

In Table 6.2 we verified that in any given year there is a strong tendency for conflict and coercion to covary. That is, when conflict is high, one can expect coercion to be high; when conflict is low, coercion tends to be low, and conflict does indeed appear to breed conflict. That conclusion, though, avoids the question of how it starts, why it escalates, and how it is contained.

In order to explore those questions, we listed the conflict scores for each year in each of the 63 nations. The conflict score in each year was multiplied by the ratio listed in Table 6.1 for that nation to identify the

TABLE 6.4   Coercion as a Stimulant to Conflict (France)[a]

Year	Conflict Score	Normal Coercion Score	Actual Coercion Score	Difference
1955	120	52	25	−27
1956	117	50	39	−11
1957	105	45	38	− 7
1958	182	78	89	+11
1959	71	31	43	+12
1960	103	44	68	**+24**
1961	**341**	147	123	−24
1962	3	1	0	− 1
1963	107	46	56	+10
1964	34	15	27	+12
TOTAL	1183		508	

[a]Ratio = .43

"normal" level of coercion one would expect to be used in containing the turmoil. The data for two nations, France and Egypt, are presented in Tables 6.4 and 6.5, respectively. France was selected as a nation experiencing high levels of conflict, while Egypt was selected because of low levels of conflict during that same time period.

In France, for example, in 1955 there were 120 acts of conflict. Thus, we would expect 52 acts of coercion if the "normal" ten-year ratio prevailed (120 × .43). The actual coercion score for France was only 25. A difference was calculated between the normal and actual coercion scores each year. For France in 1955, this difference is −27. Through 1957 there continued to be fewer acts of coercive control than one would expect. In 1958 the pattern changed, and coercive activity increased vis-à-vis the level of conflict, reaching a high in 1960. This high was immediately followed in 1961 with the peak of conflict of that decade (341 acts of conflict).

One can similarly read the data on the Egyptian experience. In a nation experiencing relatively low levels of conflict in this time period, there was an extremely high level of visible coercive control—a ratio of 3.76. Even this ratio was exceeded in 1956 and followed by the peak level of conflict the next year. This pattern of the association between coercion and conflict was repeated in a surprisingly large number of nations.

TABLE 6.5   Coercion as a Stimulant to Conflict (Egypt)[a]

Year	Conflict Score	Normal Coercion Score	Actual Coercion Score	Difference
1955	4	15	23	+ 8
1956	12	45	82	+37
1957	16	60	23	−37
1958	7	26	14	−12
1959	1	4	8	+ 4
1960	7	26	15	−11
1961	4	15	40	+25
1962	7	26	13	−13
1963	0	–	10	+10
1964	5	19	9	− 9
TOTAL	63		237	

[a]Ratio = 3.76.

There are four different patterns logically possible: (1) the year the greatest amount of conflict occurs is also the year when the actual coercion is much higher than expected, (2) the year of the greatest conflict is followed by unusually high coercion, (3) the year of greatest conflict is preceded by unusually high coercion, and (4) none of the above. The modal pattern was the third one in which peak levels of conflict had been preceded by much higher than normal levels of coercion. In almost 50 percent of the cases, this was true. The remaining nations were distributed widely in the other three patterns with none emerging as a second strong pattern.

This is a tantalizing finding. Nothing in the theoretical framework presented here would seem to explain it. One clue we have is that the modal score of conflict was 291 in the nations following this pattern in which the year of its highest level of conflict was preceded by very high coercion. It was 480 for the group as a whole, but very high scores were found in nations falling into each of the patterns. There may be justification for eliminating certain types of conflagrations. Some nations may become so torn apart with high levels of conflict that notions of norms of government control activities are characteristically different than where levels of conflict are less intense.

Concluding Remarks

The exploratory nature of the analysis here is quite apparent. We found a strong relationship between coercion and conflict (r = .72), but this does not come close to explaining the total variance. Furthermore, the unexplained variance is not simply attributable to a few highly authoritarian nations that were included in the analyses. It is a pattern that consistently holds at all levels of structural coerciveness and industrial development, and in all regional groups. To be sure, the correlation coefficient is lower in the Eastern European nations (r = .57) than in other regions of the world, but it is still positive and still fairly strong.

The model we attempted to develop also explored a different dimension of this covariance. While the general trend is for coercion to occur in the same year as conflict, this tells us nothing about the relationship when *peak* years of turmoil occur. While previous cross-national studies of conflict have analyzed the characteristics of nations that experience high levels of violence and contrast these national characteristics to those in nations that are relatively peaceful, we are asking a different question. Within a nation experiencing conflict, what stimulus appears to be associated with peak periods? While our parsiminous theoretical model has been fruitful for this exploratory data analysis, further research would seem to require a more elaborate theory.

We are not without theoretical works suggesting avenues to pursue—the Marxist analysis cites capitalism and its progress toward the increasing misery of the labor force; a revolution of rising expectations of a deprived sector of the populace; perceptions of relative discontent that reach intolerable levels; the appearance of a revolutionary movement, especially a charismatic revolutionary leader; build-up of intolerable systematic frustrations, and so on. All of these models and others have been used to analyze conflict cross-sectionally. They may also prove fruitful for analysis of turmoil within a nation.

One theoretical model that has rarely been used in cross-national research is psychological learning theory. This may offer great promise in the study of relationships between different types of conflict behavior. Bandura (1973) in particular develops a theory that offers great promise in the analysis of political conflict. One of his key points is that in the absence of other factors, the viewing of aggressive behavior is an experience that serves as a model that one may later imitate. He lists three major effects of modeling influences (Bandura, 1973: 68, 69): (1) observers can acquire new patterns of behavior through observation, (2) it can strengthen or weaken inhibitions as a function of rewarding or punishing consequences, and (3) the actions of others serve as social prompts that facilitate similar behavior in others. Item 1 simply suggests that we acquire new patterns of behavior by observing and imitating what we see. This can apply to rioting as well as to baseball playing. Item 2 suggests that when we observe pleasant consequences of the model's action, it strengthens the likelihood of imitation, while when we see aversive response, it strengthens the inhibition to engage in that behavior. Item 3 suggests that whatever the model's behavior, and whatever the consequences, the fact that one sees other people engaging in these acts, serves as a *social* prompt.

Applying this to the conflict/coercion pattern, one can point to the fact that in many nations, aggressive behaviors are widely modeled. One need not belabor the point that we see acts of aggression, many that are violent, quite regularly—whether we directly observe it or observe it through the media. In the experimental situation, Bandura found that children who viewed TV violence, when not accompanied by aversive response, engaged in imitative behavior. Perhaps this would suggest that consistent and immediate punishment should follow all public acts of aggression, so that the "model" reinforces inhibitions to such acts. However, there are other factors to consider. The major complication is that coercive actions themselves may act as a model to imitate. Bandura (1973: 92) concludes that: "It is not uncommon for people whose efforts to produce desired changes have been repeatedly thwarted to emulate coercive strategies, but in their own way, after seeing other groups successfully attain what they want through aggressive means."

A careful development of the Bandura model may generate testable hypotheses that lead to the development of increased understanding of political conflict. However, whatever model is used for further inquiry, the topic is an important one in cross-national research. Some critics have expressed the opinion that satisfactory tests of any of the models require much more detailed data than are available for research on a large number of countries. It seems premature, however, to make any such judgment. There are rich data for developing a general understanding of these phenomena.

NOTES

1. For a thorough review of this research, see T. R. Gurr (1980). If the reader wishes to go beyond the selected list of references in this chapter, attention is directed to the bibliography in this work, which contains some 700 entries.

2. Discussion of measurement problems can be found in most standard texts on research methods. An excellent analysis can be found in Kaplan (1964).

3. Representative collections of articles can be found in Gillespie and Nesvold (1971) and Feierabend, Feierabend, and Gurr (1972). Complex variables such as political democracy, political development, as well as political conflict were operationalized and subject to empirical analyses.

4. Eckstein (1980) has an extensive discussion of the role theory has played in the cross-national study of conflict. Other articles in the volume (Gurr, 1980) discuss the critical exchange among scholars in this field. The discussion is far too long to summarize here, but it can be noted that the prevailing tendency is to attempt development of more parsiminous theory, as Eckstein suggests. Gurr's work in particular can be described as pursuing this effort.

5. These data are available for distribution through the Inter-University Consortium for Political and Social Research, Ann Arbor, Michigan 48106. The data file is listed as ICPSR 5207, Feierabend, Feierabend and Nesvold, *Systemic Conditions of Political Aggression (SCOPA) Project, 1955-1964.*

REFERENCES

ANDERSON, C. W. and B. A. NESVOLD (1972) "A Skinnerian analysis of conflict behavior." American Behavioral Scientist 15: 883-910.

APTER, D. E. (1965) The Politics of Modernization. Chicago: University of Chicago Press.

AZAR, E. E. and J. B. BEN-DAK [eds.] (1975) Theory and Practice of Events Research: Studies in Inter-Nation Actions and Interactions. New York: Gordon & Breach.

BANDURA, A. (1973) Aggression: A Social Learning Analysis. Englewood Cliffs, NJ: Prentice-Hall.

BANKS, A. S. and R. B. TEXTOR (1963) A Cross-Polity Survey. Cambridge: MIT Press.

DAVIES, J. C. (1962) "Toward a theory of revolution." American Sociological Review 26: 5-19.

DEUTSCH, K. W. (1961) "Social mobilization and political development." American Political Science Review 55: 493-514.

ECKSTEIN, H. (1980) "Theoretical approaches to explaining collective political violence," in T. R. Gurr, Handbook of Political Conflict. New York: Free Press.

ELDRIDGE, A. F. (1979) Images of Conflict. New York: St. Martin's.

FEIERABAND, I. K. (1966) "Aggressive behaviors within politics, 1948-1962: a cross-national study." Journal of Conflict Resolution 10: 249-271.

――― and R. L. FEIERABEND (1971) "The relationship of systemic frustration, political coercion, and political instability: a cross-national analysis," pp. 417-440 in J. Gillespie and B. Nesvold (eds.) Macro-Quantitative Analysis. Beverly Hills: Sage.

――― and T. R. GURR (1972) Anger, Violence and Politics. Englewood Cliffs: Prentice-Hall.

FEIERABAND, I. K. and B. A. NESVOLD (1969) "Social change and political violence," in H. D. Graham and T. R. Gurr (eds.) Violence in America. New York: Praeger.

——— and R. L. FEIERABEND (1970) "Political coerciveness and turmoil: a cross-national inquiry." Law and Society Review 5, 1: 93-118.

GILLESPIE, J. V. and B. A. NESVOLD [eds.] (1971) Macro-Quantitative Analysis: Conflict, Development, and Democratization. Beverly Hills: Sage.

GILLESPIE, J. V. and D. A. ZINNES [eds.] (1977) Mathematical Systems in International Relations Research. New York: Praeger.

GRAHAM, H. D. and T. R. GURR (1979) Violence in America: Historical and Comparative Perspectives. Beverly Hills: Sage.

——— [eds.] (1969) Violence in America: Historical and Comparative Perspectives. Washington, DC: Government Printing Office.

GURR, T. R. [ed.] (1980) Handbook of Political Conflict. New York: Free Press.

——— (1976) Rogues, Rebels, and Reformers: A Political History of Urban Crime and Conflict. Beverly Hills: Sage.

——— (1970) Why Men Rebel. Princeton, NJ: Princeton University Press.

——— (1968) "A causal model of civil strife: a comparative analysis using new indices." American Political Science Review 62: 1104-1124.

——— P. N. GRABOTSKY, and R. C. HULA (1977) The Politics of Crime and Conflict: A Comparative History of Four Cities. Beverly Hills: Sage.

GURR, T. R. and M. I. LICHBACH (1979) "Forecasting domestic political conflict," pp. 153-194 in J. D. Singer and M. D. Wallace (eds.) To Augur Well: Early Warning Indicators in World Politics. Beverly Hills: Sage.

——— with C. RUTTENBERG (1967) The Conditions of Civil Violence: First Tests of a Causal Model. Princeton, NJ: Center of International Studies.

HIBBS, D. A. (1973) Mass Political Violence: A Cross-National Causal Analysis. New York: John Wiley.

HIRSCH, H. and D. C. PERRY [eds.] (1973) Violence as Politics. New York: Harper & Row.

HUNTINGTON, S. P. (1968) Political Order in Changing Societies. New Haven, CT: Yale University Press.

KAPLAN, A. (1964) The Conduct of Inquiry. San Francisco: Chandler.

KELMAN, H. C. [ed.] (1965) International Behavior: A Social-Psychological Analysis. New York: Holt, Rinehart & Winston.

KORNHAUSER, W. (1959) The Politics of Mass Society. New York: Free Press.

LERNER, D. (1958) The Passing of Traditional Society. New York: Free Press.

MARKUS, G. B. and B. A. NESVOLD (1972) "Governmental coerciveness and political instability." Comparative Political Studies: 231-244.

MIDLARSKY, M. and R. TANTER (1967) "Toward a theory of political instability in Latin America." Journal of Peace Research 4: 209-227.

NESVOLD, B. A. (1969) "Scalogram analysis of political violence." Comparative Political Studies: 172-194.

RUMMEL, R. J. (1975) Understanding Conflict and War, 4 vols. New York: John Wiley.

—— (1972) The Dimensions of Nations. Beverly Hills: Sage.

——— (1966) "Dimensions of conflict behavior within nations, 1946-59." Journal of Conflict Resolution: 65-74.

——— (1963) "Dimensions of conflict behavior within and between nations." General Systems Yearbook 8: 1-50.

RUSSETT, B. M. (1965) Trends in World Politics. New York: Macmillan.

——— (1964) "Inequality and instability: the relation of land tenure to politics." World Politics 16: 442-454.

——— H. R. ALKER, Jr., K. W. DEUTSCH, and H. D. LASSWELL (1964) World Handbook of Social and Political Indicators. New Haven, CT: Yale University Press.

SINGER, J. D. and M. D. WALLACE [eds.] (1979) To Augur Well: Early Warning Indicators in World Politics. Beverly Hills: Sage.

SKINNER, B. F. (1953) Science and Human Behavior. New York: Macmillan.

TANTER, R. (1966) "Dimensions of conflict behavior within and between nations, 1958-60." Journal of Conflict Resolution: 41-65.

VIDICH, A. J. and R. M. GLASSMAN [eds.] (1979) Conflict and Control: Challenge to Legitimacy of Modern Governments. Beverly Hills: Sage.

ZINNES, D. A. and J. V. GILLESPIE [eds.] (1976) Mathematical Models in International Relations. New York: Praeger.

Synthesis

Inquiry Problems and Future Research

CHARLES F. HERMANN

This essay reviews the two immediately preceding chapters and attempts to use them as a point of departure for some more general observations about key inquiry questions in cross-national research.[1] The Nesvold and Rosenau presentations lend themselves well to the task. In some respects they are complementary and in other ways their contrasts highlight alternative approaches. In both ways they dramatize some of the current issues in cross-national endeavors. To evaluate these two contributions, the reader will be invited to judge these articles as if they were the respective author's definitive statement on the subjects addressed—an assumption that is unlikely, but nevertheless appropriate until each researcher provides us with further analysis on the topics. In the discussion that follows, I will deal first, generally, with problems of logic and levels of analysis in cross-national research, and then deal subsequently with the subproblems of missing elements of aggregation and sequence.

Theory Development and Empirical Investigation

In examining these two contributions side by side, one is struck by the number of ways in which they are complementary. The Rosenau chapter is conceptual and speculative. It develops in broad brush strokes the outline of a theoretical interpretation of how international phenomena may contribute to a change in domestic attitudes and behaviors. The civic commitment of the citizen to the national government is postulated as being fragmented and redirected toward other entities. Interdependence of nations combined with technological advances and resource depletion is viewed as a major contributing force. Rosenau interprets the reconciliation of multiple loyalties and their effects to be dependent upon psychological processes and individual constructs for ordering the world that researchers need to identify and understand.

The large number of concepts and relationships discussed or alluded to by Rosenau stands in sharp contrast to Nesvold's primary concentration on the single relationship between the state's use of coercion and public manifestations of political conflict. What is the relationship between these two variables and what produces extremes in their occurrence? These questions are at the heart of Nesvold's inquiry. Unlike Rosenau's chapter, hers is an empirical analysis of variations in a single relationship.

Both studies need to be extended by the kind of research design represented by the other. Upon examining Rosenau, the reader may ask: Is this really true? With what evidence do you substantiate your assertion? Where are the data? After encountering Nesvold's study and discovering the global correlation of .72 between political conflict and coercion across 117 nations for each of ten years, the reader may join with the author in asking: Why is this so? What theory could account for this relationship? Is it part of a larger pattern of relationships or an artifact with limited real significance? In sum, the chapters illustrate the two essential components of cross-national research—theory development and empirical investigation.

It is apparent throughout the field of cross-national research and social inquiry generally that theoretical development and empirical investigation must complement one another (Boynton would call this coherence). Because such an observation seems obvious, it is surprising that in cross-national studies as a whole, we have had difficulty keeping the two elements intertwined. Early comparative studies were highly speculative with only scant attention paid to evidence or the canons governing its collection or use. After all, when the support for an interpretation of multiple societies depends on the direct or indirect observations of a single observer, the task of gathering empirical support for cross-national generalizations is overwhelming. By the 1960s, however, the enthusiasm among many Western scholars for data collection—national accounting data, other aggregate data, event data, perceptual data, voting data, survey data—and the means of manipulating large data files efficiently, overwhelmed most efforts at theory building.

Are we now collectively in a position to do better—to combine careful cross-national empirical analysis with thoughtful theoretical development? Perhaps, but the integration is not likely without considerable skill and a conscious commitment to conduct work in one domain that facilitates efforts in the other. Surely it is of critical importance to train graduate students and others committed to cross-national inquiry to work in both modes. Although many graduate programs offer instruction in various data collection and analysis methods, training in theory and concept development often goes no further than an introductory seminar in the philosophy of science and perhaps a course that reviews recent substantive theoretical developments in comparative or international politics. Courses in logic or mathematics, seminars on theoretical work in other social sciences, or exercises designed to encourage the student to move from observable phenomena and actual or imaginable experiences to broad generalizations are not routinely advanced. Even if a person is given the opportunity to develop capabilities in both modes, personal talent and predisposition may lead to concentration in one area or the other rather than both.

When a scholar does not perform both functions and hopes that one or more others will build upon his or her work and conduct complementary inquiries, it is imperative that the initial investigator thinks and communicates in ways that facilitate consideration of his or her contribution. If individual scholarly efforts are consciously viewed as building blocks in a cycle of theory and empirical inquiry, various requirements could be advanced to promote the process. Among such requirements, concept formation and specification of conditions certainly should be prominent. These topics bring us back to the Nesvold and Rosenau studies.

Concept Development and Condition Specification

Though the two studies illustrate complementary sides of the theory development/empirical verification concern, they are similar in their interest in multiple units at several levels. Interpretation of phenomena at one level is advanced in terms of phenomena at a different level. The national government is a unit of concern to both Nesvold and Rosenau. The former examines it as emitting coercive behaviors; the latter finds it involved in a web of interdependent relationships that reduce its ability to engage in behaviors that might resolve domestic problems. Both authors introduce subnational units, but with a surprising lack of specification. Rosenau concentrates on the citizen and "unknown others." The latter may be deceptively easy to operationalize as a "remainder" category—all the people in the world with whom a person does not interact directly. Operationalization, however, is not the same as concept development. In fact, it is not clear that Rosenau is concerned with all unknown others, but only with those to whom an individual assigns some "loyalties or sentiments." Those key descriptors of the unit remain undefined terms. Nesvold considers the behavior of subnational units that challenge the regime or its policies. The behaviors are operationalized—riots, demonstrations, terrorist actions, revolts, and so on—but the units that engage in such behaviors receive no explicit attention. In a similar fashion, Rosenau specifies interdependence as a behavior pattern outside the national government, but is rather unclear about the units generating that relationship. One is left to wonder whether interdependence as used is only between governments, between entire societies, or between various components of a society. (The latter option raises the prospect of some parts of a society being more interdependent than others).

It can be argued that an attempt to explain behavior patterns, whether they be interdependence or political conflict, will be hampered without specification of the behaving unit. When an infant with a relatively undifferentiated means of communication cries, it may not have the same implications as a crying adult. A crying adult in one culture may have a far different meaning than the same adult behavior in another society. Concept development, not just operationalization, is a critical task in any research enterprise and it becomes even more acute in cross-national inquiries. Cross-national equivalencies in units and behaviors must be established rather than assumed.[2]

Both studies struggle with another critical task—the specification of the conditions and parameters under which the postulated relationship might exist. Rosenau stipulates some conditions; Nesvold searches for them empirically. Rosenau speculates that the hypothesized relationship between the citizen and the state applies in industrialized democracies. He suggests that the relationship increases as interdependence increases. In that author's present formulation, the effect of interdependence on citizen behavior is indefinitely linear. Each and every incremental increase in interdependence is assumed to produce an effect on citizen behavior comparable to that of every other equivalent increase. Variability is introduced not as the amount of interdependence changes, but rather as the individual responds in either an accommodative or resistant mode. The alternate responses are briefly mentioned as being influenced by international crises, technological breakthroughs, inflationary cycles, political leadership, and political socialization. Only the latter intervening variable is discussed to suggest how it affects the direction of individual response. The task of specification is begun, but unfinished.

Nesvold first examines the global relationship between political conflict and state coercion and then checks to see if the relationship is affected by geographical region, structural coerciveness, industrial development, and finally, individual nations. As with Rosenau, the discussion as to why these conditions might be expected to alter the relationship is almost nonexistent.

In terms of specifying underlying conditions and limiting parameters, these chapters may reflect a continuing evolution in cross-national research. The authors are more sensitive to the need than might have been the case a decade ago in cross-national research, but a more explicit and thorough treatment is required. Zinnes (1975) describes the large volume of comparative and international work that engages in what she calls "ad hoc hypothesis testing," the simplest form of which is the exploration of a bivariate relationship—A covaries with B. Typically, the researcher offers some anecdotal suggestions as to why such a relationship is plausible before engaging in an empirical test. Missing in the vast majority of studies, however, is any recognition of the need to probe more deeply at the expected underlying logic for the association and the conditions under which it might be expected to occur, change in intensity, reverse, or disappear entirely.

In cross-national research, certainly part of this specification must concern the class of nations to which the relationship might apply and why. It is a fuller treatment of the "why" in designating conditions that we must stress in the future. The Rosenau interpretation of the individual and the state is noted as a problem of industrial democracies. Is it because they are more prone to interdependence? Is it their pluralism in the organization of interests that facilitates alternative objects of loyalty and commitment? Is it the individual's greater access to communication, information, or personal wealth?

In advancing the idea of the policy sciences, Lasswell (1971) urged his colleagues to establish the contextuality of their research. His concern with context, that of Zinnes (1975) with the inadequacy of ad hoc hypothesis testing, and the references here to conditions and parameters, share a common concern. Until the developers of theoretical works commit themselves to explication of the underlying logic, specification of conditions and parameters will remain a significant impediment to cross-national research.

Problems of Aggregation and Sequence: Multiple Levels and Complex Interactions

In examining the two studies as a set, it is possible to construct linkages between the phenomena addressed in each. In Rosenau's chapter among the effects of increasing international interdependence examined are the emergence of more issues in the public arena and the reduced effectiveness of national governments in resolving domestic public problems. How does the individual member of the polity respond to such circumstances? Rosenau suggests a person reacts in their civic role with either accommodation or resistance. Each of these broad response domains consists of many kinds of behavior and the resistance pattern certainly could include political conflict—demonstrations, riots, strikes, and so on. Moreover, national governments could respond to a reduction in their effectiveness by attempting to reduce interdependence (if that were the perceived source) by initiating new modes of problem solving, engaging in propaganda to lower citizen expectations, or increasing police powers to ensure their continuance in office in the face of domestic dissatisfaction. The last course would likely lead to more governmental coercion. Thus, Rosenau's concern with the effects of interdependence could be a source of the state coercion/political conflict relationship examined by Nesvold. Specifically, the effects Rosenau attributes to increased interdependence could intensify the state coercion/political conflict relationships.

It might also be argued that as dissident groups—who oppose a current regime for whatever reasons—seek to mobilize broad support for their cause by political conflict, the individual citizen's loyalty to the regime could be seriously affected. Some citizen's may react by a renewal of their commitment to the state, whereas others may experience exactly the kind of loss of civic attachment that Rosenau describes. Certainly if state coercion increases or if what has become the accepted or "normal" pattern of state treatment of opposition increases (Nesvold's coercion/conflict ratio), then notions of the civic self are likely to be affected. Following this line of argument, one would expect to observe some of Rosenau's competing loyalty phenomena in countries experiencing peaks in the Nesvold ratio of coercion/conflict.[3]

Though the linkages between the two sets of concerns may appear plausible, the material from each would seem to be only a partial explanation for the phenomena of concern to the other. Facing the assumed consequences of interdependence, Rosenau's citizen has multiple options of which political conflict is only one. From the perspective of Nesvold's research, interdependence may be a factor contributing to coercion or conflict but certainly it is only one source applicable to a subset of the countries examined. If, in the contemporary world, interdependence is steadily increasing, it cannot account for the fluctuations in the coercion/conflict ratio in an industrial democracy such as France.

The attempt to identify possible points of intersection between the two studies facilitates several observations. Both studies involve not only a cross-national research design but one across levels of analysis. Not only do they involve variables at different levels, but also parallel searches for sources of explanation at nonnational levels. Nesvold and Rosenau both tend to favor psychological types of explanation. Nesvold suggests learning theory. Rosenau implies some form of cognitive structure approach with his proposals for differentiated systems orientations to determine the nature of the civic self. There is no necessary reason to suspect that all cross-national studies will tend in the future toward psychological forms of explanation, but it does seem reasonable to suggest that as national variables (e.g., state performance as problem solver, state coercion) are linked to supranational (e.g., interdependence) or subnational (e.g., civic self, political conflict) variables, then the search for explanation will require theories at these other levels and conceptualizations that can bridge across them.

The juxtaposition of the two studies also suggests that the authors explicitly stipulate relationships that comprise only one set of responses in circumstances not well defined. Fragmented loyalties might arise from interdependence, but they may also result from either state coercion or political conflict. State coercion might trigger political conflict or vice versa, but both may result from third factors such as interdependence. There may be a tendency to construct explanations that are too linear to permit a reasonable interpretation of the actual political world. By linear is meant explanations of the form: A produces one type of change in B, which in turn has one outcome that results in C, and so on. If our purpose is to understand C, it may be necessary to consider the effects of A on variables other than B and the multiple factors that can influence the value of B, if it is the trigger for C. The criterion of parismony often has been introduced to avoid consideration of more complex, nonlinear interactions. We face a danger, however, of letting our thinking become simpleminded as well. By assuming we can comprehend only simple, linear relationships we may fail to understand essential social patterns. Even if actual research designs are simplified, there is no reason why one's thinking about the phenomena must be so constrained. In fact, it may even be preferable to design a more complex interpretation than to settle for one so simple that the prospects of success and acceptance are minimal.

How far considerations of complex interactions must be taken cannot be fully determined without a clear specification of the underlying logic expected for the basic relationships and a stipulation of the conditions under which they are expected to hold. This returns us to the earlier discussion.

Patterns, Puzzles, and Precision—
The Future of Cross-National Research

It would be inappropriate to conclude this essay without reference to one aspect of the discussion that surrounded the original conference presentation of the preceding chapters. The question was raised as to whether cross-national research in political science has a future. Was the surge of studies in the 1960s and 1970s that examined a large sample of nations in either a cross-sectional or longitudinal design a transitory interest? As Professor Maurice East observed in his remarks at the conference, others have suggested that cross-national research is too gross to reveal actual political dynamics, too simplistic to capture complex relationships, too insensitive to distinctive historical experiences of different polities and cultures, too dependent upon inaccurate, noncomparable data, and too focused on the aggregate national level to provide realistic explanatory theories. Though the conference reached no collective position on these issues, the author of this essay has reached a strong positive position on the question. One would hope that we have learned a good deal about cross-national political research since the early days of large data-based studies that began two decades ago. Because of this experience, we should not expect—indeed we would not wish—that the future would be an unaltered continuation of past research. If one conceives of cross-national political research more broadly as the development and examination of empirically investigatable theories about sets of nations or political phenomena located in different countries, continuation in years ahead seems certain.

Exactly how future cross-national research will take shape in the years ahead depends upon a number of factors. Some of these, such as the nature, level, and source of funding for political science research, are beyond the scope of this essay. It does seem possible, however, to identify some needed, and probable, characteristics using the Nesvold and Rosenau studies as a point of departure.

(1) Cross-national explanations will employ variables from multiple levels of analysis—supranational, national, and subnational. Perhaps in no way are the two preceding chapters more illustrative of the future of cross-national studies than with respect to their use of variables drawn from multiple levels. These more complex interpretations have implications not only for theory development, but also for research designs and data collections.

(2) Greater specification will be made of the context and the underlying logic expected to govern basic relationships specified in theories and supporting empirical research. It is unlikely that all researchers will become formal modelers or confine themselves to rigorous deduction from a set of initially given conditions and terms. That step is not necessary to achieve at a verbal level greater specification of the reasons and conditions for any hypothesized relationships. That commitment involves more than the introduction of control or mediating variables, although their use might well follow from greater efforts at identifying necessary conditions and parameters.

(3) Cross-national research will involve a greater variety of research techniques and methods. Gillespie (1971) reminded us of the distinction between the cross-national and the configurative approaches to comparative analysis. The cross-national approach formulates empirical generalizations about the entire political system using each system in a specified set as one data point and comparing them all simultaneously. The configurative approach examines one system at a time and comparisons are made sequentially. In effect, the configurative approach is a set of case studies. Both Gillespie (1971) and Russett (1970) remind us that each approach has assets and liabilities. They can and should be used as complementary strategies for theory building. Their more frequent use in tandem in the years ahead will not only strengthen each, but will facilitate bonds between comparativists specializing in aggregate data manipulations and those specializing in the study of a single country or region. Cross-national theory can be viewed as a common enterprise pursued by different but complementary strategies of inquiry.

(4) More effort will be given to concept formation and the association between acting units and their behaviors. The studies under review concentrated on the analysis of behaviors (e.g., interdependence, political conflict, system orientations, state coercion) with minimal attention to the nature of the units responsible for those behaviors. In many studies, the

focus is reversed—attributes of units are examined with minimal reference to the expected behaviors. Most cross-national studies require attention to both for a number of reasons, including designing the research so that one is able to determine whether behaviors in different countries can be treated as equivalent.

(5) Cross-national studies will offer a closer interaction between theory development and empirical investigation. It still may be unrealistic for many contributing scholars to be at one and the same time extraordinary creators of theory and talented data analysts, but there is reason to be optimistic that the contributions of each will be more accessible and usable to the other. Certainly, advancement on the previously noted four points would have that effect; so, too, would attention to both concerns in graduate education. The Rosenau and Nesvold studies provide reason to be encouraged. Certainly Rosenau discusses the issue of operationalization in his theory development chapter. To a very considerable degree, Nesvold discusses both past and prospective theoretical levels that pertain to the relationship she explores. Both scholars demonstrate a concern upon which others can expand.

These five developments are the author's proposed requirements for the future of cross-national research. Though others might disagree in whole or in part with the list, it seems reasonable to project that evolution and innovation will occur and that cross-national research will continue for the simple reason that it can fulfill a valuable set of purposes in comparative analysis. Cross-national research can reveal basic patterns that characterize sets of nations with a clarity that seems unavailable in any other way. It can, as Nesvold nicely demonstrates, offer the inquiring mind puzzles that motivate new insights and research. Furthermore, it is a powerful vehicle for increasing the precision of our knowledge both with respect to its boundaries and scope and with respect to the manner (i e., the concepts and theories) in which we express it. The continuation of cross-national research is not in doubt.

NOTES

1. The author has had the advantage of developing this essay after having heard a critique of the chapters in question by Maurice A. East (University of Kentucky), Lyndelle Fairlie (San Diego State University), and William Lineham (State University of New York at Stony Brook), as well as the general discussion by participants attending the conference on "New Dimensions in Political Science." It is impossible to acknowledge all the individual insights gained by through these interactions, but it

is undoubtedly the case that these comments have benefited by the process although I alone am responsible for this presentation.

2. MacIntyre (1973) makes the noncomparability of social concepts across cultures one of his main reasons for challenging the possibility of a science of comparative politics. As they now stand, the concepts introduced in the two proceeding cross-national studies would offer considerable ammunition for MacIntyre's arguments. For a discussion of developing empirical equivalence for concepts on a cross-national basis, see Przeworski and Teune (1970).

3. This essay will make no effort to critique the empirical analysis procedures used in the Nesvold study as that would turn the comments in the direction of a separate, noncomparable examination of her study. The intention is rather to treat the Nesvold and Rosenau research as a set from which observations about cross-national research might be developed. It might be noted, however, that Professor William Lineham, in his discussion of the Nesvold study, raised interesting questions about the design of the state coercion/political conflict ratio for cross-national research. Using as it does the raw frequency of events in both categories, the ratio does not take into consideration the effects of population. The same number of incidents of either kind in India and Iceland, for example, would suggest very different things.

REFERENCES

GILLESPIE, J. V. (1971) "An introduction to macro-cross-national research," pp. 13-30 in John V. Gillespie and Betty A. Nesvold (eds.) Macro-Quantitative Analysis. Beverly Hills, CA: Sage.

LASSWELL, H. D. (1971) A Pre-View of the Policy Sciences. New York: Elsevier-North Holland.

MACINTYRE, A. (1973) "Is a science of comparative politics possible?" pp. 171-188 in Alan Ryan (ed.) The Philosophy of Social Explanation. London: Oxford University Press.

PREZEWORSKI, A. and H. TEUNE (1970) The Logic of Comparative Inquiry. New York: John Wiley.

RUSSETT, B. M. (1970) "International behavior research," pp. 425-443 in Michael Haas and Henry S. Kariel (eds.) Approaches to the Study of Political Science. Scranton, PA: Chandler.

ZINNES, D. A. (1975) "Research frontiers in the study of international politics," pp. 87-198 in Fred I. Greenstein and Nelson W. Polsby (eds.) International Politics, Vol. 8, Handbook of Political Science. Reading, MA: Addison-Wesley.

PART IV

Cumulation and Synthesis in Integrative Models

Introduction

Two Views of Integrative Models

J. DONALD MOON

A major problem of inquiry that is increasingly being discussed in the discipline is that of integrating a vast array of research studies into a coherent whole that can be used to build theory in a subfield of the discipline. American politics is a natural place for this type of discussion to take place. The vast array of studies at the individual and institutional levels poses very real problems of integration and theory development. If we cannot come to some resolution of the problems of theory building in this subfield, then we may find it even more difficult to follow a systematic program of theory building elsewhere. In this section, we have chosen to focus on the integration of findings regarding the courts and other basic American institutions.

American politics is an ideal area to study the question of integration and its role in theory building, in part because it has always been a central preoccupation of political science in America. Over the years, the nature of our preoccupation has changed; at one time the emphasis may have been on the changing legal and constitutional form of the Republic, at another, we have stressed education for citizenship. For many years after World War II some of the most innovative and important studies focused on the political behavior of individuals. Such studies were made possible by the development of survey research methods, and they were often based upon theoretical concepts drawn from such allied disciplines as sociology and social psychology. During the past few years, however, there has been a renewed interest in the operation of political institutions, including the courts, Congress, and the presidency at the national level, and the evolving systems of representation and implementation that link national politics with state and local political systems.

This renewed interest in structures and institutions is a natural development of the recent focus on the political behavior of individuals. Having come to a much better understanding of the attitudes, knowledge, and activities of individual citizens, we should naturally wish to integrate that knowledge with our understanding of the functioning of the political system as a whole. In considering how individual behaviors aggregate to constitute the polity, our attention is immediately drawn to the principal institutions that constitute the political system and that provide the context and background to individual behavior.

We are also led to this concern with institutions by developments in American politics. This has been an important period for institutional change and reform, in which the structures of our major institutions have themselves become political issues. We have seen extensive critiques of the growth of presidential power, and the attempt to change the balance of power between the presidency and Congress. The structure and procedures of political parties, particularly the Democratic party, have come under intensive scrutiny and have been subjected to numerous alterations and reforms. The courts and their role have been the center of a major political storm. As they have legislated major changes in important areas of national life, including race relations, legislative redistricting, abortion, and police procedures, various groups have come to feel that they have exceeded their legitimate powers, and have sought to revise some of their decisions and to restrict the future scope of judicial action. Moreover, as the courts have undertaken direct responsibility for functions normally performed by the other institutions, including the management of local school systems and statewide prison systems, political institutions such as state government have become parties to these controversies.

It is not surprising that the courts should come to be the focus of so much attention, both from political scientists and political actors, given their uniquely central role in American politics. Very few political systems vest their judges with as much power and responsibility as we do, and in some measure this reflects what Vincent Ostrom calls the "design" of the American polity—the fact that we have a written constitution, and the role of the courts in interpreting it. This at least apparent centrality of the constitution to American politics gives us a substantive focal point for discussion of major questions of integration in American politics.

In the following chapter, Samuel Krislov reviews the development of theory and research in the subfield of the courts and judicial processes and raises a major question about integration in the discipline. He notes a wide range of studies and makes some linkages between these studies, as well as discovering some very real gaps in the research literature. He then goes on to outline where fruitful cumulation might occur and gives some basic guidelines for how that cumulation might be achieved. He pays particular attention to the need for coherence between basic ideas and research activities as a first step toward cumulation in the field of judicial process.

Vincent Ostrom analyzes a second key missing element in integration, that of synthesis. He argues that synthesis in American politics depends on the consideration of basic issues at the constitutional level of analysis. We must include the study of the constitutional level of analysis in order to synthesize disparate research findings on individuals and institutions. He goes on to develop an argument that provides a model for how synthesis might be achieved utilizing the constitutional level of analysis as a basis.

Together, these chapters provide powerful arguments for the need for cumulation and synthesis in the discipline. They also provide some useful starting points for this effort. They point toward future directions in thinking and research that will help us to integrate our knowledge and move the discipline toward higher levels of explanatory power on basic questions in the American politics field. As such, these chapters provide a model that can be applied across fields in the discipline.

7

Building Knowledge About the Judicial Process

SAMUEL KRISLOV

A New Approach

A new approach to the judicial process accompanied the renewed interest in social science that followed World War II. The influence of Arthur Bentley was felt in political science generally, and in the study of political influences on courts especially. The "scientific" mode of study of judicial process has been neither a success nor a failure. Some of its aspirations have been met, though usually in attenuated form; some have not achieved even modest fulfillment.

Twenty years ago, Charles Hyneman listed five faults with the study of public law, including: (1) description of court structure, (2) delineation of actual judicial processes, (3) information about techniques for control and implementation, (4) research on effects of public opinion on judicial attitudes, and (5) description of the political milieu in which the courts operate. By and large these *have* been dealt with. These friendly chidings of two decades ago no longer chafe. Our remaining problems are of a more conceptual and less descriptive variety.

The broader concern with "process" has prevailed over the more restrictive "behavior" notions. The result is a more expansive view of what is researchable, in both the behavioral and the traditional modes. Posing interesting and divergent puzzles has made the field of interest to a growing number of outsiders. The skills acquired in research have also enabled large numbers of people to find employment in court management and related fields.

Building on the work of the legal realists, the new approach explored the force of rules in decision making. Like the voting behavior studies, the new judicial behavior inquiry emphasized what judges did, not what they said. Drawing from diverse sources, including organization theory and legal anthropology, it stressed awareness of the context of litigation—its social function, and its alternatives. Such studies drastically expand the domain of inquiry—in time, in intensity, in range of appropriate evidence, and in adequacy of proof. The ten-foot shelf of upper-court decisions is no longer sufficient: Field inquiry is required; results no longer reflect simply opinions of the author or superior reasoning power. An outline of the major puzzles in this approach and some of its problems follows.

Data Collection and Its Potential:
Issues of Method

American legal scholars operate under a distinct handicap. Statistics on the judicial process are subject to more than normal ambiguity, since the federal system—with 51 jurisdictions—generates data in noncomparable conceptual categories and compilations. Under these circumstances, conclusions are few and highly questionable. For example, we are told persistently by presidents, media, and experts that litigation is growing at a threatening pace, outstripping population, engulfing the courtrooms. The evidence on this rather central question—one with profound policy implications—is tantalizingly inconclusive. There is only one attempt to pull together national data in roughly comparable catagories and this from only 44 states (though they comprise 92 percent of the national population). The U.S. courts have clearly experienced steep caseload increases, largely in areas where Congress has legislatively opened the gates to litigation. However, federal courts handle only approximately 5 percent of the cases.

Other bodies of official data pose similar problems. The Uniform Crime Reports is a partial system, collected for somewhat tendentious purposes, and its rather odd methods of tabulation make impossible many desirable analyses of the data. Sentencing data are accessible, but not in aggregate form, and probation data are simply not available in any comprehensive fashion.

Still other forms of "hard" data can be derived from published records. Most conspicuous has been the effort to use judges' votes in cases to infer motivations, particularly ideological leanings. To date, the effort has been useful mainly in analyzing larger collegial courts, but has yielded little when applied to three-judge panels, because of a strong tendency toward unanimity there, and because the few 2-1 breakdowns offer little opportunity for comparison. While the results indicate fairly durable ideological differences, they have been regarded as less than earthshaking. The techniques and findings are similar to congressional roll-call analysis, but without the interesting relationships to constituency characteristics, they have only limited potential when applied to judicial voting.

Kagan and associates (1977) have attempted to trace the evolution of state supreme courts by sampling records at discrete time intervals in different state systems. The authors suggest a three-stage evolution: from automatic review in a two-tier system, to selective review in a three-tier, to a highly selective public-law-emphasis stage. The technique has little theoretical justification and the results are not so well demonstrated as they are interesting.

There are a few rigorous, experimental studies: the Chicago jury study (Kalven, 1966); Maurice Rosenberg's (1964) pretrial study set up for, and with, the New Jersey Supreme Court; and more recent efforts such as the ABA Shreveport study of legal needs (Marks et al., 1974). Additionally, the judicial process is amenable to Donald Campbell's (1963) quasi-experimental techniques. Before-and-after studies are not possible because drastic changes, e.g., new laws or policy shifts, abruptly affect time-series. The results so far tell more about the effectiveness of specific policies than about the operations of the judicial system. In short, the difficulty in obtaining "hard" data has made these studies rare.

Most of our information on the judicial process comes from "soft" methods: history, doctrinal analysis, and our own version of ethnographic studies. Doctrinal analysis presents a powerful logic, but within a confined and sometimes fictional universe. Until about ten years ago, for example, a law student could complete a criminal law course without becoming aware of the phenomenon of plea bargaining. Precision and hard thinking in legal analysis are attractive for their neatness, often derived from ignoring untidy reality. Charles Beard spoke contemptuously of "logic chopping and the star-spangled manner," and clearly doctrinal analysis, for all its many strengths, carries with it important limitations.

But more significant, perhaps, than the predominance of such analysis is the degree to which we depend on the descriptive analyses of lawyers and judges, suitors and defendants, reports and social scientists. Descriptive analyses have all the faults (and often few of the virtues) of ethnographic studies generally. The lack of self-conscious method extends to the naive assumption that a particular study of a particular court or courts is generalizable in the particular way developed by the observer.

In general, work using soft data has also been ethnocentric. Research by Americans has stressed cultural contexts and familiarity with local conditions. Some efforts to cumulate findings are apparent, but in most cases they are undercut when defining conditions are considered. That is, when studies that appear to treat the same phenomenon are examined closely, variations of important factors are usually so great as to make generalizations suspect.

Litigation, Litigiousness, and the Definition of Controversy

Societies such as Japan, Spain, and Germany have long collected meticulous and copious court data. Those records have languished, evidence in search of a problem. They suggest the obvious. For example, caseloads have increased with population. But simple extrapolation of population growth is an insufficient explanation of increased caseloads. Population density, for example, clearly leads to more interactions, such as greater automobile accident rates per number of miles driven. Density may also lead to less easily explained growth in litigation. Zeisel et al. (1978), for instance, used square footage in department stores to predict expected tort cases and found that the factor $(1 + 1.3)$ fits the data better than a simple multiplier. They also developed a stable rank order of cities in litigation-proneness over several areas. Population changes may affect litigation; younger populations generate more criminal cases and automobile-based tort actions. The growth of middle-aged groups, particularly in urban areas, boosts bankruptcy proceedings and so forth.

Some groups may have a greater propensity to litigate than others. Von Ihering (1915) postulated a litigious personality. Kalven (1965) suggested a similar theory that marginal groups bring about the development of new law. Similarly, Oriental reluctance to resort to courts may cause low rates of litigation in China and Japan. However, Haley (1978) has recently argued that in fact, Japanese rates are reasonably high and would compare with Western rates except that elite decision makers deny access to courts whenever caseloads increase. Grossman and Sarat (1971) have shown that, assuming caseload data to be roughly comparable, most generalizations about litigation in different countries are not well founded. Since Tocqueville, at least, it has been assumed that Americans are especially litigious, but Grossman and Sarat's data place them among the high, but not the highest, litigators.

Silberman (1978) found evidence of a greater propensity for young people to litigate and suggests that aging of the cohort is not the explanation. Rather, he argues, some change in social mood has resulted in a genuine generational difference. In addition, the Zeisel study provided some support for the notion that there is a greater tendency to sue in urban areas and in impersonal situations.

Studies of individual courts (e.g., Friedman and Percival, 1976; MacIntosh, 1978) do not seem to indicate any trend toward litigiousness, but the problem of whether those courts perform the same social function limits the degree of generalization possible. Juan Toharia (1974), using Spanish data, indicates that while legal disputes have outstripped population, other sources of resolution, e.g., arbitration, are available, causing the litigation rate to drop.

The collection of more careful comparative data has now begun. Friedman and Percival have initiated an era of over-time studies. More important potentially are studies that provide direct information on motivations and calculations of litigators and potential litigators.

Funneling of Litigation

While controversy is endemic in human interaction, going to court is hardly an inherent human reaction. Settlement and compromise are, of course, possible resolutions. Turning to nonlegal or extralegal structures is another.

Clearly lawyers play a key role in such matters. Their presence is apparently litogenic—the higher the number of attorneys in a community, the greater the litigation rate. However, the causality is by no means clear. Quasi-experiments, as in altering lawyer's fees through law, take place, but only a few studies, and those inconclusive, have been attempted. Studies show great variation in lawyers' propensity to encourage clients to litigate and in their belief that a candid appraisal of the client's chances should influence that client's decision to sue. Studies have demonstrated that litigating philosophies of prosecutors and other government attorneys significantly affect social policy and their support or denial of specific rights.

Organized groups have learned to litigate to secure their programs. Some, such as the American Civil Liberties Union and Sierra Club, are programmatic, with no overt economic interest. But organized interest groups of every kind are active (Vose, 1958; Krislov, 1962). Interesting material on the functional bias of courts toward various groups has been developed empirically (but also in challenging form) by Black (1976) and Galanter (1974). Black suggests that in every society, an upper-class person committing an offense against a lower-class person will be treated more leniently than in the opposite case. Crimes against persons known to the offender will also be treated more leniently than will offenses against strangers. Galanter notes that organized groups that repeatedly litigate have great advantage in our legal system.

In recent years, the movement toward socialized legal representation has begun. Representation of the poor, through the Legal Services Corporation, has provided access to legal services for social strata formerly unable to afford them. Prepaid legal services plans have been developed by unions, university students, and other groups. To the degree that these groups have high potential for, but low actual rates of, litigation these new services have potentially great impact. The services are largely too new to have been evaluated in significant ways. However, the National Legal Corporation completed a study showing its delivery of legal services is quite comparable to the private sector. Whether these structures and the emergence of interest groups willing to participate in, and contribute to, test-case litigation have altered the number of cases or the tendency to litigate is a matter for further inquiry. It is, however, interesting to note that, while throughout most of the first three-quarters of this century activist litigating groups of both the general interest, ACLU-type or the more particularist, Nader-type were "liberal" in their orientation, right-wing groups are now vigorously litigating.

Within organizations, too, lawyers have different concepts about goals of litigation. The early OEO Legal Services (predecessor to the Legal Services Corporation) was wracked by arguments about "band-aid" work of high salience to clients (like divorce) but not of social moment (like a juicy constitutional law test case). While recognition of the importance of meeting the needs of the poor on a day-to-day basis has carried the day, some differences in strategies and emphasis still prevail.

Economists of law have shown formally what had been more or less understood; namely, that delay (or queuing) is one means by which the legal system allocates scarce court time. Alternatively, demand for a service priced below its cost tends to rise beyond capacity to deliver. Courts are something like public highways; almost without limit under usual conditions, as fast as one is created, use quickly exceeds supply. Reducing delay encourages greater use, with inevitable increase in delay, just as reducing highway congestion encourages purchase of cars.

When rapid decisions are sought, or a specialized law is desired, arbitrators or private judges can be used. In general, such arrangements abound, and in advanced societies, are apparently used more often than formal court proceedings. However, these arrangements are subject to control by public courts and necessarily tend to parallel those of public law.

The reasons lawyers are turned to, as well as the attorneys' calculations and preferences, are now being studied in an ongoing Wisconsin study of litigation and in a new inquiry at the appellate level, both commissioned by the Department of Justice's Office for the Improvement of Justice. The complexities of all this have yet to be charted, though the general outlines are clear enough.

In general, the judicial process has been mapped fairly well. The Columbia Project on Effective Justice traced tort cases in New York City, from notification of intent to file to completion. Only 1 percent of the original population of cases reached the formal decision stage. Among cases actually coming to trial, slightly over 50 percent were settled by the parties (Hunting and Neuwirth, 1962). Whether these percentages hold in different locales or times, or in more formalized business cases, is not known. However, experts assume the general configuration to be correct.

Much the same picture emerges in criminal proceedings, with only a fraction of known complaints to the police even listed as crimes. In only about a tenth of these crimes is an alleged perpetrator identified, and in only a fraction of that number are formal charges made. Because there are many programs that involve community diversion (corrective programs, nominally voluntary, as a substitute for formal proceedings), few cases are tried, though the vast majority that do go to trial result in convictions. (Conviction rates of up to 90 percent are not uncommon.) Inasmuch as trials are something of a last resort, since diversion and plea bargaining are alternatives, most trials are "dead-bang" cases in which the prosecution, dealing from strength, is totally confident and the defense finds no way to secure better terms from the prosecutor.

Plea bargaining was fully described by social scientists and lawyers as early as the 1920s. Roscoe Pound, Felix Frankfurter, and Raymond Moley were leaders in rigorous studies of local court systems that developed the information almost accidentally. Moley suggested that if Ali Baba's forty thieves were arrested in a modern American city only four would be sentenced. Today that number would be closer to one. Oddly, the facts about startlingly low conviction rates were perhaps subconsciously suppressed, though data were published and available, until the President's

Crime Commission revived the issue in 1967. With the simultaneous parallel publication of the American Bar Foundation's studies of "actual" versus "nominal" behavior of police and prosecutors, a new wave of realism began.

Plea bargaining has remained controversial. Some view it as degrading that criminals (more properly, alleged criminals) may haggle with the legal order. Others see coercion involved in agreeing to plead guilty in exchange for expected lighter punishment, and as incompatible with the notion of justice. Others seek a system where guilty pleas are never accepted and trial is always required.

However, many regard such bargaining as inevitable, even desirable, since it allows professionals to evaluate the strength of the evidence and the character of the accused on common scales. Some experiments in abolition of plea bargaining (e.g., Denver) have reported good results, but in Alaska the evaluators found the negative aspects of the reform out-weighed the good.

The Importance of the Court of Original Jurisdiction

The case method of the law schools focuses almost exclusively on appellate courts and legal rules. Harvard Dean Christopher Columbus Langdell believed understanding a case completely meant knowing that area of law completely. "Flower in the Crannied Wall, I pluck you out of the Cranny. If I could understand you, root and all, I would know what God and Man is." Both Wordsworth and Langdell are now seen as hopeless romantics.

The legal realists accepted and extended Holmes's insight that general principles do not decide concrete cases. Llewellyan, for example, showed that the common law, like common sense, had equal and opposite proverbs or maxims to explain equal and opposite results. The "fact skeptics," led by Jerome Frank, emphasized the difficulty both of proving "facts" and of selecting the "relevant" facts.

The lower courts' power derives, in the initial stages of a case, from the process of fact finding and, in its final stages, from the application of generalized rules. Jack Peltason (1963) and Walter Murphy (1958) have made important contributions in delineating the organization theory and bureaucratic analysis of courts. Judge Charles Wyzanski (1952) (who refused an appointment as appellate judge precisely because he thought the lower courts were more important) and Bernard Botein (1952) have written, from a subjective viewpoint, about what judges do. Studies, such as those of Mileski (1971) and Feeley (1979), on lower local courts, and of Dolbeare (1967), on a district federal court, have enriched knowledge of day-to-day operations and pressures.

Intracourt Relations

The way judges interact has been one of their most closely guarded secrets. The reaction to *The Brethren* (Woodward and Armstrong, 1979) was composed of one part shock among the naive that judges are human, two parts chagrin among judge worshippers that this humanity is revealed in a mass-market book, and three parts distaste for an ignorant, dull, and semicompetent volume. But the furor is typical and reflects deeply felt attitudes.

Given judges' preoccupation with privacy, one might anticipate that processes of interaction would be poorly understood. But rather the opposite is true. While there is a spate of gossip, which is not completely accurate (witness again *The Brethren*), the basic processes have been well-charted empirically, theoretically, and historically.

Two basic approaches have developed. (1) Through archival material, scholars put together notebook or diary records of past judicial decisions (e.g., Kluger, 1976; Murphy, 1964; Ulmer, 1972). (2) Through voting patterns of the sort referred to earlier—smallest space analysis, bloc voting techniques, scaling, and the like—putative relationships are suggested (see e.g., Schubert, 1974). Studies of chief justices and their leadership techniques (Danelski, 1960; Ulmer, 1964) paralleled these studies. Atkins (1972) has been a leader among those who extended such inquiries to examination of chief judges in U.S. Courts of Appeals. Fair (1971) and others have worked on state courts.

There are serious difficulties with each technique. Archivists depend on the evidence of those who choose to leave their entrails to be read. Some, like Justice Black, feel such records should die with the judges; others simply fail to collect such materials. At present, we rely heavily on the Stone and Burton records, though those of stout heart and strong stomach have been working on the Frankfurter papers. One need not view the Supreme Court from a Rashomon perspective to realize re-creation of the past presents all the difficulties of historical method. Indeed, it is widely known that the current chief justice and his colleagues have differed over vote counts and the chief's position on important cases—an important issue, given the power of the chief to assign the writing of the opinion when he or she is a member of the majority. Historians are not likely to "settle" matters on which the sources disagree. If a major "source" is reticent, and reluctant to pass on perceptions, archives tell only a partial truth.

The patterns discovered in voting statistics are all too often treated as divine truth. There are, of course, many techniques for manipulation of data, which produce different patterns, but the interpretations are almost always ad hoc, not grounded in any theory. These techniques are often arbitrary in determining significance, not only because they ignore conventional rules for rejecting the null hypothesis, but also because they provide no concept comparable to the probability that a distribution occurs by chance, which undergirds most conventional statistical tests.

Methodological problems with judicial voting studies abound. The "prediction" of judicial votes has been justly criticized as no more than low-level forecasting (Sibley, 1967), and as disguised extrapolation (Becker, 1964). Other work has concentrated on what Danelski has precisely pinpointed as "descriptive" statistics—the specification of a small number of factors that presumably influence the attitudes of the modern justices.

The failure to consider political content, the preoccupation with ordering, and the frequent use of tautological variables have produced massive disinterest in judicial voting. This is unfortunate, for the potential of the techniques has not been attained. For example, no one has explored the division in John Marshall's court, though his insistence on reporting decisions as unanimous will make serious analysis difficult. But a century of voting records does exist and has not been exploited. Extending scales, factors, or dimensions backward in time, and indicating when they cease to be applicable will probably tell us much more about "the judicial mind" than the relatively neat picture currently projected. Even the Canadian and Australian systems, heavily influenced by the American experience, are only roughly describable using current terms and methods.

At any rate, the external examination of judicial behavior has proceeded without much concern for courts' internal workings. The most important work in the area, Murphy's *Elements of Judicial Strategy* (1964), combines external empirical and theoretical analysis with heavy emphasis on tactics revealed by historical studies. His forerunners, Beveridge (1916) and Mason (1956), lacked the systematic notions developed by, as one best-selling novelist has put it, "a vulgar political scientist" (Murphy, 1979).

Others have attempted more limited synthesizing efforts. Schubert (1974) used linguistic analysis of opinions to contrast Jackson's conservative votes and liberal rhetoric. Ulmer (1972) used Burton's papers to reconstruct the Court's internal workings. More recently, Provine (1979; see also Ulmer 1979) has used these papers to "disconfirm" behavioral findings, including some of Ulmer's.

It is reassuring that some of our best work has been in areas such as assignment of opinions where the information is less open to study then other points of inquiry. Ingenuity (e.g., in use of game theory) has made up for scarcity of access.

Compliance and Impact

The efficacy of court decisions is in one sense amazing. A number of riots have ended on delivery of a piece of legal paper. But it is also evident that the ultimate and basic physical force necessary to achieve efficacy is external to the court system. Furthermore, as we have emphasized, higher courts seldom issue specific orders, contenting themselves with generalized principles and remanding the vast bulk of cases for "action not inconsistent with this decision."

The problem of what a court decision is worth has generated increasing interest in the past few decades. While the initial concern was with "compliance" (Krislov, 1971), or conscious obedience, most subsequent discussion has been cast in terms of the less specific "impact." The extension of this concern into the administrative sphere has been called "implementation" (Pressman and Wildavsky, 1973). Research has focused on higher court/lower court relations, the frequency of higher court intervention, and the freedom of lower courts to act (Murphy, 1958, 1959; Krislov, 1968). Motivations for citizen compliance have been studied in both sociological (Krislov, 1972) and economic terms (Brown and Stover, 1977). Becker and Feeley (1973) collected useful materials, while Wasby (1970) codified the literature. Frank (1958) interpreted the issue of compliance as one of attention and control (along lines similar to Neustadt's later interpretation of the presidency) and concluded that courts have handicaps in struggles to gain compliance.

Major studies have examined postdecision consequences of court decisions. Muir's brilliant *Prayer in the Schools* (1967) explains individual responses—conformity or opposition—in terms of cognitive theory. Conflicting literature on efforts to regulate the police has had impact on popular debate (especially the work of Kamisar, 1979, and Cannon, 1979). Effects of recent court deicisions on prisons were described in detail by Harris and Spiller (1976). Most impact studies are atheoretical or proceed from atypical frameworks, making comparisons artificial.

Ross has used quasi-experimental measurement in a number of studies (e.g., Campbell and Ross, 1968). Other studies have also attempted to identify correlates of policy acceptance or rejection using acceptance as both the dependent and independent variable. Socialization to comply has also been studied, and is closely intertwined with the individual's sense of the purpose, fairness, and legitimacy of laws. Societies evolve in complex ways, with respect to both the machinery and the methods of inculcating obedience (Schwartz and Miller, 1964; Andenaes, 1966).

Other Branches

"Courts are not the only agency of government that should be assumed to have the capacity to govern," Harlan Fiske Stone noted, in a famous dissent. This notion complements older concerns about the legitimacy of sharing power. The current emphasis on judicial capacity dovetails nicely with such normative questions, which have often been posed in terms of assumed incapacities—courts' unrepresentativeness, class bias, and lack of speed or ability to handle technical concerns well.

Legal scholars have recognized the inherent limits of judicial power, the courts' lack of enforcement and fiscal powers, and their incomplete jurisdiction over some vital social concerns (see Jackson, 1955; Curtiss, 1947). Curtiss referred to the Supreme Court as a "tenant at sufferance," easily controlled by Congress and the president. Dahl (1957), in an overly influential study, has emphasized the fact that Congress and the executive have usually been able to reverse or modify Supreme Court judgments rather rapidly. Caspar (1976) has challenged the Dahl thesis as highly timebound. Adamany (1973) and Funston (1975) have developed evidence linking Dahl's notions to critical elections and shifts in basic national political coalitions.

The inherent power of the political branches over the appointment of judges and the jurisdiction of courts has generated sophisticated political history (Warren, 1935; Pritchett, 1961; Murphy, 1962; Westin, 1962). The appointment power and its consequences have been examined at the federal level by Goldman (1978) and Slotnick (1979), among others. Varying state appointment systems have been charted by Jacobs (1966), Ulmer (1964), and Nagel (1973), who find that system characteristics account for surprisingly small differences in judicial appointments. It has also been shown that a surprisingly large percentage of judges are appointed by governors, whether or not the selection system is one of election or appointment, because judges do not conveniently leave the bench precisely at the expiration of their terms.

Jurisdictional power and change, delineated by Warren (1935) and by Frankfurter and Landis (1928) in basically legalistic terms, have been treated in broader terms by Casper and Posner (1974). Schmidhauser and Berg (1972), Scigliano (1971), and Pritchett and Murphy have studied direct conflict between the Court and Congress.

The challenge to the competence of the court system has, as noted earlier, been most thoroughly articulated by Horowitz, who finds the limits inherent and ineluctable. Others, such as Fiss (1979) and Sarat (1980), have been somewhat more sanguine. Horowitz's empirical evidence consists of four after-the-fact case studies, all "confirming" his argument. No more convincing effort has been mounted and his critics' arguments are, if anything, less empirically based.

Normative Study and Policy Applications

The relationship of norms and ideas to other factors in the judicial process remains the most challenging and perplexing research area. Because such factors lie at the heart of law, this question seems more urgent than other concerns. Fuller (1964) argued that notions of justice and procedure define law, and that Austin-Kelsen approaches were not merely morally obtuse, but empirically misleading. His viewpoint now is virtually the party line of the Berkeley Law and Society Group, and is defended by an imposing array of names—Selznick, Skolnick, and Nonet (see e.g., the Auerbach-Skolnick exchange, 1966). Another well-known argument is Kluckhohn's (1951) view that values constitute a field of inquiry that can be studied objectively, without commitment or normative conclusion.

The debate about norms and values has been enriched by normative legal philosophers, who attempt to derive values from neutral principles. The Kelsen line of inquiry has, through Hart's influence on Dworkin, led to a complex reasoning that legal rules are eminent in a society. Dworkin (1979) both follows and breaks with his intellectual mentors, suggesting that principles are not just available for subjective justification but may be almost impossible for decision makers to resist.

Closely related to Dworkin's is the work of Tribe (1980), who argues that definitions of end or purpose are ultimately necessary in any specification of judicial function. Thus functionalists such as Ely (1980) and Choper (1980) are seen as naive in their emphasis on judicial machinery. (The argument is analogous to Fuller's and other idealists' defense of democracy against Popper and other instrumentalists.) In any event, Tribe posits, as the seventh of his "models" of constitutional law, "structural due process," based on values and ends, already part of the social and legal order.

Additionally, normative philosophers—conspicuously Rawls (1971) and Nozzick—have drawn exciting and precise normative conclusions based in part on empirical research. To date, however, this work has been used to justify policy preferences rather than to illuminate the judicial process.

The legal anthropologists have been most successful in identifying norms. They have developed interesting notions about the mediation process, its linguistic patterns, and its symbolic functions (see Buckle and Buckle, 1979; Gulliher, 1973). Such notions are perhaps most easily discernible where conflicts follow fairly standard patterns. The legal anthropologists have also traced specific norms that influence decisions. This is, again, more evident in societies whose patterns are less like our own, or whose value orderings are more nearly universal and monotonic. An alternative explanation may well be that "success" occurs because we lack rival interpreters and specific information needed to develop competing interpretations.

The decline of internecine warfare between traditionalists and neobehaviorists has broadened the study of legal phenomena. Packer's (1968) distinction between "due process" and "crime control" models of justice has inspired many empirical studies. Indeed, his formulations and those of Rawls are two very rare examples of overstudied and overreplicated conceptual schemes.

Inevitably, normative clarification and empirical generalization trail off into policy recommendations. Courts need help and have been more receptive in recent years to studies and outside advice. The applied policy approach—visible most emphatically in such journals as *Judicature* and *Justice Systems Journal*—has many attractions including the possibility of actually contributing to social development. Its major drawback is shared with most multidisciplinary approaches. It tends to lose focus, to find its problems in small, social complications rather than developing cohesive theoretical tendencies. Since we have already lamented the weakness of theory in the area, we must note that the concern for normative and policy elements usually aggravates that failing.

Conclusions

In the main, our knowledge, though much more extensive, is no more firmly based than it was three decades ago. Even assuming the accuracy of our individual studies, contingencies and circumstances remain generally unspecified and produce conclusions of doubtful validity.

Social scientists are adept at "transmuting" soft data into lawlike generalizations, attributed to "the literature." Berenson and Steiner (1964) is the ultimate example. Soft insights can also provide guidance for tight design, adequate sampling, and precise hypothesis. This remains our hope and is occasionally the basis of our achievement.

If the new paradigms have lent themselves to constructive puzzle setting, they have been generally less successful at moving us toward any sort of cumulativeness. There is considerable closure in the factor analysis/ spatial analysis of judicial ideology; some have labeled it largely tautological. But most other work involves differences in method, assumptions, or conditions that make the heaping together of studies highly questionable. Heroic assumptions are made of comparability of studies, and these assumptions are usually suppressed in the conclusions. Later scholars easily demonstrate differences, and the very process of cumulation is discredited.

Even worse, we are often unable to specify the operative conditions of our studies to permit replication. Though we aspire to laboratory method, we seldom work with control groups, yet we have neither accepted nor substituted for economists' sophisticated use of error terms and other techniques that attempt to compensate for chance error and other corruptions of canonical method that inhere in our loose approaches.

A striking failure of work in the judicial process has been our inability to define, except ostensibly, our subject matter. This produces no great problem within a single society where variations are minor—Louisiana's court system is more similar to that of Arkansas or California than to that of Paris. The problem arises when we wish to generalize over different countries and, a fortiori, when we look at non-Western societies or preindustrial eras.

Then, too, the multidiscipline, multi-issue concerns that have dominated the study of public law have increasingly proven distracting. The law-and-society perspective increasingly makes discourse with anthropologists or economists of law easier than with international relations specialists or students of political behavior. The concern with social science was to have united the field; it has often proved distracting. It was expected to set common theoretical problems; it has set scholars off in wildly different directions.

But on balance, the questions addressed seem both more significant and more promising than the issues of simple doctrinal exploration. Even normative issues seem more vigorously and directly approached. With the meeting of more descriptive needs and greater understanding, the foundation for tighter theoretical sophistication may have been laid. Without it, these efforts of several decades will be quickly regarded as useless and trivial.

REFERENCES

ADAMANY, D. (1973) "Legitimacy, realigning elections and the Supreme Court." University of Wisconsin Law Review: 790-846.

ANDENAES, J. (1966) "The general preventative effects of punishment." University of Pennsylvania Law Review 114: 949-962.

ATKINS, B. (1972) "Decision-making rules and judicial strategy on the United States Courts of Appeals." Western Political Quarterly 25: 626-642.

AUERBACH, C. and J. SKOLNICK (1966) "An exchange." Law and Society Review 1: 91-110.

BECKER, T. (1964) Political Behavioralism and Modern Jurisprudence. Chicago: Rand McNally.

——— and M. FEELEY [eds.] (1973) The Impact of Supreme Court Decisions. New York: Oxford University Press.

BERELSON, B. and G. STEINER (1964) Human Behavior: An Inventory of Scientific Findings. New York: Harcourt, Brace, Jovanovich.

BEVERIDGE, A. M. (1916) The Life of John Marshall. Boston: Houghton Mifflin.

BLACK, D. (1976) The Mobilization of Law. New York: Academic.

BOLAND, B. (1980) "Fighting crime: the problem of adolescents." Journal of Criminal Law and Criminology 71: 94-97.

BOTEIN, B. (1952) Trial Judge. New York: Simon & Shuster.

BROWN, D. and C. STOVER (1977) "Court directives and compliance." American Politics Quarterly 5: 465-480.

BUCKLE, L. and S. BUCKLE (1979) Bargaining for Justice. Lexington, MA: D. C. Heath.

CAMPBELL, D. T. (1963) "From description to experimentation: interpreting trends as quasi-experiments," in C. W. Harris (ed.) Problems in Measuring Change. Madison: University of Wisconsin Press.

——— and R. H. LAURENCE (1968) "The Connecticut crackdown on speeding." Law and Society Review 3: 33-76.

CANNON, B. (1979) "The exclusionary rule: have critics proved that it doesn't defer the police." Judicature 62: 398-409.

CAPPELLETTI, M. and J. GARTH [eds.] (1978-1979) Access to Justice. Italy: A. Giuffrè.

CASPER, G. and R. POSNER (1974) "A study of the Supreme Court's caseload." Journal of Legal Studies 3: 339-375.

CASPER, J. (1976) "The Supreme Court and national policy making." American Political Science Review 70: 50-63.

CHOPER, J. (1980) Judicial Review and the National Political Process. Chicago: University of Chicago Press.

CURTISS, C. P. (1947) Lions Under the Throne. Boston: Houghton Mifflin.

DAHL, R. (1957) "Decision making in democracy." Journal of Public Law 6: 279-295.

DANELSKI, D. (1960) "The influence of the chief justice in the decisional process of the Supreme Court." Presented at a meeting of the American Political Science Association.

DOLBEARE, K. (1967) Trial Courts in Urban Politics. New York: John Wiley.

DWORKIN, R. (1979) Taking Rights Seriously. New York: Oxford University Press.

ELY, J. H. (1980) Democracy and Distrust. Cambridge, MA: Harvard University Press.

FAIR, D. (1971) "State intermediate appellate courts." Western Political Quarterly 24: 415-424.

FEELEY, M. (1979) The Process is the Punishment. New York: Russell Sage.

––– (1969) "A comparative analysis of state Supreme Court behavior." Minneapolis, University of Minnesota. (unpublished)

FISS, O. (1979) "The forms of justice." Harvard Law Review 93: 1-58.

FRANK, J. (1949) Courts on Trial. Princeton, NJ: Princeton University Press.

FRANK, J. P. (1958) The Marble Palace. New York: Knopf.

FRANKFURTER, F. and J. LANDIS (1928) The Business of the Supreme Court. New York: Macmillan.

FRIEDMAN, L. and R. PERCIVAL (1976) "A tale of two courts." Law and Society Review 10: 267-301.

FULLER, L. (1964) The Morality of Law. New York: Oxford University Press.

FUNSTON, R. (1975) "The Supreme Court and critical elections." American Political Science Review 69: 795-811.

GALANTER, M. (1974) "Why the haves come out ahead." Law and Society Review 9: 95-160.

GLAZER, N. (1975) "Toward an imperial judiciary?" Public Interest 41: 104-123.

GOLDMAN, S. (1978) "Profile of Carter's judicial nominees." Judicature 62: 246-254.

GROSSMAN, J. and A. SARAT (1971) "Political culture and judicial research." Washington University Law Quarterly: 177-207.

HALEY, J. A. (1978) "The myth of the reluctant litigator." Journal of Japanese Studies 4: 359-390.

HARRIS, M. and D. P. SPILLER (1976) "After decision." American Bar Association. Commission on Correctional Facilities and Services, Resource Center on Correctional Law and Legal Services, Washington, D. C.

HART, H.L.A. (1961) The Concept of Law. New York: Oxford University Press.

HOROWITZ, D. (1977) The Courts and Social Policy. Washington, DC: Brookings.

HUNTING, R. and O. NEUWIRTH (1962) Who Sues in New York City. New York: Columbia University Press.

HYNEMAN, C. (1959) The Study of Politics. Urbana: University of Illinois Press.

JACKSON, R. (1955) The Supreme Court in the American System of Government. New York: Oxford University Press.

JACOBS, H. (1966) "Judicial insulation." University of Wisconsin Law Review: 801-819.

KAGAN, R. et al. (1977) "The business of state Supreme Courts." Stanford Law Review 130: 121-156.

KALVEN, H., Jr. (1966) The Negro and the First Amendment. Chicago: University of Chicago Press.

KAMISAR, Y. (1979) "Closing arguments in the debate." Judicature 62: 336-350.

KLUCKHOHN, C. (1951) "Values and value orientations," in T. Parsons et al. (eds.) Toward a General Theory of Action. Cambridge, MA: Harvard University Press.

KLUGER, R. (1976) Simple Justice. New York: Knopf.

KRISLOV, S. (1968) Supreme Court and Political Freedom. New York: Free Press.

——— (1959) "Constituency versus constitutionalism: the desegregation issue and tensions and aspirations of southern attorney generals." Midwest Journal of Political Science 3: 75-92.

——— et al. (1972) "The Amicus Curiae brief." Yale Law Journal 72: 694-721.

MacINTOSH, W. V. (1978) "Litigation in St. Louis county." National Academy of Sciences, Washington, D.C. (unpublished)

MARKS, F. R. et al. (1974) The Shreveport Plan: An Experiment in the Delivery of Legal Services. Chicago: American Bar Foundation.

MASON, A. T. (1956) Harlan Fiske Stone. New York: Viking.

MILESKI, M. (1971) "Courtroom encounters." Law and Society Review 5: 473-538.

MOLEY, R. (1974) Politics and Criminal Prosecution. New York: Arno Press.

MUIR, W. (1967) Prayer in the Public Schools: Law and Attitude Change. Chicago: University of Chicago Press.

MURPHY, W. (1979) The Vicar of Christ. New York: Macmillan.

——— (1964) Elements of Judicial Strategy. Chicago: University of Chicago Press.

——— (1962) Congress and the Court. Chicago: University of Chicago Press.

——— (1959) "Lower court checks on Supreme Court power." American Political Science Review 153: 1017-1031.

——— (1958) "Civil liberties and the Japanese exclusion case." Western Political Quarterly 11: 3-13.

NAGEL, S. (1973) Comparing Elected and Appointed Judicial Systems. Beverly Hills: Sage.

PACKER, H. (1968) The Limits of Criminal Sanction. Stanford: Stanford University Press.

PELTASON, J. (1963) Federal Courts in the Political Process. New York: Random House.

PRESSMAN, J. and A. WILDAVSKY (1973) Implementation. Berkeley: University of California Press.

PRICHETT, G. H. (1961) Congress vs. the Supreme Court. Minneapolis: University of Minnesota Press.

PROVINE, D. M. (1979) "Case selection in the United States Supreme Court." Presented at a meeting of the American Political Science Association.

RAWLS, J. (1971) A Theory of Justice. Cambridge, MA: Harvard University Press.

ROSENBERG, M. (1964) The Pretrial Conference and Effective Justice. New York: Columbia University Press.

RYAN, J. P. and A. ALFINI (1980) American Trial Judges. New York: Free Press.

SCHMIDHAUSER, J. and L. BERG (1972) The Supreme Court and Congress. New York: John Wiley.

SCHUBERT, G. (1974) The Judicial Mind Revisited. New York: Oxford University Press.

SCHWARTZ, R. and J. MILLER (1964) "Legal evolution and societal complexity." American Journal of Sociology 70: 159-169.

SCIGLIANO, R. (1971) The Supreme Court and the Presidency. New York: Free Press.

SIBLEY, M. (1967) in J. Charlesworth (ed.) Contemporary Political Analysis. New York: Free Press.

SILBERMAN, M. (1978) "The study of legal change." Law and Society Association Paper. Beverly Hills: Sage.

SLOTNICK, E. E. (1979) "Changing role of the Senate judiciary committee in judicial selection." Judicature 62: 502-510.

TOHARIA, J. J. (1974) Cambio Social y Vida Juridica en Espana. Madrid: Edicusa.

TRIBE, L. (1980) "The puzzling persistance of progress-based constitutional theories." Yale Law Journal 89: 1063-1080.

ULMER, S. S. (1979) "Selecting cases for Supreme Court review." Presented at a meeting of the American Political Science Association.

——— (1972) "The decision to grant certiorari as an indicator to decision on merits." Polity 4: 429-447.

——— (1964) "Leadership in the Michigan Supreme Court," in G. Schubert (ed.) Judicial Behavior. Chicago: Rand McNally.

VANDERBILT, A. T. (1949) Men and Measures in the Law. Ann Arbor: University of Michigan Press.

Von IHERING (1915) The Struggle for Law. Chicago: Callaghan.

VOSE, C. (1958) "Litigation as a form of pressure group activity." American Academy of Political and Social Science Annals 319: 20-31.

WARREN, C. (1935) Congress, the Constitution and the Supreme Court. New York: Macmillan.

WASBY, S. (1970) The Impact of Supreme Court Decisions: Some Perspectives. Homewood, IL: Dorsey.

WESTIN, A. (1962) "Corporate appeals to Congress for relief from Supreme Court ruling." Presented at a meeting of the American Political Science Association.

WOODWARD, B. and S. ARMSTRONG (1979) The Brethren. New York: Simon & Shuster.

WYZANSKI, C. (1952) "A trial judge's freedom and responsibility." The Record of the Association of the Bar of the City of New York 7: 280-309.

ZEISEL, H. et al. (1978) Delay in the Court. Boston: Little, Brown.

8

A Forgotten Tradition

The Constitutional Level of Analysis

VINCENT OSTROM

This chapter will attempt to provide some basic theoretical ideas that may be useful for increasing synthesis in the study of political institutions. I proceed on three assumptions. First, political science is concerned with the study of government. Second, government is a matter of human design and choice. Third, the level of choice that applies to the specification of the terms and conditions of governance is one of constitutional choice (Ostrom, 1980).

At the constitutional level of analysis, one is concerned with basic questions of why human beings have recourse to political institutions, and what options are available. One is also concerned about what implications follow from alternative possibilities and what criteria are used, or what purposes are served, in the choices that are made among the alternative possibilities. Thus, political theory has a special relevance for the constitutional level of analysis. The constitutional level of analysis has a fundamental role in clarifying the design of structural arrangements that apply to the play of the games of politics. The play of a game is determined by the rules of the game; and the rules establishing the terms and conditions of governance are constitutional in character. The constitutional level of analysis, then, informs the operational level of analysis of who gets what, when, and how (Lasswell, 1936).

The American political system was created as the result of a series of relatively self-conscious efforts in design. This design reflects considerations of a distinctive nature that are not characteristic of the organization of all political systems. In particular, the designers of the American system of government used a federal, rather than a unitary, conception as the proper structure for a democratic polity. Yet we confront the puzzling circumstance that the dominant tendencies among American political scientists in the last century have been: (1) to reject the theory upon which the design of the American political system was based, (2) to accept the logic of a unitary state governed in accordance with principles of a Westminster-type parliamentary system as the appropriate model for the organization of a democratic society, and (3) to adopt the methodology of the natural sciences as the appropriate way to study political phenomena. The stance taken by political analysts in the twentieth century poses rather fundamental questions about the relationship of knowledge to the design and construction of political experience. Are artifacts created by design to be studied as though they were natural phenomena? Or, does the study of artifacts require that the intentions, conceptions, and calculations of the designers be taken into account in understanding the nature of an artifact. These questions pose important theoretical and methodological problems for political scientists.

In developing this chapter, I shall turn first to the design of the American constitutional system. I shall then turn to the twentieth-century break with that tradition. Finally, I shall explore the issue of how to construe the essential characteristics of the American political system.

The Design of the American Constitutional System

The American Declaration of Independence, as a founding document, serves as a general preamble to the various experiments in constitutional choice that occurred both within the states and in the larger community shared by the several states. The Declaration opens with a presumption that a people, in dissolving the bonds that have connected them with another people, owe an explanation to the rest of mankind for the action being taken. Choice exists and choice is grounded in reason. A reasoned explanation is due to others.

The grounds and criteria justifying the Declaration of Independence are stated in the following language:

We hold these Truths to be self-evident, that all Men are created equal, that they are endowed by their Creator with certain unalienable Rights, that among these are Life, Liberty, and the Pursuit of Happiness—That to secure these Rights, Governments are instituted among Men, deriving their just Powers from the Consent of the

Governed, that whenever any Form of Government becomes destructive of these Ends, it is the Right of the People to alter or to
abolish it, and to institute new Government, laying its Foundation
on such Principles, and organizing its Powers in such Form, as to
them shall seem most likely to effect their Safety and Happiness.

In this statement, basic presuppositions are postulated about the human
condition. That condition implies both being and becoming. Governments
are instituted among human beings to realize potentials. That which is
instituted is artifactual in nature. It is created as a conscious effort in
design using principles articulated through forms to accomplish specifiable
purposes. The criterion that is appropriate to the exercise of governmental
prerogatives is the informed consent of the community of people who are
being governed. Whenever governments as artifacts are destructive of the
ends for which they are instituted, The Declaration asserts the "Right of
the People" to engage in processes of constitutional decision making with
a view to altering or abolishing an existing government or of instituting a
new government. The design of institutions of government is a subject of
choice where human beings can draw upon knowable principles and design
structures in appropriate forms to further human aspirations.

Alexander Hamilton makes a similar observation about the problem of
design in the opening paragraph of *Federalist* 1:

It has been frequently remarked that it seems to have been reserved
to the people of this country, by their conduct and example, to
decide the important question, whether societies of men are really
capable or not of establishing good government from reflection and
choice, or whether they are forever destined to depend for their
political constitutions on accident and force. If there be any truth in
the remark, the crisis at which we are arrived may with propriety be
regarded as the era in which that decision is to be made; and a wrong
election of the part we shall act may, in this view, deserve to be
considered as the general misfortune of mankind [Hamilton, Jay,
and Madison, n. d.: 3].

Hamilton's observation is much more problematical than the Declaration's
assertion of the "Right of the People to alter or to abolish" an existing
government "and to institute new Government." Experience with organizing a government under the Articles of Confederation had, so far as
Hamilton was concerned, proved to be a failure. The task proclaimed in
the Declaration was both more problematical and more revolutionary in

the sweep of human history than had been anticipated. A federal union was necessary to the maintenance of peace on the North American continent. Otherwise, a multitude of states could be expected to repeat the experience of Europe in warring upon one another. Their constitutions would then be determined by accident and force. But, confederations had proved a failure. It was necessary to go back to first principles in devising a federal system of government where its structure of concurrent governments would extend to the person of citizens in their individual capacities and be limited by constitutional rules as enforceable laws (see relevant discussions especially in *Federalist* 8, 15, and 16).

The Americans were, thus, to determine whether institutions of government could be designed by reflection and choice or whether it was the fate of mankind to be governed by institutions over which they had little or no control. If Hamilton was correct, the American experiment in constitutional choice represented an epochal development in the human political experiment that was of substantial significance for a political science. Political science would contribute to the design of political institutions fashioned on the basis of reflection and choice.

Madison in *Federalist* 14 takes a similar position when he observes that the American Revolution implied a major break with the past. Madison articulates this contention in the following words:

Had no important step been taken by the leaders of the Revolution for which a precedent could not be discovered, no government established of which an exact model did not present itself, the people of the United States might, at this moment, have been numbered among the melancholy victims of misguided councils, must at best have been laboring under the weight of some of those forms which have crushed the liberties of the rest of mankind. Happily for America, happily, we trust, for the whole human race, they pursued a new and more noble course. They accomplished a revolution which has no parallel in the annals of human society. They reared the fabrics of governments which have no model on the face of the globe. They formed the design of a great Confederacy, which it is incumbent on their successors to improve and perpetuate. If their works betray imperfections, we wonder at the fewness of them. If they erred most in the structure of the Union, this was the work most difficult to be executed; this is the work which has been new modelled by the act of your convention, and it is that act on which you are now to deliberate and to decide [Hamilton, Jay, and Madison, n. d.: 85).

In presenting their arguments in *The Federalist,* both Hamilton and Madison explicitly assert that they draw upon a body of knowledge identified as a science of politics. They make systematic use of the theory inherent in a science of politics to conduct their analysis and present their arguments. In *Federalist* 9, for example, Hamilton observes that there have been those throughout history who have "decried all free government as inconsistent with the order of society" (Hamilton, Jay, and Madison, n. d.: 48). However, he goes on to observe that innovations have occurred in the design of republican institutions of government that enhance their viability. In doing so he explicitly states:

> The science of politics, however, like most other sciences, has received great improvement. The efficacy of various principles is now well understood, which were either not known at all, or imperfectly known to the ancients. The regular distribution of power into distinct departments; the introduction of legislative balances and checks; the institution of courts composed of judges holding their offices during good behavior; the representation of the people in the legislature by deputies of their own election; these are wholly new discoveries, or have made their principle progress towards perfection in modern times. They are means, and powerful means, by which the excellences of republican government may be retained and its imperfections lessened or avoided [Hamilton, Jay, and Madison, n. d.: 48-49).

After having recited these contributions of political science to the design of republican institutions, Hamilton then goes on to advance the contention that a new principle—that of federalism—might be added to the list of new discoveries in a science of politics. It is this principle that provided an important element in the design of the new constitution and was also the primary source of objections to the new constitution.

Both Hamilton and Madison draw upon a structure of axiomatic reasoning that enables them to explain why particular provisions were made in the proposed constitution and what consequences can be expected to follow. In doing so, they are using the logic of theoretical reasoning as a fundamental tool that enables human beings to use their capacity to reason, and thus, to inform choice. Theory is used both to engage in positive analysis to clarify the implications that follow from particular structural characteristics and to clarify normative criteria used in the design of a constitution. Examples of positive analysis include Hamilton's clarification of the implications that follow when governments presume to govern other collectivities rather than reaching to the person of the individual (*Federalist* 15 and 16) or Madison's clarification of the oligarchical tendencies inherent in the size of deliberative assemblies, whether of a direct democracy or of a representative republic (*Federalist* 55 and 58).

Considerations of design also require reference to normative criteria, or considerations of value, in selecting among alternative possibilities. Criteria relevant to human choice generally and to constitutional choice in particular are given explicit attention in *The Federalist*. Madison warns that "choice must always be made, if not of the lesser evil, at least of the GREATER, not the PERFECT, good" (Hamilton, Jay, and Madison, n. d.: 260). In *Federalist* 37, he explains the tradeoffs that occur in the design of governmental institutions with reference to such values as energy in government, stability, safety, and republican liberty. In *Federalist* 31, Hamilton gives quite explicit attention to the use of moral and jurisprudential reasoning to considerations of institutional design.

Having contended that serious mistakes had been made in the constitution of the first American confederation, neither Hamilton nor Madison argue that their formulations are infallible. Rather they argue that both the proponents and the opponents of the new constitution "ought not to assume an infallibility in rejudging the fallible opinions of others" (Hamilton, Jay, and Madison, n. d.: 226). Language, by its application to classes of events, implies simplification and vulnerability to error. Moreover, in the case of the formation of human institutions, people use words to express ideas whose referents are not the objects of nature but relationships among human beings. The design of human institutions thus depends upon the use of language to conceptualize arrangements that exist and have meaning only in human thought and experience. Greater ambiguities inevitably exist in the use of language as a tool for reasoning about human institutions than about material conditions.

Given these limitations, both Hamilton and Madison contended that the appropriate test for the conceptions being acted upon in formulating the design of the Constitution of 1787 was to try the experiment and see whether concepts yielded the consequences that were anticipated. If the plan of the convention contained errors based upon inadequate experience and understanding, those errors "will not be ascertained until an actual trial shall have pointed them out" (Hamilton, Jay, and Madison, n. d.: 235). Hamilton, in the concluding essay of *The Federalist* (n. d.: 574) quotes David Hume to the effect that:

> To balance a large state or society . . . , whether monarchical or republican, on general laws, is a work of so great difficulty, that no

human genius, however comprehensive, is able, by the mere dint of reason and reflection, to effect it. The judgments of many must unite in the work; experience must guide their labor; time must bring it to perfection, and the feeling of inconveniences must correct the mistakes which they *inevitably* fall into in their first trials and experiments.

In the course of elaborating the design of a system of government where the exercise of governmental prerogative would be subject to the rule of law, Americans in the revolutionary era were engaged in a novel experiment in human governance of special significance for a science of politics. Thomas Hobbes (1651: ch. 18) had earlier argued that those who exercise the prerogatives of government are the source of law, and, as such, are above the law. They cannot be held accountable to law. Hobbes's theory of sovereignty assumed that the unity inherent in a system of law derived from having a single ultimate source of law. This implies that those who exercise governmental prerogatives have indivisible authority that is not subject to limits.

The American experiment in constitutional choice was based upon radically different conceptions. These conceptions held that the prerogatives of government could be limited by a rule of law provided that several conditions could be met. First, a constitution need be distinguished from ordinary law. A constitution supplies the rules of law applicable to the conduct of government, while ordinary law applies to relationships among individual members of a society. This distinction can be maintained so long as the processes of constitutional decision making are separated from the processes of governmental decision making. A constitution, according to Madison, is "established by the people and unalterable by the government and a law [is] established by the government and alterable by the government" (Hamilton, Jay, and Madison, n. d.: 348).

Given the special juridical status of a constitution as law applicable to the organization and conduct of government, the terms and conditions of constitutions might then incorporate those provisions that facilitate the maintenance of a rule of law. This poses a puzzling problem. Laws are without meaning unless they can be enforced. A distinguishing characteristic of government is that those who exercise the prerogatives of government have access to powers of coercion usually symbolized as the sword of justice. Enforcing rules of law upon those who exercise the prerogatives of government implies the enforcement of law upon the enforcers. Conceptualizing a solution to this problem was no small task.

In the American case, this task of establishing rules of law that applied to rulers was accomplished by specifying limits to all exercise of governmental prerogatives through the distribution of authority to diverse decision structures. A separation of powers with reciprocal veto capabilities implies that the authority of each set of governmental decision makers is subject to limits and that no single center of ultimate authority exists in the American system of government. A sharing of powers within the constraints of reciprocal veto positions is necessary in establishing the legal and political feasibility of any course of collective action. In addition, the prerogatives of government are subject to limits that recognize the correlative constitutional rights of individuals both to act separately and collectively in the performance of governmental functions without interference by governmental authorities.

Constitutional provision is also made for both the direct and indirect participation of citizens in decision-making processes of government. Citizen participation through elections is well recognized among political scientists, but we also need to recognize that making provision for trial by jury involves the direct participation of citizens in the judicial process where the implementation of law is being determined.

Finally, both Hamilton and Madison recognize that constitutional provisions and a distribution of powers, "in such a manner as that each may be a check on the other—that the private interest of every individual may be a sentinel over the public rights" (Hamilton, Jay and Madison, n. d.: 337), is insufficient to maintain the enforceability of constitutional law. There comes a point where the maintenance of a constitutional order depends upon the limits enforced by the decisions that citizens take. This is recognized when Hamilton observes:

> Everything beyond this must be left to the prudence and firmness of the people; who, as they will hold the scales in their own hands, it is to be hoped, will always take care to preserve the constitutional equilibrium between the general and the State government [Hamilton, Jay, and Madison, n. d.: 193].

This observation need not be limited to relationships between the national and state governments but might apply to other constitutional equilibria. Madison even anticipates that enterprises of ambition, such as a military coup, might be successfully resisted in the American constitutional system (*Federalist* 41). Hamilton implicitly recognizes the right in individuals to resist enactments of Congress and seek judicial remedies against legislative usurpation of constitutional powers in his discussion of judicial review in *Federalist* 78.

Formal constitutional limits are necessary in creating opportunities for citizens to impose limits and gain access to the exercise of governmental prerogatives. But these necessary conditions are not sufficient. The necessary and sufficient conditions can be met only when citizens share a common understanding of the nature and requirements of a constitutional order and are willing to pay the price of enforcing limits upon officials. In short, the American experiments in constitutional choice cannot be expected to work without reference to the way people, as artisans, make use of constitutional limits as appropriate instruments for their own governance.

The Break with the Federalist Tradition

By the end of the nineteenth and the beginning of the twentieth century, any sense that the American system of government represented a fundamental experiment of epic proportions had been abandoned. Political preoccupations were with machine politics and boss rule, and the fundamental thrust of reform efforts was with the simplification and strengthening of the governmental apparatus. Preoccupation with a range of new problems led to pervasive efforts to question and to reject prior formulations.

The attack upon the theory used in the design of the American constitutional system took different forms. There were those, like Charles A. Beard (1913), who attacked the economic motivations of those who had the greatest influence in framing the constitutional system, and thus cast doubt upon the system as anything other than a self-serving arrangement by a propertied class. There were others, like Frank Goodnow, (1900), who rejected constitutions as formalisms having little significance for the way that governments worked. Efforts by other peoples in Latin America and Europe to use the American constitutional formula often resulted in failure. These failures were construed as evidence that constitutions have little, if any, practical significance. There were still others, like Woodrow Wilson, who believed that the early American constitutional experiments were misguided efforts on the part of those who failed to understand the essential nature of the political process. Wilson's argument has probably been the most influential among political scientists. I shall pursue that argument further.

Wilson saw his own generation as opening a new era of constitutional criticism. His was the first generation, Wilson argued, not subject to an unquestioning adoration of the Constitution. Instead, it had freed itself of the shackles of deference and had the privilege to engage in "the first season of free, outspoken, unrestrained constitutional criticism" (Wilson, 1885: 27).

Wilson was persuaded that the constitutional structure designed in the eighteenth century had become little more than a formal facade that concealed the fundamental reality of American politics. His thesis was that "the actual form of our present government is simply a scheme of Congressional supremacy" (Wilson, 1885: 28), that could no longer be "squared" with traditional constitutional theory.

> All niceties of constitutional restriction and even many broad prin-
> ciples of constitutional limitation have been overridden, and a
> thoroughly organized system of congressional control set up which
> gives a very rude negative to some theories of balance and some
> schemes for distributed powers, but which suits well with conve-
> nience, and does violence to none of the principles of self-govern-
> ment contained in the Constitution [Wilson, 1885: 31].

Wilson rejects what he refers to as the "literary theories" and "paper pictures" of the Constitution reflected in the writing of John Adams, Alexander Hamilton, and James Madison. He argues that "those checks and balances have proved mischievous just to the extent to which they have succeeded in establishing themselves as realities" (Wilson, 1885: 187). He further asserts that "this balance of state against national authorities has proved, of all constitutional checks, the least effectual" (Wilson, 1885: 34).

These structures were contrary to the essential nature of government. Wilson argues that "the leading inquiry in the examination of any system of government must, of course, concern primarily the real depositaries and the essential machinery of power" (Wilson, 1885: 30). He then goes on to assert a basic presupposition in his political science that "there is always a centre of power." The task of the scholar then is to determine "where in this system is that centre? In whose hands is self-sufficient authority lodged and through what agencies does that authority speak and act" (Wilson, 1885: 30). If one sets aside formalities and looks at the "practical conduct" of government, Wilson advances the thesis that "the predom-inant and controlling force, the centre and source of all motive and of all regulative power, is Congress" (Wilson, 1885: 31).

The controlling principle in Wilson's political theory is that "the more power is divided the more irresponsible it becomes" (Wilson, 1885: 77). His preferred solution is a unitary system of government following the model of the British Parliamentary system in which Parliament, as the representative body, exercises the supreme authority of government. The requirements of self-government can be met if Parliament as the representative body is raised "to a position of absolute supremacy" (Wilson, 1885: 203).

Elsewhere Wilson (1885: 181) asserts:

> No one, I take it for granted, is disposed to disallow the principle that the representatives of the people are the proper ultimate authority in all matters of government, and that administration is merely the clerical part of government. Legislation is the originating force. It determines what shall be done; and the President, if he cannot or will not stay legislation by the use of his extraordinary power as a branch of the legislature, is plainly bound in duty to render unquestioning obedience to Congress. And if it be his duty to obey, still more is obedience the bounden duty of his subordinates. The power of making laws is in its very nature and essence the power of directing, and that power is given to Congress.

Wilson's political science does not address the same questions as were addressed in *The Federalist*. Wilson rejects form as having little if any practical significance in the conduct of government. Instead, form is, as Bagehot (1867) contended, the exterior facade of government that conceals the reality of power that operates behind the facade. In taking this position, Wilson opens himself to many ambiguities.

On the occasion of the fifteenth printing of *Congressional Government* in 1900, Wilson, for example, found it necessary to call the reader's attention to extensive changes that had taken place in "our singular system of Congressional government" (Wilson, 1885: 19). The war with Spain had resulted in important changes "upon the lodgment and exercise of power within our federal system" (Wilson, 1885: 22). Increasing power of the president was bringing a fundamental change in the American system of government. Wilson (1885: 23) concludes his preface by observing:

> It may be, too, that the new leadership of the Executive inasmuch as it is likely to last, will have a very far-reaching effect upon our whole method of government. It may give the heads of the executive departments a new influence upon the action of Congress. It may bring about, as a consequence, an integration which will substitute

statesmanship for government by mass meeting. It may put this whole hopelessly out of date.

The "people's parliament" had become "government by mass meeting." The heads of the executive department were exercising a "new influence upon the action of Congress" rather than being "bounden in duty to render unquestioning obedience to Congress." The power of making laws was no longer "the very nature and essence of the power of directing" (i.e., the power of government). Instead, "the new leadership of the Executive" will "substitute statesmanship for government by mass meeting."

Any close student of *The Federalist* would appreciate that Wilson was using a radically different mode of political analysis than that used in the design of the American constitutional system. Madison's thesis that "the accumulation of all powers . . . in the same hands, whether of one, a few, or many, and whether hereditary, self-appointed, or elective, may justly be pronounced the very definition of tyranny" (Hamilton, Jay, and Madison, n. d.: 313) is beyond Wilson's comprehension. Instead, Wilson character-izes such government as "responsible" government because people can then know whom to hold accountable. It never occurs to Wilson that the "new leadership of the Executive" will be anything other than "statesman-ship." The possibility of tyranny is alien to his thinking.

The characterization of a unitary authority that exercises ultimate supremacy in all matters of government as a responsible government poses an interesting problem in a theory of sovereignty. To exercise unlimited and ultimate authority in all matters of government implies that no effective remedies are available to hold the supreme authority accountable. Hobbes recognized this clearly in formulating his theory of sovereignty. Yet Wilson, in offering a coherent argument, was confronted with the necessity of specifying the remedies that were available for enforcing responsibility. He would unquestionably have responded that Parliament is responsible to the people. But if Parliament is supreme in all matters of government, can it also be responsible to the people? Or if it is to be responsible to the people, is it supreme in all matters of government?

Wilson's conception of constitutional decision making was radically at variance with that of Hamilton and Madison. Constitutions for Wilson involve the choice of a broad, general form of government rather than specifying rules that establish the terms and conditions of government. Once the general form of government is selected, the basic constitutional task is accomplished, and then the more difficult task of organizing and running a government begins. Wilson (1887: 207) was critical of the American experience when he observed:

> Once a nation has embarked in the business of manufacturing constitutions, it finds it exceedingly difficult to close out that business and open for the public a bureau of skilled, economical administration. There seems to be no end to the tinkering with constitutions.

Wilson's preoccupation with the "realities" of power as determined by practice and the independence of those realities from became the basis for a new political science that was radically different from the political science that had been used to design the American constitutional system. What exists is justified by its existence. There are no generally recognized normative criteria for evaluating the performance of government apart from being in effective control. The study of political science can be a value-free endeavor to determine who exercises power in human societies. The methods of the natural sciences can be used to discover the realities of political power.

The question remains as to how political scientists are to construe the American experiment in constitutional choice. I shall turn to that problem next.

How Do We Construe the Essential Characteristics of the American Political System?

Two fundamentally different conceptions of political experiences emerge in the formulation of those who engaged in the founding of the compound structure of the American republics, and those who have engaged in the study and practice of politics in the twentieth century. Twentieth-century scholars view themselves as being sufficiently free from commitments to engage in an objective, value-free assessment of the realities of power. They advance the contention that form makes little or no difference. Government, as it were, is the result of shifting coalitions, historical accidents, and basic underlying forces within a society that *cause* political developments to occur.

Those who participated in the founding of the American republics, by contrast, argued that human beings could create governments by reflection and choice using knowable principles to create appropriate forms so that people might exercise essential control over the conduct of government.

Governments are artifacts that human beings can *design* and *use* so as to serve their aspirations and purposes, subject to control by the community of people being served.

The latter argument is of fundamental importance for political science if political scientists are to be more than contemporary historians preoccupied with the lore of power. If people can create and maintain governments of their own choosing, presumably their artisanship will depend upon the use of a science that can specify relationships between conditions and consequences in establishing the terms and conditions of government. Such knowledge might then be used to select particular terms and conditions that will meet the design criteria for creating an appropriate system of "good" government.

The design of institutions of government would then reflect two types of calculations. One is the calculation of the probable consequences that follow from specifiable conditions. The other is the criteria to be used in selecting from among alternative possibilities. These criteria will then be used in evaluating alternative institutional designs and thus become the basic values or objectives to be realized as a consequence of the choices made and acted upon.

The design of any artifact then is never value-free. Rather, the creation of any artifact depends, first, upon a knowledge of technique and, second, upon choice in which criteria of selection apply to the choices made. The knowledge of techniques is grounded in science. Criteria of selection are grounded in moral considerations pertaining to human preferences and values. Since any artifact is a product of both forms of calculation, a proper understanding of its meaning or significance requires reference to the knowledge of techniques and criteria of selection that were entailed in its creation and use.

In the case of a political science, this implies that an appropriate beginning point is to consider the arguments of those who undertake the fundamental tasks of designing and creating governmental institutions. Such arguments provide explanations for the techniques used and the criteria utilized in formulating the particular design. The operation of the system can then be evaluated where the criteria of choice are used as evaluative criteria to assess performance, and the appropriateness of technique can be determined by its instrumental quality in yielding the desired results.

The capacity to conduct such an inquiry depends on a knowledgeable understanding of the nature of political phenomena, the primary ingredients used in political artisanship, and the way these ingredients work to yield the results they do. All forms of human organization are artifacts that contain their own artisans. Organizations are used to order human relationships in the conduct of joint activities and enterprises. Order is created by reference to rules. Since rules are not self-formulating, self-applying, or self-enforcing, they depend upon the agency of some who exercise the prerogatives of rulership with reference to others. Rules imply both rulers and ruled. The creation and maintenance of a system of rule depend upon a radical inequality between those who are rulers and those who are subject to rule. Instruments of coercion are necessary ingredients in any system of rule and provide an opportunity for those who are rulers to dominate the allocation of values in a society and exploit others to their own advantage. Fundamental tensions exist in all human societies when the prerogatives of rule are used not to sustain a mutually productive relationship among members of a society, but to allow some to exploit others.

The possibility of devising a system of rule in which rulers are themselves subject to the rule of law was the essential nature of the American experiments in constitutional choice. To attempt to realize such a possibility poses design problems of a substantial magnitude. Authority must be distributed in a way that all authority is subject to limits and no one, or no one set of decision makers, is permitted to gain dominance over the rest.

Since rules are not self-applying and self-enforcing, any system of constitutional rule depends upon a knowledgeable use of the prerogatives of government and citizenship to maintain and enforce limits inherent in a system of constitutional law. Knowledge, both of techniques and design criteria, is thus essential to the conduct of the American experiments in constitutional rule. This knowledge provides appropriate criteria to evaluate performance and methods that can be used for officials to check and limit one another, and for citizens to maintain proper limits in their relationships with officials. Any such structure of relationships is vulnerable to the development of coalitions that attempt to dominate all decision structures. The viability of a system of constitutional rule depends, in turn, upon awareness of these exposures and the willingness of others to resist such usurpations of authority.

As we approach the close of the second century of the American experiments in constitutional choice, we need to reconsider the arguments of those who participated in the design of those experiments and their twentieth-century critics who dismissed their arguments as "literary theories" and "paper pictures" unrelated to the realities of political power.

The appropriate level of analysis for this purpose is that relevant to constitutional choice. We still confront the question of

> whether societies of men are capable or not of establishing good government from reflection and choice, or whether they are forever destined to depend for their political constitutions on accident and force [Hamilton, Jay and Madison, n. d.: 3].

The question still has profound significance for the human race. Perhaps it is time that we return to the constitutional level of analysis and take account of arguments and normative assumptions as they are relevant to an assessment of performance in construing the American experiments in constitutional choice. To develop a lore about the realities of power without knowing how that lore relates to design possibilities and performance criteria is to ignore the basic question of whether societies of men are capable of creating and maintaining self-governing institutions from reflection and choice.

REFERENCES

BAGEHOT, W. (1876) [1964] The English Constitution. London: C. A. Watts.

BEARD, C. A. (1913) [1965] An Economic Interpretation of the Constitution of the United States. New York: Free Press.

HAMILTON, A., J. JAY, and J. MADISON (n.d.) [1964] The Federalist. New York: The Modern Library.

HOBBES, T. (1651) [1960] Leviathan. Oxford: Basil Blackwell.

GOODNOW, F. J. (1900) Politics and Administration: A Study in Government. New York: Macmillan.

LASSWELL, H. D. (1936) [1958] Politics: Who Gets What, When, How. New York: Meridian.

OSTROM, V. (1980) "Artisanship and artifact." Public Administration Review 40 (July/August): 309-317.

--- (1974) The Intellectual Crisis in American Public Administration. Birmingham: University of Alabama Press.

--- (1971) The Political Theory of a Compound Republic. Blacksburg, VA: Center for Study of Public Choice, Virginia Polytechnic Institute and State University.

WILSON, W. (1887) "The study of administration." Political Science Quarterly 2 (June): 197-222.

--- (1885) [1959] Congressional Government. New York: Meridian.

Synthesis

The Problem of Reflexivity in
Theory Building

J. DONALD MOON

In the history of political thought, a number of different conceptions of politics have been advanced, but there are two that stand out in sharp opposition to each other. Both are important to any discussion of the role of integration in theory building. On the one hand, there is the reductionist idea that the political sphere involves simply the play of social, economic, or even biological forces, and that political events and processes can be explained (and explained away) as simply the more or less mechanical outcome of these forces. On the other hand, the political may be seen as a realm of human freedom, as that sphere of social life in which people can collectively and, to a certain degree, autonomously determine the conditions and terms of their common life. The latter conception might be called the "classical" conception; it is central to the political theories of Plato and Aristotle, expressing part of what Aristotle meant in speaking of politics as the master science, or what Plato meant in characterizing the art of statesmanship as the art of directing all of the other arts. It is a view that came to seem naive in the modern world, and some have suggested that its abandonment marks the historical change from philosophical and normative political theory to the scientific study of politics.

Just as modern natural science arose along with a view of nature as a realm of necessity, of the operation of blind causal forces external to human purposes, so modern social science was predicated upon the same conception of society. Social change, institutions, and events came to be seen as following laws of their own, and social outcomes were seen not as reflecting human choices and purposes, but the operation of these laws. And if at first people thought only of economics in these terms, it was not long before they applied these ideas to politics as well. As Ostrom points out, governments came to be seen as "the result of shifting coalitions, historical accidents, and basic underlying forces within a society that cause political developments to occur."

But this radically determinist view, as Ostrom argues in his chapter, was not the conception of politics entertained by the founders of our republic, nor is it an adequate perspective from which to approach the constitutional level of political analysis. At the constitutional level, political institutions may best be seen as artifacts, as the result of human design and planning. This does not mean that in politics we are free to create institutions according to our own fancy: The very focus on *design* calls attention to the constraints under which we work in creating political institutions. Even free artistic expression is constrained—and enabled—by the properties of the media in which the artist works, and this is even more true of politics. For in the design of a constitution, we not only give expression to our basic values and principles, but we also set up those structures that we expect will best realize our values. Constitutional design, then, requires knowledge of the causal relations that determine the consequences of different institutional arrangements, for it is only on the basis of such knowledge that we can choose those structures whose consequences will be most desirable, given the situation in which we find ourselves.

To conceive of politics as, in part, a sphere of human freedom as the founders did, is not at all to abandon the scientific pespective. This was clearly brought out in the discussion following Ostrom's presentation of his paper at the conference. In her prepared remarks for the conference, Marjorie Hershey contrasted Ostrom's account of the apparently successful design of our national political institutions with recent efforts to reform the Democratic party. These reform attempts, she pointed out, were exercises in the design of political institutions, and were at least ostensibly intended to enhance popular control of public policy. But they could not be said to be successful in this, as they facilitated the expression of extreme views, and so discouraged the development of majoritarian positions by the party. Thus, they weakened the party as an institution of accountability in the larger political system. Assuming the sincerity of the reformers, these examples bring out the critical role played by our knowledge of the effects of different institutional structures in the design of political and social institutions. It is precisely the task of political science to develop such knowledge. An advantage of the "design" perspective, as Edwin Fogelman pointed out, is that it keeps political science focused on the real world, and on significant issues of political life.

The conception of politics as involving at least a potential, albeit constrained, sphere of autonomy raises the obvious question: How must the political system be organized if this potential is to be realized? Ostrom advises us to look at the *Federalist* for an answer to this question, and the answer we will find there, he argues, is that the political system must be based upon an explicit constitution, which specifies the governmental institutions and practices necessary to such a system. The *Federalist* also presents the principles to be employed in designing these institutions and in outlining their structures. I would like to raise a prior question: How can a constitution, conceived as the "law applicable to the organization and conduct of government," have an effect on future behavior? Evidently, such a law can be effective as a guide to the conduct of political actors only if it is precise enough to specify what they are to do, and only if there is a procedure to reach common understandings about what the law requires. It is because of this that the American experiment in political organization has led to such an important role for the courts and the judicial system generally in American politics, for it is the courts that are principally charged with the task of making the required constitutional interpretations.

While the courts may provide authoritative interpretations of the constitution, they do not by themselves guarantee that the constitution will be efficacious. For this to happen, the courts must actually be guided by the constitution (as it has developed into a body of constitutional law) in making their decisions. This raises a central issue that bedevils the judicial process and the study of the judicial process: What is the force of rules in judicial decision making? In what ways and to what extent do normative and ideational elements control the outcome of judicial decisions? And this, of course, is a central focus of much of the research on judicial process in America, and a major concern of Krislov's chapter.

This issue arises against the background of one extreme position, which is associated with the legal realists, and which might be seen as akin to the reductionist view of politics I discussed above. According to this position, legal reasoning is so elastic that it does not pose a major constraint on the decisions judges reach. This means that legal decisions cannot be explained in terms of their consistency with a prior body of law, either because the notion of consistency is not well defined in this context, or because the range of decisions that would be consistent is so wide that legal reasoning would not lead to a determinate result. In order to explain judicial decisions, then, one would have to invoke extralegal factors such as the ideology and class background of the judge, the historical context within which litigation occurs, or the political milieu of the courts.

The theory of constitutional government as Ostrom presents it depends upon the rejection of this skeptical position, and it requires that there be a close relationship between judicial decisions and constitutional (or other relevant) law. If legal outcomes are significantly affected by extralegal factors, then even if the legal decisions are effective in influencing political actors, it cannot be said that the constitution is effective in controlling behavior. While the constitutional structure created by the founders may have consequences for the operation of the political system, these consequences might then be largely unintended and, in any event, they would not occur in the manner contemplated by the theory.

Unfortunately, we have not been able to determine the relationship between constitutional law and judicial decision. As Krislov points out, understanding the relative weights of legal and extralegal factors has been one of the principal preoccupations of the new, scientific approach to the judicial process. But, while this approach has been enormously successful in certain respects, this central issue has proven to be intractable. In general, Krislov finds, the study of judicial process has suffered from many of the same difficulties that have plagued other areas of social inquiry. One of the main problems is to find general categories that can be used in describing and presenting particular cases, and in formulating theories and generalizations. Without such categories, it is hard to see how the problems of comparability of cases, cumulation of findings, and replicability, which Krislov details, can be solved. But because social phenomena are constituted in part by the concepts and self-understandings of social actors, and because these concepts and self-understandings vary with time and place, it is enormously difficult to find catagories that are sufficiently general. Thus, it has not been possible to establish such apparently simple or straightforward relationships as that between litigiousness and population size. Even if we have a clear idea of population size, the very concept of "litigation" is culturally variable, and so measures of litigiousness in one society or at one time may not be comparable to such measures in another society or time.

One of the problems with using empirical evidence to study the force of rules in judicial decision making is that we may need further conceptual clarification of what it means to follow a rule, or to apply a rule to a particular instance. This is suggested by recent controversies in constitutional law. Some scholars, such as Dworkin and Tribe have argued that the constitution specifies a set of substantive values and commitments that the government must pursue, and it is part of the task of the courts to discover the true meaning of these constitutional values, and to see that they are made effective in the cases that come before them. Against this view there are a number of scholars who argue that the constitution specifies only the procedures that government must follow in enacting laws, and that the courts are therefore limited to scrutinizing these procedures. When people disagree so deeply about what adherence to the constitution requires on the part of judges, and about the scope of legitimate judicial concern under the constitution, it is hard to imagine how we could begin an empirical study of the force of law in determining judicial outcomes.

One of the reasons these issues are so important is that there is a very close relationship between political legitimacy and the operation of the courts in this country. Empirical evidence that the courts do not decide cases principally on the basis of the law, but that extralegal factors largely determine judicial outcomes, not only undermines the courts as an institution that is supposed to act on the basis of law, but also tends to undermine the legitimacy of the political system as a whole. That is because the legitimacy of the political system depends in part upon its claim to be a constitutional system, to subject the behavior of political actors controlling the government to the rule of law, and because it is the role of the courts to interpret and apply the law to the other actors in the system. If the courts themselves do not act in accordance with the law, then the claim of the system to be constitutional is seriously undermined.

This point was stressed during the discussion following the presentation of Krislov's paper. Ronald Weber called attention to the tendency among many commentators and students of the Supreme Court to "worship" it, citing hostile reactions to the kind of "revelations" found in Woodward and Armstrong's *The Brethren*. He argued forcefully that it was the duty of scholars to examine the courts as objectively as possible, and that this required that they free themselves from the kind of "reverence" of the court that is part of our political culture. Only in this way can we expect to discover the extent to which the courts really play the role in our constitutional system that the theory of constitutionalism assigns to them. A critical and distanced attitude is required if we are to discover the relative influence of legal and extralegal factors in determining the outcome of judicial decisions.

At this point John Sprague asked whether there might be a possible conflict between our obligations as scholars and our obligations as citizens. Shouldn't we draw back from "debunking" the courts in order to preserve their legitimacy? Is it possible that the political system depends upon the widespread acceptance of a myth regarding judicial behavior? Several participants responded to Sprague's question by arguing that the greater danger to democracy arose from such myths, that false expectations would inevitably become disappointed, and that this would lead to the institutions involved experiencing a loss of legitimacy.

These discussions illustrate the paradoxical role of social and political scientists in relationship to their subject matter. As students of politics, we attempt to develop theories that will describe and explain political life, but it is possible that these theories, by being communicated to political actors, may affect their behavior in such a way as to change the phenomena we study. The reflexive relationship in which we stand to our subject is reflected in our dual roles as political scientists and political actors, and it makes the ideal of scientific objectivity and neutrality profoundly ambiguous. For, on the one hand, the ideal of objectivity is essential to the very notion of knowledge and the search for knowledge: It would be self-contradictory for a scholar to allow his or her ideals and aspirations to distort his or her perceptions and explanations to the world. On the other hand, recognizing the reflexive character of social scientific inquiry, the ideal of an objective, impartial form of scientific knowledge becomes problematic, inasmuch as our knowledge becomes part of the very world we study, and so cannot simply be said to "reflect" that world.

The dilemma of reflexivity is nicely brought out in the conclusion to Ostrom's chapter, where he points out that the operation of a constitutional system depends upon the citizenry's possessing certain knowledge about the operation of the system, which can be used by citizens "to maintain proper limits in their relationships with officials." The real danger that Ostrom sees in the "new political science" epitomized in the work of Woodrow Wilson is that, by coming to be accepted by the citizens as descriptive of our political system, it would deprive them of the very knowledge they require in order to maintain the system! The choice of theories is not merely a scientific problem of the truth content of the theories involved, but also a practical problem with implications for the moral basis of the political system itself.

The reflexivity of social science should not be confused with a second way in which social science may affect social life, that is, through the conscious application of social science knowledge to achieve various goals. In her prepared remarks for the conference, Susan White stressed the responsibilities of social scientists that result from the attempt to use social science instrumentally, as a kind of social engineering. This occurs when, to use White's examples, social science is used to predict the deterrent effects of certain punishments, or to design programs and facilities to rehabilitate criminals. Such instrumental applications of knowledge are clearly central to the "design" approach to political institutions, and because they invariably involve' treating people in certain ways, often with the objective of manipulating them, they raise deep ethical questions that the social scientist cannot in good conscience avoid. In this respect, however, our position is like that of the natural scientist, who must also be concerned with the uses to which his or her discoveries may be put.

The design approach that Ostrom advocates has the enormous advantage of focusing our attention on both of these aspects of the relationship between political science and political life. By viewing human organizations as "artifacts that contain their own artisans," he stresses the reflexive nature of political science and the role of human knowledge and concepts in constituting social and political reality. At the same time, by focusing on the design of such organizations and the consequences of their operation, he calls our attention to the possible instrumental uses of political knowledge to alter social arrangements to achieve particular goals and values. By raising questions at the constitutional level of analysis, he provides a framework for understanding that may be adequate to the reflexive character of our political knowledge and to a conception of politics as a realm of collective self-determination. But, as Krislov's analysis demonstrates, we have much to learn about the operation of our constitutional system before that framework becomes a genuine theory.

About the Contributors

G. R. BOYNTON is Professor of Political Science and Director of the Laboratory for Political Research at the University of Iowa. From 1972 to 1974, he served as Director of the Political Science Program of the National Science Foundation. His most recent publication is *Mathematical Thinking About Politics* (1981).

DAGOBERT L. BRITO is Director of the Murphy Institute of Political Economy and Professor of Economics at Tulane University in New Orleans. He is listed in the 1982-1983 volume of *Who's Who in America*, and has authored numerous articles, which have appeared in *Public Choice*, *American Economic Review*, *Econometrica*, *Public Finance*, *International Economic Review*, and the *Quarterly Journal of Economics*. His current research interests include dynamic strategy models and behavioral and economic foundations of arms races.

JUDITH A. GILLESPIE is the Director of the Program in Educational Policy and Change, Department of Political Science, Indiana University, Bloomington. Her chief interests are in the fields of political theory and curriculum development. She is the former editor of *Teaching Political Science* and the author of several textbooks and research monographs in political education. She is the executor of the John V. Gillespie Memorial Fund, which provides fellowships for advanced graduate students at Indiana University.

CHARLES F. HERMANN was born on June 19, 1772. He served for fourteen years in His Majesty's Navy after having been found drunk in a bar near the docks at Bristol. Slipping off ship one night in Boston, he sought political asylum in the United States. After attending Harvard Medical School, Hermann became the first White House Fellow serving President John Quincy Adams. He left that position in disgrace, however, when he allegedly lost fourteen papers of secret transcripts of Adams-Hayes conversations. Leaving politics, he became a ski bum and later a Formula I race car driver. A racing accident left him badly in need of a brain transplant, but he attempted to perform the operation himself using his old Harvard training. Having bungled the job, he pursued the only career left open to him given his remaining mental abilities—a professor of political science specializing in the comparative study of foreign policy.

BARBARA J. HILL is a research assistant at the University of Illinois and a doctoral candidate at Indiana University. She is the author of a recent article in the *Journal of Conflict Resolution* and regional, national, and international conference papers. In the spring of 1982, she was awarded the first John V. Gillespie Memorial Fellowship, for the academic year 1982-1983. Her current research interests include the investigation of different forms of international conflict resolution techniques, a game-theoretic model of international conflict dynamics, and the interrelationships between theories of federalism and international relations theory.

MICHAEL D. INTRILIGATOR is Professor of Economics at the University of California, Los Angeles, where he is also Professor of Political Science and Associate Director of the Center for International and Strategic Affairs. His recent publications include *Econometric Models, Techniques, and Applications* (1978) and numerous articles that have appeared in the *Journal of Conflict Resolution, Public Choice,* and *Mathematical Social Sciences.* He is co-editor, with K. Arrow, of the *Handbook of Mathematical Economics* (1981); with Z. Griliches, of the *Handbook of Econometrics* (1982); and with B. Brodie and R. Kolkowicz, of *National Security and International Stability* (forthcoming). His current research includes work on nuclear proliferation, on the behavioral and economic foundation of arms races, on mathematical economic theory, and on applied econometrics.

BRIAN L. JOB is Associate Professor in the Department of Political Science at the University of Minnesota. He received his Ph.D. from Indiana University (working with John V. Gillespie and Dina A. Zinnes). His research has focused upon forecasting in international crises, international alliances, and the causes of war. His articles have appeared in a variety of journals including the *American Journal of Political Science, International Studies Quarterly,* and the *Journal of Conflict Resolution.*

DAVID L. JONES is a research programmer and consultant at the Computing Services Office, University of Illinois, and is a Ph.D. candidate in Political Science at Indiana University. His research focuses on formal models of international conflict. He has presented papers at the Midwest Political Science Association Meetings, and has coauthored a paper that appeared in the *Journal of Conflict Resolution,* and a number of research papers from the Center for International Policy Studies, Indiana University.

SAMUEL KRISLOV is Professor of Political Science at the University of Minnesota. He has served as President of the Midwest Political Science Association and the Law and Society Association, and as Chairman of the Committee on Research in Law Enforcement and Justice of the National Research Council. A Guggenheim Fellow in 1979-1980, he has also received awards from the Ford, Bush, and Russell Sage Foundations.

STEPHEN J. MAJESKI is Assistant Professor in the Department of Political Science at Syracuse University. The *Journal of Conflict Resolution* recently published an article he co-authored with David Jones. Currently, his research interests include the following: investigation of mathematical models of the U.S. defense expenditure process, examination of different aspects of arms race models, and certain general methodological issues of model specification and estimation.

J. DONALD MOON is Associate Professor of Government at Wesleyan University. He has published "The Logic of Political Inquiry" in the *Handbook of Political Science,* and essays in *Political Theory,* the *Journal of Politics, Philosophy of the Social Sciences,* and other journals. He is currently working on problems relating to environmentalism and the legitimacy of the liberal-democratic welfare state.

BETTY A. NESVOLD is Professor of Political Science and Associate Dean of the College of Arts and Letters at San Diego State University. Her research has focused on cross-national studies of conflict and violence, has been supported by the National Science Foundation. Her articles have appeared in *Comparative Politics, American Behavioral Scientist,* and the *Journal of Conflict Resolution.* With John V. Gillespie, she coedited *Macro-Quantitative Analysis,* a Sage publication. She has served as President of the Western Political Science Association and Treasurer of the American Political Science Association.

ELINOR OSTROM is Chair of the Department of Political Science and Co-Director of the Workshop in Political Theory and Policy Analysis at Indiana University. Her research interests are in the study of urban service delivery and the effects of institutional arrangements on citizens, elected officials, bureau chiefs, and street-level bureaucrat behavior. She is the author of *Urban Policy Analysis: An Institutional Approach* and the editor of *The Delivery of Human Services: Outcomes of Change.*

VINCENT OSTROM is Professor of Political Science and Co-Director of the Workshop in Political Theory and Policy Analysis at Indiana University, Bloomington. His principal publications include *The Political Theory of a Compound Republic* and *The Intellectual Crisis in American Public Administration.*

JAMES N. ROSENAU is Director of the Institute for Transnational Studies at the University of Southern California. His recent publications include *The Dramas of Political Life* (1980), *The Scientific Study of Foreign Policy* (1980), *The Study of Global Interdependence* (1980), and *The Study of Political Adaptation* (1981). He is also editor of *In Search of Global Patterns* (1976) and coeditor of *World-System Structure* (1981).

BARBARA SALERT is an Associate Professor of Political Science at Washington University, St. Louis, Missouri. She was a graduate student of John Gillespie and received her Ph.D. from Indiana University in 1975. Her work focuses on problems of political violence and protest movements. She is the author of *Revolutions and Revolutionaries: Four Theories* (1976) and coauthor of *The Dynamics of Riots* (1980).

DINA A. ZINNES is Merriam Professor of Political Science at the University of Illinois, Urbana. She is the author of *Contemporary Research in International Politics* and articles in *International Studies Quarterly,* the *Journal of Conflict Resolution,* and the *American Political Science Review.* Currently, she is serving as President of the Midwest Political Science Association and managing editor of the *American Political Science Review.* Her current research interests are mathematical models of international politics, forecasting international crises, and wartime coalition behavior.

DATE DUE